IMPORTING THE LAW IN POST-COMMUNIST TRANSITIONS

This book, one of the very first monographs on the Hungarian Constitutional Court available in English, is a unique study of the birth of a new legal system after the collapse of communism in Central and Eastern Europe. It shows that the genesis of the new legal order was determined by massive Western involvement and an unprecedented level of exportation and importation of law. Anchored in a detailed comparative study of German and Hungarian constitutional case law on human dignity, this book argues that law importation was a deliberate strategy carried out by the Hungarian Court in the early years of its operation. It explains how the circumstances of the transition and the background of the importers determined the choice of German case law as a model and how the Court used it to construct its own version of the right to human dignity. It highlights the Hungarian Court's instrumentalisation of imported law in order to lay the foundations of a new conception of fundamental rights. While focusing on the Hungarian experience, this book engages with international debates and provides an original theoretical framework for approaching the movement of law from the importers' perspective.

Volume 1 in the series, Human Rights Law in Perspective

Human Rights Law in Perspective

General Editor: Colin Harvey

The language of human rights figures prominently in legal and political debates at the national, regional and international levels. In the UK the Human Rights Act 1998 has generated considerable interest in the law of human rights. It will continue to provoke much debate in the legal community and the search for original insights and new materials will intensify.

The aim of this series is to provide a forum for scholarly reflection on all aspects of the law of human rights. The series will encourage work which engages with the theoretical, comparative and international dimensions of human rights law. The primary aim is to publish over time books which offer an insight into human rights law in its contextual setting. The objective is to promote an understanding of the nature and impact of human rights law. The series is inclusive, in the sense that all perspectives in legal scholarship are welcome. It will incorporate the work of new and established scholars.

Human Rights Law in Perspective is not confined to consideration of the UK. It will strive to reflect comparative, regional and international perspectives. Work which focuses on human rights law in other states will therefore be included in this series. The intention is to offer an inclusive intellectual home for significant scholarly contributions to human rights law.

Volume 1 Importing the Law in Post-Communist Transitions

Catherine Dupré

Importing the Law in Post-Communist Transitions

The Hungarian Constitutional Court and the Right to Human Dignity

CATHERINE DUPRÉ

·HART·
PUBLISHING
OXFORD – PORTLAND OREGON
2003

Hart Publishing
Oxford and Portland, Oregon

Published in North America (US and Canada) by
Hart Publishing c/o
International Specialized Book Services
5804 NE Hassalo Street
Portland, Oregon
97213-3644
USA

Hart Publishing is a specialist legal publisher based in Oxford, England.
To order further copies of this book or to request a list of other
publications please write to:

Hart Publishing, Salter's Boatyard, Folly Bridge,
Abingdon Road, Oxford OX1 4LB
Telephone: +44 (0)1865 245533 or Fax: +44 (0)1865 794882
e-mail: mail@hartpub.co.uk
WEBSITE: http//www.hartpub.co.uk

British Library Cataloguing in Publication Data
Data Available
ISBN 1–84113–131–8 (hardback)

Typeset by Hope Services (Abingdon) Ltd.
Printed and bound in Great Britain on acid-free paper by
Biddles Ltd, www.biddles.co.uk

*This book is dedicated to
my grandparents*

Series Editor's Preface

This is the first book in the series *Human Rights Law in Perspective*. I am pleased to be able to launch the series with this comprehensive study. As Dr Dupré notes, there is much interest in the work of the Hungarian Constitutional Court. This monograph is a welcome and significant addition to the existing literature. Although the focus is on the Constitutional Court, Dr Dupré also maps the birth of a new legal order in Hungary and the theoretical framework she develops for explaining law importation will be of general interest.

The book addresses the development of the right to human dignity and the way that law importation was used to construct a new foundation for fundamental rights in Hungary. As Dr Dupré argues, the Hungarian Constitutional Court was a prolific importer of foreign law in the early stages of the transition. But the process of law importation in Central and Eastern Europe went far beyond the courts, as she notes. By 'law' she means rules, principles, standards of constitutionality, institutions or methods of adjudication. The German model, in particular, was employed extensively in the process of overcoming the past.

Law importation is placed at the centre of the transition in Hungary. Hard questions are asked in this book. Dr Dupré focuses on the perspective of the importer in an attempt to understand the legal and non-legal reasons for the process. Who were the exporters and importers? What models were most extensively used and why? How was the Hungarian Constitutional Court able to import foreign law in the way it did? These are all questions thoroughly examined in this book. Dr Dupré argues that although the Constitutional Court used the language of globalisation or *ius commune* the law it imported was more specific. Faith was placed in the new language of law and the Constitutional Court proved to be a persuasive institutional actor in Hungary. The idea of a judicial dialogue played some part in this, but it appears that the Court also had to speak the right language and this largely meant opening a legal path to the West. She maps the adoption of foreign law as a modern substitute for natural law in the transition and highlights the fact that the Constitutional Court was in a strong position to introduce liberal values into the constitutional system. This is traced to an argument about a European, and even global, legal enterprise. Dr Dupré is sceptical about rhetorical claims surrounding the globalisation of rights. For example, two points she makes stand out. First, that the globalisation of rights in the post-communist transitions was a one-way process with little attempt in the West to learn from the protection of social rights. Secondly, her phrase 'not global but German' highlights the particular nature of law importation in Hungary. Although the judges talked of global law, they had a specific example in mind which could solve the problems they faced in constitutional adjudication. As this book explains, the strategy worked, in the narrow sense that the Court was able to construct the foundations of a new constitutional order underpinned by liberal values. In the longer term Dr Dupré is less certain about this approach.

   The transitions in Central and Eastern Europe must be viewed in their specific contexts. However, they continue to attract detailed scrutiny and some lessons may be learned. While Dr Dupré focuses on Hungary, questions are raised and answers provided which are of general relevance. This impressive work is a significant contribution to the debate and it is a pleasure to be able to include it in this series.

Colin Harvey
December 2002

Summary Contents

Contents

Acknowledgements

This research was conducted over a period of 10 years during which time I lived in five different countries and learnt three languages. The project started germinating when I was still an undergraduate student and first encountered comparative constitutional law at the Max Planck Institute in Heidelberg. It subsequently became the subject of my *Diplôme d'Études Approfondies* (DEA, equivalent to a LLM) dissertation and of the PhD proposal that I submitted to the European University Institute (EUI), where I undertook most of the research on which this work is based.

As this was such a new field, I have often felt the isolation of long term research as I was venturing into constitutional adjudication in post-communist countries. On the completion of this book I realise, however, that I have benefited from the support of several people without whom this monograph would never have been completed and I wish to thank them here in a roughly chronological order.

I am grateful to the French Ministry of Culture and Education for the financial support (*bourse Lavoisier*) that I received at the EUI for two years of my doctoral research. The EUI was probably the only place where I could have carried out such an extravagant project at the time in such a delightful environment. I am particularly grateful to Professor Philippe Schmitter for sitting on my PhD panel, as well as for his support at the very end of my thesis which gave me strength to go on with this project.

This book would not have been possible without the Max Planck Institute in Heidelberg, where I was always welcome to use its fantastic library. In particular, I am grateful to Christoph Benedict for reading my PhD dissertation and commenting on my analysis of German case law. I am also grateful to Lutger Radermacher for reading and commenting on some of the draft chapters of this book and for his very kind suggestions for improving some of the footnotes.

I wish to address sincere thanks to the Hungarian Constitutional Court and its members, constitutional judges and their advisors, whose openness provided me with invaluable insight into this exceptional period of foundation. The president of the Court, László Sólyom, always managed to find time to discuss issues with me, as did his colleagues Justices Antal Ádám, Tamás Lábady, Imre Vörös and János Zlinsky. I also found a lot of friendly support in the triumvirate of the first advisors to the president: Péter Paczolay, Gábor Halmai and Botond Biskey. The librarian of the Court, Ms Judit Petróczi, helped me find my way around Hungarian literature and materials.

I wish to thank Professor Georg Brunner (Institut für Ostrecht, Cologne University) for his encouragement and very friendly assistance with understanding

Hungarian case law. During my time at the University of Birmingham, I received invaluable support and encouragement from Professor David Feldman. I am also particularly grateful to Professor Istvan Pogany (University of Warwick) for his friendly support with this huge enterprise and for his perceptive and helpful comments on draft versions of some chapters. Last but not least, I was very glad that Richard Hart accepted my proposal and I have greatly appreciated his patient support while I was writing this book.

This work has involved much linguistic effort, including learning Hungarian and translating human dignity cases. I wish to thank particularly warmly Judit Nagy-Darvas, my remarkable Hungarian teacher, who happened to be in Florence for one year when I started this research in 1994.

I am also very grateful to three Hungarian lawyers who were fellow research students at the EUI between 1995 and 1998. Péter Munkacsi very kindly sent me the first Hungarian cases available in English and helped me to find resources in the Library of Parliament in Budapest. Orsolya Farkas and János Volkai contributed with great patience and kindness to this work and made sure that my translations and interpretations did not deviate from the original Hungarian of the constitutional cases.

This book, however, would not have materialised without the support and assistance of Dr Stephen Skinner (University of Warwick). This study has generated many thousands of words, but I still lack the right ones to express my gratitude to him.

List of Tables

Table of Cases

Introduction

A T THE END of the summer of 1989, the first wave of 'tourists' from Eastern Europe travelled to the West. In autumn 1989, the collapse of the Berlin Wall marked the end of almost half a century of communist dictatorships and inaugurated a new era. A period of intensive changes started to reshape the political and institutional architecture of Europe. The dismantling of the Soviet Union provoked the emergence of new independent states and the disappearance of others, after reunification or secession. Everywhere, in response to these changes, new constitutions were enacted or old constitutions were substantially amended.

Central and Eastern Europe, the study of which had waned and was essentially left to sovietologists and other specialised research centres, attracted fresh interest and, indeed, this caused a welcome excitement in the academic community. The scale of the changes affecting virtually all academic disciplines opened dazzling research perspectives—in particular for comparative lawyers. All disciplines were challenged to propose an explanation for this incredible and unforeseen phenomenon, leading to developments in the areas of, for example, élite studies, institutional studies, micro/macro economics, political and legal theory. Every school of thought endeavoured to tackle the end of what had been the main division of the world for the previous 50 years, an ideological divide under which a generation was born, that it had always known and accepted as an ineluctable feature of the world.[1] The lives of the older generation, those who had known the world before the emergence and the development of two opposing blocs, had also been transformed and shaped by the division. The shock caused by the unexpected and complete demise of the Soviet empire was such that one of the first academic interpretations of this phenomenon was to call it 'the end of History.' However, the world recovered from this great transformation and new states, institutions, international structures and life in general went on, as indeed did History.

The collapse of communism was fascinating because it radically transformed the world and Europe in particular. Yet for such a massive change, it took place in a relatively peaceful way. This was particularly true of the years 1989–90 and of the way the process of change was initiated. Of course, we cannot forget the

---

[1] J Elster, C Offe and UK Preuß start their book on *Institutional Design in Post-communist Societies: Rebuilding the Ship at Sea* by pointing out that: 'The breakdown of the European regimes of state socialism and the subsequent efforts to establish a new social order in its former domain are arguably the most consequential, as well as most fascinating, historical events in the authors' adult lifetime' (Cambridge, Cambridge University Press, 1998), 1.

dismantlement of Yugoslavia and the extreme violence of the Balkan wars, the military repression of Tchechen rebels, nor the fact that in Romania the change of regime culminated in the execution of the Ceausescus and that very violent strikes and demonstrations were among the main features of the Romanian transition. On the whole, however, the generally peaceful and controlled character of the shift from communism may be appreciated in relation to the unfulfilled fears of a third world war and nuclear Armageddon that the Cold War had (maybe not without reason) entertained. Perhaps we Westerners were relieved to observe that the changes in Central and Eastern Europe did not affect the comfort of our daily lives. In contrast with what had happened in previous democratic transitions in Southern Europe, as well as in South America, the military did not play a major role, nor did it represent a major threat. The post-communist revolutions were, as it seemed at first, initiated and conducted by the people themselves. Dissidents played a leading role in this process, together with civil society, maybe particularly in countries like Poland, East Germany and Hungary. In fact the post-communist revolutions seemed to fit into a sort of ideal representation of revolution where the people pooled their efforts and resources to throw out 'bad' communist dictators in order to replace them with democratically elected leaders.

After the first and most spectacular changes, the realisation began to dawn that perhaps these revolutions were far more complex than they first appeared, and since then it has become increasingly difficult to define them in general terms, or even to define them under the sole term of 'revolution.' Indeed, one of the difficulties of understanding the changes is reflected in the lack of one satisfactory term to label them.[2] The people involved in these changes often preferred not to use the word 'revolution' to refer to the events of the 1990s. In countries such as Czechoslovakia and Hungary, this term was very soon qualified, as in 'velvet revolution' or in 'refolution,' in an attempt to represent the idea of the gradual and perhaps moderate character of the changes, in contrast to the usual sense of 'revolution,' which historically has been associated with extreme violence and brutality, as in the French or Bolshevik revolutions.[3] In Hungary, the years 1989–90 are more commonly referred to as '*rendszerváltás*' ('change of system'), which translates well into German as '*Systemwechsel.*' Rudolf Tökés captured the particular nature of the Hungarian changes with the phrase 'negotiated revolution' which is also the title of his book.[4]

The term 'transition' is perhaps the lowest common denominator, but although it indicates a gradual move from one set of circumstances to another, it remains non-specific and it does not fully indicate the particular character of

    [2] See the reflections of J-Y Potel on this, *Les Cent Portes de l'Europe Centrale et Orientale* (Paris, Les Editions de l'Atelier, 1998), 45–46.
    [3] TG Ash, *We the People: The Revolution of 89 Witnessed in Warsaw, Budapest, Berlin and Prague* (London, Granta Books, 1990), 14.
    [4] R Tökés, *Hungary's Negotiated Revolution: Economic Reform, Social Changes and Political Succession* (Cambridge, Cambridge University Press, 1996).

the changes in Central and Eastern Europe. At first, this term was adequate because the collapse of communism was seen to be a shift from the lack of democracy to democracy. However, it soon became clear that it was not only a matter of abandoning the so-called 'peoples' democracies,' but also a matter of economic transformation and fundamental ideological reconstruction. The simple term 'transition' actually embraced all aspects of the definition of a state: ideology, society, politics, economics and law. It is therefore an apparently simple term that must be understood as encapsulating a wide range of elements.

This book is concerned with the legal dimensions of the changes as they are reflected in a new constitution and one of its essential post-communist features, constitutional adjudication. This legal analysis is nevertheless undertaken in the context of the wider aspects of 'transition' in Central and Eastern Europe. In the absence of better terms and rather than trying to create a more accurate neologism to describe the collapse of communism and its consequences, I will use both 'transitions' and 'changes' with no implied difference in meaning.

1. THE STUDY OF TRANSITIONS: A DISCIPLINARY CROSSROADS

Post-communist transitions have now given birth to a new kind of academic, the 'transitologist'; but back in 1989, there was no particular discipline designed to concentrate on these changes and the first commentators came from a wide range of areas.

Some scholars came from Soviet studies, that is an area essentially concerned with the Soviet Union in its political and economic dimensions, and secondarily with other countries of the communist bloc. The sovietologists certainly suffered from the inability of their discipline to predict the fall of the Iron Curtain and they were momentarily discredited as a result. Even so, they had invaluable knowledge of the Soviet Union. They were familiar with the social and cultural situation there, they often had contacts and links with (post)-communist bodies, they spoke Russian and, as a result, they could gain access relatively rapidly to what was happening in the former Soviet bloc.

Another significant group of academics comprised the observers of democratic transitions in other parts of the world, such as South America and Southern Europe. With their experience and knowledge of post-totalitarian democracies, they turned to post-communist systems, probably eager to test their hypotheses and to extend their empirical field of studies.[5] Their main difference from

---

[5] See PhC Schmitter, G O'Donnell and L Whitehead (eds), *Transitions from Authoritarian Rule: Prospects for Democracy* (Baltimore, Johns Hopkins University Press, 1986); JJ Linz and A Stepan, *Problems of Democratic Transition and Consolidation: Southern Europe, South America and Post-Communist Europe* (Baltimore, Johns Hopkins University Press, 1996) and A Przeworski, *Democracy and the Market, Political and Economic Reforms in Eastern Europe and Latin America* (Cambridge, Cambridge University Press, 1991).

the sovietologists was perhaps that, despite lacking specialist knowledge, they possessed a conceptual frame through which they could understand (and assess) what was happening. This allowed a clarification of the post-communist turmoil: they identified the components of the transitions and the various steps of this process.

Lawyers too were active contributors to the study and observation of post-communist transitions. Their role was slightly different in that they were perhaps more involved in the mechanics of transformation by providing advice, technical expertise and assistance, crash courses in, for example, human rights, the rule of law and the separation of powers. Back home, they often reported in law journals (as well as to their colleagues and students), in a descriptive and informative manner, on what they had seen in the East. However, in contrast to political science, there does not yet seem to be a strong and clearly organised group of lawyers who could be identified as specialising in post-communist legal developments. Those lawyers who have shown an interest in this area have rather done so by extending a pre-existing interest in a specific branch of law, such as constitutional law, company law or family law for example, to the post-communist context. Similarly, post-communist law has now been integrated into the study of European (Union) law as the enlargement issue and its related problems have come to include the issue of the Union's external borders and what lies beyond them.

On its own, none of the disciplines outlined above (or of the other disciplines that I may have omitted here) can claim to possess 'the truth' about post-communist transitions; nor can any discipline claim to understand fully and to be able to explain (let alone to predict) the changes that are taking place. Each discipline has developed a partial explanation which is often only valid for the particular group of countries considered in a given study, such as the Visegrad states, the Baltic states, the Balkan states (with a subdivision to include the ex-Yugoslavia) or the Central European states. More recently, the *summa divisio* in the approach to post-communist states has been between the states which can join the European Union soon, and all the others.

These various groupings of states illustrate scholarly efforts to cope with the immensity of the field, the sheer number of countries involved and the complexity of related issues which make it impossible to claim genuine knowledge and understanding of the whole phenomenon of post-communist transitions. Even the categories themselves, mentioned above as examples, are questionable as to their content and their extent: they will inevitably include a disturbing case which does not fit with the rest of the category, but which nevertheless cannot be excluded. In other words, despite apparent resemblances between countries in a group, it is almost impossible to develop a meaningful explanation that applies to more than one country. The more we know and the more the 'post-communist transitions' develop, the more it becomes difficult to have an overview and to restrict the field of study to a neat set of countries or indeed to a single discipline.

2. A CASE STUDY: THE HUNGARIAN CONSTITUTIONAL COURT

If determined to go on with the study of post-communist transitions, we are forced to restrict the scope of observation. The option of a case study thankfully rescues us from this inextricable and frustrating situation; but the selection of the case studied needs to be qualified. It would be an exaggeration to claim that the choice of Hungary and the Hungarian Court at the outset of this study was entirely guided by objective and theoretical criteria, as this would negate the role of coincidences and chance in this undertaking. Having said that, Hungary was a very suitable choice for a case study and Hungarian constitutional law is fascinating in more than one way. Furthermore, Hungary probably embodied the mildest form of communism in Central and Eastern Europe and the Kádár regime with its 'goulash communism' had significantly relaxed the dogmas of Moscow. Unlike some other communist countries, Hungary under communism was not completely cut off from the West and it managed to maintain privileged links with liberal democracies and with West Germany in particular. As a result, one can consider that Hungary was more or better prepared for the change of regime. In fact, some commentators date the beginnings of change back to 1956. Challenges to the Kádár regime itself, which culminated in 1988 when he had to leave the Politburo, stretched back to the 1970s. The famous samizdat movement started in the 1980s and was crucial in stimulating political opposition. When Kádár died in July 1989 aged 77, on the day of Imre Nagy's rehabilitation by the Hungarian Supreme Court, it was clear that this would open the way to more fundamental changes. In September 1989, Hungary was the first communist country to open its border with the West in order to allow 12,000 East German 'tourists' to cross over into Austria.

The relatively mild character of the communist regime in Hungary, together with a relative openness to the West, were also noticeable at the legal level. In 1975, Hungary signed the Helsinki Agreement and modified the 1949 Constitution. In 1983, a further constitutional amendment created the Council for Constitutional Law. Although it did not challenge the principle of unity of powers, which was at the heart of the communist legal system and meant that the law-maker was not subject to any controls, it was the first attempt to introduce some review of the constitutionality of norms. Commentators noted that this reform only enacted a mild version of the proposals which had been put forward at the time by Hungarian academics, thus indicating that significant constitutional reforms were already the subject of discussion in legal circles.[6]

---

[6] Gy Antalffy, 'Modification de la constitution en Hongrie' [1984] *Revue de Droit Hongrois* 5–19; I Kovács, 'Du droit public hongrois au droit constitutionnel socialiste hongrois' [1987] *Acta Juridica Academiae Scientiarum Hungaricae* 321–344; G Rácz, 'Einführung der Verfassungs-normenkontrolle in Ungarn' [1984] *Juristenzeitung*, 879; A Takács, 'Problems of the Protection of the Constitution, with Special Regards to the Constitutional Law Council' [1987] *Acta Juridica Academiae Scientiarum Hungaricae* 165–92.

The Hungarian Constitutional Court (*az alkotmánybíróság*), on which this study is focused, came into existence seven years later, in 1990 and arguably benefited from the earlier reflection which accompanied the creation of the Council for Constitutional Law. Although a number of aspects of the Constitutional Court were still awaiting refinement when it started working in January 1990, it was already clear that the Court was going to be powerful: during its first term under its president László Sólyom it was commonly described as the most powerful constitutional court in the world. This is due to its wide-ranging competences which mean that anyone can easily file a petition about virtually any constitutional issue, with subsequent proceedings being very informal. In addition to its impressive range of powers, the Court was staffed by a number of judges who wished to participate in the elaboration of a new legal system and the transition towards liberal democracy.

Not surprisingly in the early stages of the transition, constitutional case law was extremely abundant and dealt with numerous political-constitutional crises, many of which were major steps in the Hungarian transition. Inevitably, sensitive political questions were referred to the Court, such as, to name a few, the powers of the President of the Republic, the death penalty, the very controversial legislation on compensation for actions taken by the communist regime, freedom of speech and the status of the media, the restitution of Church property, the restitution of Jewish possessions and other property, freedom of enterprise, background checks for those in public office (lustration law), the controversial package of economic reforms (named as the Bokros package after the Minister of the Economy who drafted it), compensation for past injustices and the review of international treaties (with an eye on possible EU membership).[7]

Finally, the Hungarian Constitutional Court was one of the very first post-communist courts to translate some of its significant rulings into English, which was of course an extremely useful starting point for this study.[8] It has since then attracted a considerable amount of academic attention in the West—and in Hungary too—and it is now a relatively well-known Court.[9] In addition, the

---

[7] Most of the cases listed above were translated in L Sólyom and G Brunner (eds), *Constitutional Judiciary in a New Democracy: The Hungarian Constitutional Court* (Ann Arbor, University of Michigan Press, 2000).

[8] These translations were available in the Max Planck Institute of Comparative and Public International Law in Heidelberg where I started my bibliographical research for this project in December 1993.

[9] On the Hungarian Court in English, see, eg L Sólyom and G Brunner (eds), *Constitutional Judiciary in a New Democracy: The Hungarian Constitutional Court* (Ann Arbor, University of Michigan Press, 2000) and L Sólyom, 'The Hungarian Constitutional Court and Social Change' (1994) 19 *Yale Journal of International Law* 223. The first studies of the Court, outside Hungary, were however published in German. See, eg T Lábady, 'Über die Richtungen der Weiterentwicklung der Verfassungsgerichtsbarkeit' [1991] *Wichtigste Geseztgebungsakte Osteuropas, Monatashefte für Osteuropäisches Recht* 368 and G Brunner, 'Zweieinhalb Jahre ungarische Verfassungsgerichtsbarkeit' (1993) 32 *Der Staat* 287. See also I Pogany, 'Human Rights in Hungary' [1992] *International and Comparative Law Quarterly* 676 and 'Constitutional Reform in Central and Eastern Europe: Hungary's Transition to Democracy' (1993) 42 *International and Comparative Law Quarterly* 332.

judicial reasoning developed by the Constitutional Court, albeit extremely complex at first sight, was absolutely fascinating due to its creativity and it soon became clear that the Court was a very prolific importer of foreign law.

Human dignity was introduced in almost all post-communist constitutions in Central and Eastern Europe and it clearly had a very strong symbolic dimension.[10] In the Hungarian Constitution, it heads the chapter on fundamental rights and freedoms. Due to its openness, human dignity soon became a key argument for petitioners, as well as for constitutional judges and it was a central aspect of a large number of cases decided by the Hungarian Court. Moreover, a significant proportion of these cases were on fundamental issues which arguably determined the elaboration of the new legal system. They included cases on trade unions, on capital punishment, on the public prosecutors' powers and on compensation for actions by the former communist regime. In most of them, the human dignity (*az emberi méltóság*) argument played a decisive role in the Court's reasoning. It was a right used by the Court from the beginning, since its eighth ruling in 1990 and throughout the transition. The repeated reliance on human dignity enabled the Court to develop an elaborate construction of this right and to use it as the basis for a system of protection for the other new fundamental rights set out in the Constitution. Finally and crucially, the interpretation of human dignity in Hungarian case law is a clear example of law importation, the source of which can be identified as German constitutional law.

3. INVENTING A METHOD

In the early 1990s, post-communist studies were at an embryonic stage and it was not a subject commonly taught in (French) law schools. At that time, literature in the West was almost nonexistent. Gradually a few broad introductions to the new legal systems were published in some law journals, but even then they remained exceptional and only very general information could be gleaned after a meticulous comparative literature survey. Beyond that, virtually nothing specific on the detailed aspects of the elaboration of new legal systems after the collapse of communism was available in Western languages. In a language other than Hungarian, the first book on the Hungarian Court and its case law was an edited collection of cases, written in German, which came out in 1995.[11] In English, this precious book only came out in 2000, that is two years after I defended my PhD. The first foreign language monograph on the Hungarian

[10] C Dupré, 'Le droit à la dignité humaine, emblème de la transition constitutionnelle?' in K Tóth (ed), *System Transformation and Constitutional Development in Central and Eastern Europe* (Kecskemét, Károli Gáspár Reformed University Press, 1995), 51.

[11] L Sólyom and G Brunner (eds), *Verfassungsgerichtsbarkeit in Ungarn, Analysen und Entscheidungssammlung* (Baden-Baden, Nomos Verlag, 1995).

Constitutional Court, essentially concerned with its competences and the various remedies available before it, was published in German in 1998.[12] These volumes were very nicely complemented by a book marking the anniversary of the first nine years of constitutional adjudication in Hungary, edited by Gábor Halmai and published in Hungarian and English in 2000.[13]

Consequently as a result of the dearth of literature in a language other than Hungarian and in response to the novelty of this field and of the introduction of constitutional adjudication in Hungary, four priorities guided this research. Firstly, I decided to focus on one small aspect of the wider reality of building a new legal system, ie one single constitutional right. The lack of translations meant that in order to do this I had to learn Hungarian (at least enough to be able to read the constitutional rulings) because I was and remain convinced that this was the best way to understand the reasoning of the Court and to follow its development.

My second priority was not to read Hungarian constitutional case law in isolation from the context in which it was developed, so I regularly travelled to Budapest and spent time there. In this way I was able to meet those directly involved with the cases, mainly the judges themselves, as well as their assistants. I extended this narrow circle to include outsiders at the Court and met other people generally involved in the constitutional changes, mainly academics, and occasionally members of parliament and civil servants. Meetings and interviews with them would, as I first thought, provide me with the missing pieces of this gigantic jigsaw puzzle. Although I kept meeting my interlocutors at regular intervals, as the case law and my own research developed, I soon realised that I could not make any direct use of these interviews, however fascinating and rich in information they were. As a result, information gathered in this way is not directly used here, although it has often completed my understanding of cases. By extension, I was also keen to take into account the context of academic debates on these issues in Hungary itself. Regrettably, the greater part of my linguistic efforts had to focus on the cases, thus leaving aside the Hungarian literature published on the Constitutional Court. This was, however, compensated to some extent by my meetings with the key players involved and by the fact that a number of important articles written by Hungarian academics were also published in English, French or German.[14]

---

[12] G Spuller, *Das Verfassungsgericht der Republik Ungarn, Zuständigkeiten, Organisation, Verfahren, Stellung* (Frankfurt/Main, Peter Lang, 1998). Although it is not primarily concerned with the Court, the book *Righting Wrongs in Eastern Europe* by I Pogany (Manchester, Manchester University Press, 1997) contains extensive analysis of Hungarian constitutional case law, particularly on compensation issues.

[13] G Halmai (ed), *The Constitution Found? The First Nine Years of the Constitutional Review on Fundamental Rights* (Budapest, INDOK, 2000).

[14] See for instance the work of A Ádám, G Brunner, G Halmai, I Pogany, A Sajó and L Sólyom to name but a few (in alphabetical order) to which I refer throughout this study and which are listed in the Select Bibliography.

My third priority was to understand the preexisting socialist law and particularly the socialist concept of rights, which was necessary to comprehend the early stages of the transition. If its future was uncertain, its origins were perhaps easier to approach. Furthermore, as the transition was also arguably a reaction to communist ideology and its law, an understanding of these was a useful step towards elucidating key constitutional changes. Literature on communist law was (comparatively) more easily available and in particular the constitutions of the Hungarian People's Republic proved to be a rich source of information, although it had to be treated with caution.

Fourthly, observing constitutional case law over a period of time was crucial to understanding its developments. Hungarian constitutional judges are elected for a term of nine years, renewable once. The Court started functioning in January 1990, that is only a few months after the amended Constitution was adopted and before the election of the new parliament in Spring of that year. After some initial changes, the composition of the Court remained fairly stable during its first term of nine years, with the judges gradually leaving and being replaced by new ones towards the end of this period. The election of six last new judges in 1998 marked the end of what has been called 'the first Constitutional Court', as well as the end of the period of observation for this study.

Although this study is essentially legal and rooted in the comparison of law, it has also found sources of inspiration in other disciplines without drawing from them any particular methodology or conceptual framework. It was born from comparative research and reflection and it is centred on the analysis and the interpretation of human dignity case law.

This study rests on two levels of comparison. The first is spatial: as human dignity was imported from German constitutional case law, Hungarian cases could only be properly understood by undertaking a close comparison with the German model. The comparison with German law is drawn from the perspective of the Hungarian interpretation of human dignity: it highlights the similarities and questions the differences. This is achieved by referring alternately to the two systems in order to follow the various features of the interpretation of human dignity by the Hungarian Court. This close comparison confirms that the Hungarian Court imported German law. The comparison also makes it possible to measure the scope of this importation and to question the differences existing between the two interpretations of human dignity. The second level of comparison is temporal and involves considering the socialist conception of rights which had prevailed until 1989 and which in many ways was still lingering in the new legal system during the early years of transition. This comparison is based on the constitutional provisions themselves, as well as on various academic studies of the communist understanding of rights. The combination of these two levels of comparison shows that law importation corresponded to a strategy of constitutional adjudication set out by the Court to deal with the change of systems.

An essential aspect of this study is the adoption of a particular perspective of comparison that I call the importer's perspective.[15] This perspective considers the movement of law from the inside, ie from the point of view of those who import the law of a foreign country and it questions the reasons for importing that law. The differences existing between the original model and the form it takes after its importation are not used to assess that importation in terms of good/bad or success/failure; instead, they become a starting point to reflect on the logic and the scope of law importation. This perspective of comparison makes it possible to go beyond the usual dichotomy of differences/similarities put forward by many comparative legal studies. This perspective also takes into account the wider context in which this importation is taking place and which is often lacking from comparative studies.

4. LAW IMPORTATION

4.1. Context

One of the striking characteristics of the transformation process was that it was not left to the people of post-communist countries. Never before in history had the drafting of constitutions and the adoption of national legal systems attracted so much attention from outside the countries concerned. Indeed, the post-communist countries adopted their new constitutions, organised their general elections and planned their budgets in the spotlight of considerable international scrutiny.

International involvement was arguably as wide as it was deep, reaching almost every single aspect of the new institutions. Individual states which were closer to the former communist bloc for historical and geographical reasons were perhaps the first to be actively involved in the changes. Very soon afterwards, they were joined by international bodies including human rights, economic and military organisations. The European Union was shaken by the collapse of the COMECON countries which had previously determined its Eastern borders. As soon as it became certain that the tanks of the Soviet empire were not going to strike back, the question of the integration of the post-communist states into the European Union emerged.

As a result of the external involvement in the reconstruction of their post-communist systems, these countries were flooded with advice and guidance as to how to build the best democracy possible in the shortest time. An unprecedented movement of law accompanied the early years of the transitions and it is

---

[15] C Dupré, 'The Perspective of Law Importation: the Hungarian Experience' in A Harding and E Örücü (eds), *Comparative Law in the 21st Century* (The Hague, Kluwer Law International, 2002), 267.

argued in this book that this is best understood in terms of the export/import of law. The exporters were experts from the West: individual countries (European and American) and institutions (the European Union and the Council of Europe, as well as the International Monetary Fund, the World Bank and other economic and financial bodies). The importers were lawyers, politicians, academics and students who, in one way or another (having to write the Constitution, to enforce it or to interpret it) were involved in the construction of new liberal institutions. Arguably, law importation was one of the main characteristics of these transitions: in order to become liberal democracies, post-communist countries imported the institutions and the law of the democracies of the West.

4.2. Strategy

This study is anchored in the analysis of the importation of the right to human dignity by the Hungarian Constitutional Court. However, rights are not the only 'law' imported and the term 'law' has to be understood in its widest meaning as encompassing a rule, a principle, a standard of constitutionality, an institution (or some of its characteristics) or a method of adjudication, etc. Law importation only designates the law of a foreign country, that is the law of a legal system which does not bind the importer. In that way, as I explain in chapter 2, it differs from mechanisms of incorporation or reception of international law for the purpose of compliance with its requirements.

Arguably, law importation undertaken by constitutional judges is almost a paradox, in that their scope of adjudication is meant to be constrained by the Constitution, the supreme law of the land, which they have to protect and guarantee. However, the Hungarian Court has routinely relied on imported law as an adjudication strategy and this is particularly clear with the right to human dignity, as explained in chapter 3. As shown in chapter 4, the judges carefully chose a suitable foreign model. In this example, it was German constitutional law for the interpretation of human dignity. While being imported, that is incorporated in its new environment, the foreign law underwent a considerable transformation. Chapter 5 demonstrates that the scope of the transformation is such that it amounts to an instrumentalisation of the foreign model on the basis of which the Court developed its own, autonomous concept of human dignity. The aim of importing foreign law is highlighted by the particular use of the imported right, and as explained in chapter 6, this involved overcoming the communist legacy and introducing a new type of rights.

4.3. The Genesis of a New Legal System

The use of imported law in Hungarian case law differs from that of comparative law to which (constitutional) courts have sometimes referred, in that it is presented as the law of 'modern constitutions.' In other words, imported law is associated with norms universally shared and accepted. Chapter 7 argues that this discourse on law importation can be likened to a modern form of natural law and that it overlaps with a justification drawn from the globalisation of law. Used in this manner, imported law provided the new values and constitutional benchmarks which were needed to reconstruct the legal system on a liberal ideological basis. The conclusion reflects on the long-term vulnerability of law importation, which in the short term had proved a very powerful tool of transformation.

Anchored by choice and by necessity in the study of one apparently small aspect of the transitions from communism, this book is ultimately a reflection on the coming into existence of a new legal order and I hope that it will encourage further research on legal developments in post-communist countries and stimulate debate on the development of law.

PART I

IMPORTING WESTERN LAW

The aim of this first part is to highlight two features of the post-communist transitions: the huge ideological transformation and the great time pressure under which the changes were undertaken.

A principal motivation of the transitions in Central and Eastern European countries, as explained in chapter 1, was to abandon communist ideology and to endeavour to rebuild these states in accordance with the tenets of liberal democracy and free market economics. Communist ideology had underpinned these countries' foundations for over 50 years, determining not only their type of regime but also their very structure, the workings of their economies and of their law. By the late 1980s, the planned economy of many of them had deteriorated to the point of national bankruptcy, so when the ageing party leaders reluctantly resigned from power, the entire system—political, constitutional and economic—fell apart.

Post-communist countries faced the daunting challenge of having to reconstruct almost every single aspect of their systems in very little time in order to avoid more havoc and to preserve some stability. This task of reconstruction was not left to the post-communist countries alone but was accompanied by a massive involvement of the West, thus provoking an unprecedented movement of export/import of law and institutions. Western experts travelled to Central and Eastern Europe to provide advice and assistance with the design of a new set of liberal democratic institutions, as well as to make sure that the nascent democracies were complying with liberal requirements. Lawyers, politicians, intellectuals and, more generally, all those involved with the changes in post-communist countries were left with little choice other than to follow the Western model and their new legal systems were largely built on the basis of law imported from the West. This importation was not a mechanical or a passive response to Western exportation and chapter 2 endeavours to unravel and to explain this complex and unique process which was one of the major characteristics of post-communist transitions.

1

New Constitutions After Communism

———⟫•∘•⟪———

THE COLLAPSE OF communist regimes in Central Europe affected the entire former communist bloc and changes in one country were very much influenced by those taking place in another. The role of the Soviet Union and the *perestroika* conducted by Gorbachev were especially influential on the fate of its brother countries. Apart from the USSR, the domestic politics and events in countries such as Poland, Czechoslovakia or Hungary were also followed with great attention and were similarly influential on the politics of other communist states. Yet, each single state reacted differently and followed its own path of transformation. Attempting to group them into rigid categories according to the type of transition would require a number of over-simplifications and would be counterproductive.

Nevertheless, this chapter will highlight a number of features that the post-communist countries shared because they had all been subject to Soviet influence for the past half a century. The imposition of communism despite individual variations led to broadly similar patterns, which ultimately caused these regimes to collapse. The age of communist rulers is one shared feature that is commonly cited. Their permanence in power, once a sign of stability, began to be questioned by reformers within the party itself and by the population. Most of the leaders, clinging to power, failed to understand the need to introduce significant reforms and gradually lost touch with people's aspirations. The dire state of the economy was also a source of concern throughout the communist bloc. Even in the countries which had fared comparatively well, such as Hungary, it became clear that very substantial reforms were badly needed. The combination of deteriorating living conditions, the lack of basic freedoms (such as freedom to travel and freedom of expression) and resentment against leaders who were increasingly disconnected from reality, meant that the population could no longer put up with the regimes under which they lived. In a few countries, such as Poland and Hungary, this provoked the emergence of an embryonic civil society which gradually developed and gained self-confidence. In other countries, such as the German Democratic Republic, Romania and Czechoslovakia, sustained repression and political censorship would unleash violent reactions against the communist regimes.

This chapter focuses on the Hungarian transition and presents it in the broader context of post-communist transitions. In many ways, Hungary was probably the communist country that was the least unprepared for the changes: the Kádár regime had considerably softened its grip on the population and on the economy and this had led to a gradual emergence of some alternative political thinking and a more pronounced opening to the West. The collapse of the regime was nevertheless rapid, necessitating the quick replacement of the ideological foundations of the legal system and of the Constitution in particular.

1. FROM COMMUNISM TO LIBERAL DEMOCRACIES: IDEOLOGICAL TRANSITIONS

Communist regimes collapsed in fairly similar conditions, which can be summarised as simultaneity, time pressure and surprise. The post-communist transitions were simultaneous in two ways: first, they took place at the same time in the early 1990s and secondly, the collapse of the political regime brought with it the collapse of the economic system, with both then having to be rebuilt concurrently. The element of time pressure was due to the sheer size of the communist bloc: when it collapsed, it created a massive shock which prompted the need for a rapid response to secure some stability in the region, as well as some control. Finally, the element of surprise: the total collapse of communist regimes in Central and Eastern Europe was largely unexpected and unpredicted both in the West and in the East. The massive scale of these changes was also reflected at the ideological level.

1.1. A Great Transformation . . .

The ideological nature of transitions in Central of Eastern Europe distinguishes them from other democratic transitions elsewhere.[1] They were not about improving democracy or replacing the leaders of the communist parties, but, for the most part, were instead about introducing democracy on the basis of a diametrically opposed ideology, namely liberalism. Communism had shaped these states and had determined political and, importantly, economic decisions for the previous half century. As a result, post-communist countries faced a double process of transition: one at the economic level, the other at the political level. Unlike previous democratic transitions in Southern Europe or South America,

---

[1] On post-communist transitions, see, eg J Batt, S White and S Lewis (eds), *Developments in East European Politics* (Basingstoke, MacMillan Press, 1993); K v Beyme, *Systemwechsel in Osteuropa* (Frankfurt/Main, Suhrkamp, 1994); K Dawisha and B Parrott (eds), *The Consolidation of Democracy in East-Central Europe* (Cambridge, Cambridge University Press, 1997); P Kendé and A Smolnar (eds), *La Grande Secousse en Europe de l'Est, 1989–1990* (Paris, CNRS, 1990); JJ Linz and A Stepan, *Problems of Democratic Transition and Consolidation: Southern Europe, South America and Post-Communist Europe* (Baltimore, Johns Hopkins University Press, 1996); G Pridham and T Vanhaven (eds), *Democratization in Eastern Europe, Domestic and International Perspectives* (London, Routledge, 1994) and G Stokes, *The Walls Came Tumbling Down* (Oxford, Oxford University Press, 1993).

the countries of Central Europe did not enjoy the 'luxury' of an intermediate stage to consolidate democracy before liberalising their economies. Due to the poor state of communist economies, economic reforms were initiated at the same time as political reforms,[2] which made the transition processes extremely complex, as well as vulnerable.

The failure of the communist regimes also had very far-reaching repercussions on the law and more particularly on constitutions, as well as on the political institutions which had been shaped to comply with and to reflect communism. In most countries, these institutions were abolished after the end of communist rule and were replaced by new ones based on the principles of liberal democracy. These two sets of principles—communist and liberal democratic—could not have been more antagonistic and in fact, communism was to a great extent a reaction to the latter, which prevailed in what were called bourgeois democracies. The influence of ideology on law is visible at several levels. While communist constitutions organised their various political institutions according to the principle of unity of power, embodied by the one-chamber parliament rhetorically representing the unity of the workers, liberal constitutions are rooted in the principle of separation. Also, while before 1989 the communist party generally monopolised political representation and leadership, after 1989 pluralism of political parties became one of the compulsory elements of transformation. Additionally, the scope and the nature of constitutions is completely different in communist systems and in liberal ones. Under communism, constitutions were provisory in nature and aimed towards the establishment of a socialist society. As a result, they were amended as many times as necessary to reflect the progress accomplished towards that goal.[3] In contrast, the conventional wisdom about liberal constitutions is that they are the supreme law of the land, that they guarantee the stability of democracy and should therefore only be amended with great caution. Post-communist transitions had to undertake a great transformation, involving the creation of new institutions and anchoring them in a new set of principles, which were in total contrast to those which so far had prevailed. The scope of this transformation was probably increased due to the fact that the demise of communism was largely

---

[2] In many cases, as JJ Linz and A Stepan pointed out: 'Indeed, despite frequent obeisance to this simultaneity imperative, domestic and foreign activists and advisors often *privileged* economic change first. Solid research is just beginning on the question of sequence in post-Communist politics, but on theoretical (and now historical) grounds we believe that more consideration should have been given in post-Communist cases to the cost of neglecting political reforms, especially state reconstruction.' The authors warned against what they called the 'inverted legitimacy pyramid,' whereby the creation of a free market is expected to legitimate the creation of a democratic society: *Problems of Democratic Transition and Consolidation, Southern Europe, South America and Post-communist Europe* (Baltimore, Johns Hopkins University Press, 1996), 435.

[3] An illustration of this logic is provided by Gy Antalffy in relation to the Hungarian constitutional amendment of 1972: 'The 1972–73 amendments are related to the requirements of the future development and improvement of the socialist democracy. Their necessity is self-evident since the deepening of socialist democracy, its harmonisation with the development of society are requirements which regularly present themselves. It is the satisfaction of these requirements which leads to the amendment of legal rules at the highest level, as well as the constitution itself': 'Modification de la constitution en Hongrie' (1984) 1–2 *Revue de Droit Hongrois* 9, author's translation from French.

unexpected. As J Elster, C Offe and U K Preuß noted in their book, *Institutional Design in Post-communist Societies*:

> There is a somewhat ironical symmetry of cognitive failure: while the official doctrine of state socialism *included* a theory about the necessary eventual demise of democratic capitalism which has so far *not* occurred, social science in the West had no established theory about the crisis and breakdown of state socialism before it actually *did* occur.[4]

Economic and constitutional reforms were periodically implemented in the communist bloc. At the end of the 1980s, communist parties and, in particular, a younger and reform-minded generation of politicians within them, were aware of the need for changes, but at the time drastic reforms, such as rethinking the very basis of the regime, were not on the agenda. As a result, the scope of the change was largely unexpected and unpredicted by both the Western and the Eastern blocs. With the Cold War and especially after the Soviet repression of the Hungarian revolution in 1956 and the Prague Spring in 1968, both sides of the Iron Curtain had got used to the partition of Europe and it seemed that nothing would put an end to it. With the fall of the Berlin Wall, all the fundamental assumptions and realities on which Europe had been built since the War collapsed. The West became aware of what was happening in Central and Eastern Europe at the last minute. In Central and Eastern Europe, communist politicians, as well as their political opponents, who were mostly asking for moderate improvements, had not imagined that their entire system would founder. Their response was nevertheless extremely rapid.

1.2. . . . Taken in Giant Steps

Considering the intensity of the changes that were introduced, the breakdown of communism and its subsequent replacement by democratic institutions took place in a very short lapse of time. Indeed, it barely took more than a couple of years to change the basis on which communist countries had lived for over 40 years and that had been established after a long and destructive war. The complete dissolution of the communist bloc and the integration of most of the former communist countries into liberal international institutions took less than five years. The visible and indeed well-known beginning of the process was the official breach of the Berlin Wall on 9 November 1989. Yet, not even a year later, in August 1990, Hungary and Czechoslovakia decided at Visegrad to join their efforts with a view to becoming members of the European Union. On 3 October of that year, East Germany ceased to exist and was absorbed into the Federal Republic of Germany. A few months later, on 25 February 1991, the Warsaw Pact was officially dissolved. This was followed in June 1991 by the dissolution of COMECON and the year finished in December with the dissolution of the

---

[4] J Elster, UK Preuß and C Offe, *Institutional Design in Post-communist Societies: Rebuilding the Ship at Sea* (Cambridge, Cambridge University Press, 1998), 2.

Soviet Union itself. In 1993, the criteria for the admission of former communist countries into the European Union were decided at the Copenhagen summit. In 1997, the Barcelona summit decided to accept Poland, Hungary, the Czech Republic and Slovakia into NATO.

Although the European Union has not yet been enlarged to include some of the former communist countries, the rules for enlargement were set out at the Luxembourg summit in 1997. The Council of Europe is probably the international institution which was most rapidly joined by post-communist states. Finally, from 1990, when the Lithuanian Soviet Republic proclaimed its independence from the USSR, to October 1994 when the Republic of Macedonia was recognised as an independent state, several new states emerged out of the ruins of the Soviet Union and of the former Czechoslovakia and Yugoslavia.

The election of new governments and the subsequent adoptions of new constitutions took less than two years. The beginning of this process can be dated to September 1988 with the election of Gorbachev as the president of the Supreme Soviet of the Soviet Union. In June 1989 in Poland, Solidarity won the first partially free elections, in July Jaruzelski was elected to the presidency and a month later the Diet asked Mazowiecki to form a new government. On 10 November, Todor Jivkov resigned from his functions as leader of the Bulgarian communist party, which he had occupied since 1954 and on 10 December 1989, Gustav Husak resigned in Prague. 1989 ended with the theatrical execution of the Ceausescus on 25 December and with Petre Roman becoming the first post-communist prime minister in Romania. Also in that month, Vaclav Havel was elected to the presidency of the Czech Republic. In 1990, a round of the first free and pluralist legislative elections for nearly half a century was held in most of the communist bloc and completed the process of replacement of the leading élites. It then took about three more years to establish new constitutional mechanisms in these countries.

2. NEW CONSTITUTIONS UNDER THE RULE OF LAW

Hungary was the first state to amend its constitution on 23 October 1989. Two years later Romania enacted a new constitution on 21 November 1991. 1992 saw the adoption of new constitutions in Bulgaria (July), Slovakia (September), Poland (October) and in the Czech Republic (December). Post-communist constitutions are all different in the sense that they reflect national particularities and identity.[5]

---

[5] See, eg S Holmes, 'Conception of Democracy in the Draft Constitutions of Post-Communist Countries' in B Crawford (ed), *Markets, States and Democracy* (Boulder, Westview Press, 1995), 71–81; AED Howard (ed), *Constitution-making in Eastern Europe* (Washington, Woodrow Wilson Center Press, 1993); R Ludwikowski, 'Searching for a New Constitution in East Central Europe' [1991] *Syracuse Journal of International Law and Commerce* 90–170; E Stein, 'International Law in Internal Law: Toward Internationalization of Central-Eastern European Constitutions?' (1994) 88 *American Journal of International Law* 427–50.

Unlike the communist constitutions, which tended to follow a very similar pattern under Moscow's close supervision, post-communist constitutions adopted different formats and some of them were 'only' interim amendments, as in Poland and Hungary. However, the unity of these constitutions consisted in their adoption of the essential principles of liberal democracy which were proclaimed in most preambles and in the introductory chapters on 'general provisions'. The context in which post-communist transitions took place together with the massive involvement of the West led the Central and Eastern European countries to follow largely the model of Western democracies and to enshrine their principles in the new constitutions.

2.1. The Rule of Law as a Founding Principle

The perspective of the rule of law is that most frequently adopted to analyse the transitions in Central and Eastern Europe.[6] However, the exact meaning of this formula is not to be found in one specific legal system and tradition. The concept of the 'rule of law' exists under various names in different legal systems (notably '*État de droit*' or more frequently '*Rechtsstaat*', translated in Hungarian as '*jogállam*') and is understood differently. Post-communist countries are no exception.

The 'rule of law' is probably the phrase that best summarises the idealistic spirit of the post-communist constitutions. This principle, explicitly enshrined in a prominent position in all constitutions, signalled the end of communism and of one party rule. Furthermore, as a clear commitment to developing liberal democracies on the model of those existing in the West, the rule of law epitomised the aim of the transitions. All post-communist constitutions emphasised the importance of the rule of law. Article 2 of the 1997 Polish Constitution declares that: 'The Republic of Poland is a democratic state governed by law implementing the principles of social justice.'[7] Similarly, the preamble of the 1991 Bulgarian Constitution proclaims that:

> We, the national representatives of the Seventh Grand National Assembly, in our aspiration to express the will of the Bulgarian People . . . proclaim our resolve to create a democratic, law-governed and social state, for which we adopt the present constitution.[8]

---

[6] Among others see R Hoffman, J Marko, F Merli (eds), *Rechtsstaatichkeit in Europa* (Heidelberg, CF Müller Verlag, 1995), and J Priban and J Young (eds), *The Rule of Law in Central Europe* (Dartmouth, Ashgate Publishers, 1999). The rule of law is also one of the recurring themes of the *East European Constitutional Review*.

[7] Unless otherwise indicated, English translations of post-communist constitutions, except for the Hungarian Constitution, are extracted from the updated inserts in AP Blaustein and GH Flanz (eds), *Constitutions of the Countries of the World* (New York, Oceana Publications, 1977).

[8] The preamble of the Czech Constitution is phrased in a very similar way: 'We the citizens of the Czech Republic in Bohemia, Moravia and Silesia . . . resolved to abide by all the tested principles of a legal state adopt through our freely elected representatives this Constitution of the Czech Republic.'

Article 1 reinforces this declaration and indicates that Bulgaria is a republic with a parliamentary system of government. This is largely the same in all post-communist constitutions, with references to the rule of law being made at the beginning, in the preamble and in the very first articles. Perhaps one spontaneous and popular understanding of the rule of law was a negative one, that is to say that it was no longer the rule imposed by one man, one party or by the Soviet Union as had been the case until then. In other words, the 'rule of law' had a particularly strong appeal because it contained the hope (and promise) that individuals' lives were not to be dictated by the communist ideology. The rule of law marked the end of the nominal dictatorship of the proletariat, which had been claimed to be the organisational basis of these countries. Article 1 of the Slovak Constitution makes this explicit:

> The Slovak Republic is a democratic and sovereign state ruled by law. It is bound neither to an ideology nor to a religion.[9]

Furthermore, the rule of law had an implicit and yet obvious meaning: it was the law that people had demonstrated for and fought for. In other words, it was the law sought by the people instead of the law imposed by the Soviet Union. It was the law people could identify with and therefore accept. Although they disturbingly echo the socialist emphasis on popular sovereignty, most constitutions complement their provisions on the rule of law with declarations that sovereignty rests with the people. In some constitutions, the rule of law principle is associated with the 'rule of laws', as in Article 4.1 of the 1991 Bulgarian Constitution, which provides that:

> The Republic of Bulgaria is a state based on the rule of law. It is governed according to the constitution and the laws of the country.

Similarly, Article 1.3 of the 1991 Romanian Constitution expands the notion of the rule of law by reference to other principles and fundamental rights:

> Romania is a social and democratic *state of law* in which human dignity, the rights and liberties of citizens, the free development of the human personality, justice, and political pluralism represent supreme values and are guaranteed. (emphasis added)

Often the importance of the rule of law is linked to explicit claims of the supremacy of the Constitution, as in Article 5.1 of the Bulgarian Constitution, which declares that: 'The constitution is the supreme law, and no other law may contradict it.'[10]

---

[9] Its preamble, however, states that: 'We, the Slovak Nation, mindful of the political and cultural heritage of our ancestors and of hundreds of years' experience in the struggle for our national existence and our own statehood, in the spirit of Saint Cyril and Saint Metod, and the spiritual heritage of the legacy of the Great Moravian Empire, based on the natural right of nations to self-determination together with the members of the national minorities and ethnic groups living on the territory of the Slovak Republic, in the interest of lasting and peaceful cooperation with other democratic states. . . .'

[10] See also Art 8 of the 1997 Polish Constitution: 'The constitution is the supreme law of the Republic of Poland.'

Article 2.2 of the Slovak constitution develops this idea and provides that:

The state authorities shall act only on the basis of the Constitution and to the extent and in the manner which will be stipulated by law.

The rule of law reflected the aspirations of the new regimes to become democracies and it tied in with the idea (often expressed with it) of sovereignty: it was their own law that post-communist constitutions were committed to enact and to safeguard. The rule of law implied a hierarchy of norms at the top of which was the constitution, often described as the supreme law of the land. Furthermore, the principle of the rule of law was intended to ensure that state power was limited: it has to act under the rule of law, it has to respect the rights of individuals and a constitutional court was created to (among other things) settle disputes about the competences of state organs[11]. The rule of law principle was arguably the most important principle guiding the elaboration of new constitutions, but it was not of course the only principle. Political pluralism, ie multiparty democracy, together with free, equal and secret elections, although not the subject of this book, were essential in creating the possibility for liberal democracy.

2.2. Separation of Powers

The principle of the separation of powers is guaranteed by all post-communist constitutions. It is sometimes enshrined in a special provision,[12] but more often it flows from their general structure, together with explicit mention of the independence of the judiciary. In this context, the separation of powers can be understood as being the opposite of the principle of centralisation of powers, or unity of power, according to which, under communism, all the power was vested in a single party. Post-communist constitutions were structured following the division of state powers as known in Western liberal democracies: the legislature, the executive and the judiciary. The Bulgarian Constitution of 1991 clearly identified the various branches of power in Article 8: 'The power of the state is divided between a legislative, an executive, and a judicial branch.'

In addition, constitutions clearly spelled out the respective roles and powers of the executive and the legislature, often elected for a different duration (four to five years). One essential and novel element of the separation of powers was the creation of an independent judiciary. A separate section of post-communist con-

---

[11] Constitutions, and in particular those inaugurating a democratic era, are often characterised by some idealism. The new institutions, however, do not necessarily (nor immediately) function in such a perfect way. This is particularly true for post-communist institutions, the actual functioning of which has not always matched the spirit in which they were established.

[12] Such as Art 10.1 of the 1997 Polish Constitution which explicitly bases the system of government on 'the division and balance between the legislative power, the executive power and the judicial power'.

stitutions, variously labelled 'Judicial Power' (Slovakia and Czech Republic), 'Judicial Authority' (Romania), or 'Judicial Branch' (Bulgaria), set out guarantees for judges' independence and the extent of their power. Article 141 of the 1992 Slovak Constitution, introducing the section on the judiciary, illustrates the cautious drafting of such provisions:

1—The jurisdiction over the Slovak Republic is exercised by independent and impartial courts of justice.

2—The jurisdiction is separated from other state bodies on every level.

Furthermore, post-communist constitutions very generally asserted that judges are only subject to the laws. This was often complemented by guaranteeing that judges shall not be removed from office except in extraordinary instances provided by law, such as criminal convictions, and by providing for incompatibilities as in Article 82 of the Czech Constitution:

1—Judges are independent in the exercise of their function. Their impartiality must not be endangered by anyone.

2—A judge may not be recalled or transferred to another court against his will; exceptions arising, in particular, from disciplinary accountability shall be stated in a law.

3—The office of judge is not compatible with the office of the President of the Republic, a member of Parliament, or any other office in state administration. The law specifies which other activities are incompatible with the exercise of the judicial function.

This provision on the incompatibility between the office of a judge and that of president, far from stating the obvious, reveals that the independence of the post-communist judiciary was not taken for granted and was a very fragile principle. Some years later, S Bartole examined the various options explored for the creation of a post-communist judiciary and he observed that constitutional choices in relation to the judiciary still reflect the difficulty of overcoming past experiences.[13]

2.3. Individualism

Individualism was one of the most important innovations of the post-communist constitutions. Exacerbated by the monumental issue of the privatisation of the economy, which very soon became the priority of the transformation process, the new spirit of individualism extended far beyond enterprise and property. The state which so far had stretched to almost the entire economic, social and cultural life of the nation spectacularly withdrew from most of these in the early years of transition, thus making space for private individuals and private entrepreneurs.

[13] S Bartole, 'Organising the Judiciary in Central and Eastern Europe' (1998) 7 *Eastern European Constitutional Law Review* 62.

Often individualism is associated with, or indeed absorbed in the wider idea of liberalism. The distinction between the two terms is important. One of the aims of the post-communist constitutions was to transform the former People's Republics into liberal democracies and, more broadly, to embrace the political ideology of liberalism. However, at the constitutional level, this was translated by the priority given to individuals as opposed to society or the collectivity, as had been the case under socialist rule. Furthermore, words can be deceptive: that is, liberties and rights in post-communist constitutions are not entirely new, as socialist constitutions did acknowledge and list a number of them.[14] The novelty of the rights granted in the post-communist constitutions is that they are centred on individuals.[15] They are no longer rights exercised in the interest of socialism and that were granted by the party, in order to shape society and to comply with the objectives of the planned economy; instead, they are rights that individuals can exercise *against* the state. In other words, because they are intended to protect individuals and they allow them the liberty to conduct their lives in their own and various ways, they recognise and protect the existence of individuals.

It is true, however, that at the beginning of the transition, a lot of emphasis was put on free elections and free speech as being essential foundations of liberal democracies. Yet, as some lawyers ironically noticed, leaders of communist parties too had always been elected under the previous regime. In that context, the right to free speech was probably the real novelty after decades of state censorship. More importantly, the right to free speech can also be understood as a further and essential recognition of individuals who have a constitutionally protected right to demonstrate their existence and to voice their opinion against the state and the government's politics.

Significantly, most post-communist constitutions highlight their new conception of rights by enshrining human dignity. Despite the little academic attention that it has so far attracted,[16] human dignity, it is argued here, promotes the constitutional recognition of individuals who are at the centre of the new legal systems. Human dignity in the post-communist constitutions has (at least) a double dimension. First, human dignity, which is often referred to in the preamble or in the first article, sets out the aim or the promise of a better life that

---

[14] Most of these rights fell into the group of social rights and they were mainly implemented through state structures, such as workplace conditions and provisions. They included rights such as the right to work, a pension, a holiday and to education. See I Kovács, *Les libertés démocratiques de la République Populaire Hongroise* (Budapest, Association des Juristes Hongrois, 1953); J Halász, *Socialist Concept of Human Rights* (Budapest, Akadémiai Kiadó, 1966); M Katona Soltész (ed), *Human Rights in Today's Hungary* (Budapest, Mezon, 1990), and G Brunner (ed), *Before Reforms, Human Rights in the Warsaw Pact States, 1971–1988* (London, Hurst and Company, 1990). Chapter 6 will consider this issue in more detail.

[15] For a general survey of the new rights, see I Pogany (ed), *Human Rights in Eastern Europe* (Aldershot, Edward Elgar Publishing, 1995).

[16] See the conference held in Montpellier and organised by the European Commission for Democracy through Law on *The Principle of Respect for Human Dignity*, 2–6 July 1998 (Strasbourg, Council of Europe Publishing, 1999).

the new regimes will endeavour to make possible. For instance, the preamble of the Czech Constitution makes this particularly clear:

> We, the citizens of the Czech Republic in Bohemia, Moravia and Silesia at the time of the renewal of an independent Czech state, faithful to all the good traditions of the ancient statehood of the lands of the Czech Crown and the Czechoslovak statehood, *determined to build, protect, and develop the Czech Republic in the spirit of the inviolable values of human dignity and freedom* as a homeland to equal, free citizens . . . (emphasis added)

In this sense, it is the emblem of the transition, the compass that politicians should bear in mind when steering the process of transformation.[17] Human dignity has a very broad and open-ended nature: it is the founding value which ties in with related aspirations, such as freedom, peace, democracy or tolerance. Human dignity has not one single and precise definition, but it is part of a set of ideals that post-communist constitutions aimed to achieve at the start of the transitions. Human dignity reflects a certain type of society that post-communist states aim to foster and safeguard.[18] In this sense, human dignity clearly has a rhetorical dimension understood in the most positive way and on its own, it crystallises the aspirations and dreams which sustained the nascent political opposition before becoming one of the constitutional leitmotivs throughout the region. Significantly, *Equal Dignity* was the title of a book written by János Kis, a Hungarian philosopher who was one of the founders of the samizdat movement and who later became the chairman of the Alliance of Free Democrats.[19] The openness of the human dignity provision in post-communist constitutions sharply contrasts with the predetermined and imposed goal of communist constitutions, which were designed to foster the development of socialist society. Human dignity, which has no narrow and rigid definition, can also be understood as a sort of guarantee or reassurance that post-communist societies are free to decide for themselves.

Secondly, the other aspect of human dignity's double dimension is that it is often the first right mentioned at the beginning of new constitutional chapters on rights and freedoms.[20] This privileged position makes it the most important

---

[17] C Dupré, 'Le droit à la dignité humaine, emblème de la transition constitutionnelle?' in K Tóth, (ed), *System Transformation and Constitutional Development in Central and Eastern Europe* (Kecskemét, Károli Gáspár Reformed University Press, 1995), 51.

[18] The Romanian Constitution makes a more precise use of dignity in that it associates it with the nature of the state. Article 1.3 reads: 'Romania is a social and democratic state of law in which human dignity, the rights and liberties of citizens, the free development of human personality, justice and political pluralism represent the supreme values and are guaranteed.' Although it might not yet have any concrete implications, this provision is potentially an extremely powerful tool if put in the hands of (activist) judges.

[19] J Kis, *L'égale dignité* (Paris, Seuil, 1989).

[20] See, eg Art 12.1 of the Constitution of the Slovak Republic: 'The people are free and equal in their dignity and rights. The basic rights and freedoms are inalienable, imprescriptible and irreversible.' Also, Art 3 of the Ukrainian Constitution: '1—The human being, his or her life and health, honour and dignity, inviolability and security are recognised in Ukraine as the highest social values. 2—Human rights and freedoms and their guarantees determine the essence and the orientation of

of the fundamental rights. As in preambles, human dignity is an indication of the significance and scope of other constitutional rights. Again, human dignity is not narrowly defined but loosely associated with other rights or values, such as freedom or equality. The fact that the meaning of human dignity is kept open and is not qualified in any way seems to indicate that rights have no other function than to protect individuals and to foster their well-being. In this sense, human dignity embodies a dramatic conceptual U-turn: it breaks with the communist approach to rights, according to which the exercise of rights was linked to that of duties, with both of them being intended to develop communist society. The very strong emblematic nature of the human dignity provisions in post-communist constitutions clearly signals the beginning of a new era, where the relationship between the state and individuals is informed by a conceptual basis which radically differs from that prevailing under communism.

2.4. Constitutional Courts

These new fundamental principles are reflected and guaranteed in post-communist constitutions by the creation of a new set of institutions, even if some of them in fact operated with various degrees of success. The function of the Central Committee of the Communist Party, which formerly monopolised actual political power and was the main decision-making centre, was abolished. It was replaced by an executive power shared between a government and a president of the Republic, whose range of competences and mode of election or appointment varies from one constitution to another.[21] The judiciary was separated from governmental control and its independence is guaranteed in most constitutions. Ombudsmen have been created to tackle individual complaints about the state and the administration in specific areas. Constitutional courts, which were systematically introduced in post-communist constitutions, were by far the most important of the new institutions and they deserve more attention here because they are the hub of the newly introduced constitutional principles. They have also often played a generally positive role throughout the region in the transition towards liberal democracy.[22]

the state. The state is answerable to the individual for its activity. To affirm and ensure human rights and freedoms is the main duty of the state.'

[21] On the presidents, see R Taras (ed), *Post-communist Presidents* (Cambridge, Cambridge University Press, 1997).

[22] H Schwartz's book is one of the few substantial surveys of post-communist constitutional courts, *The Struggle for Constitutional Justice in Post-Communist Europe* (Chicago, Chicago University Press, 2000). Other studies include: the proceedings of a conference organised by the Venice Commission of Democracy through Law and held in Brioni, Croatia, 23–25 September 1995, *La Protection des Droits Fondamentaux par la Cour Constitutionnelle* (Strasbourg, Editions du Conseil de l'Europe, 1996); H Schwartz, 'The New East European Constitutional Courts' in AED Howard (ed), *Constitution-making in Eastern Europe* (Washington, Woodrow Wilson Centre Press, 1993), 163; G Brunner, 'Development of a Constitutional Judiciary in Eastern Europe' (1992) 6 *Review of Central and East European Law* 535 and G de Vergottini (ed), *Giustizia costituzionale e sviluppo democratico nei paesi dell'Europa centro-orientale* (Torino, G Giapichelli, 2000).

Constitutional courts created by post-communist constitutions were very generally modelled on the German court, with the exception of Romania which followed the French model and introduced a less powerful court. Formally, courts appear in a separate section of the new or revised constitutions (Hungary, Romania and Bulgaria), or they are included in the section on the judiciary (Poland, Czech Republic and Slovakia). They comprise between nine (Romania) and 15 (Czech Republic) judges whose appointment is the result of a careful political compromise in which all important state organs and political authorities are involved. For instance, in the Czech Republic, judges are appointed by the president of the Republic with the approval of the senate (Art 84). In Romania, three judges are appointed by the Senate, three by the president of the Republic, and three by the Chamber of Deputies. In Bulgaria, four judges are elected by the National Assembly, four by the president and four by 'a joint meeting of the justices of the Supreme Court of Appeals and the Supreme Administrative Court' (Art 147).

A further common feature of constitutional judges is their legal expertise: all constitutions require a law degree and professional experience of varied length (ten years in the Czech Republic, 15 years in Slovakia and Bulgaria and 18 years in Romania). In addition, some constitutions provide for a minimum age (40 years in Slovakia) and requirements of 'high professional and moral integrity' (Bulgaria, Art 147(3)) or that a judge be a 'citizen of good repute' (Czech Republic, Art 84(3)). The independence of constitutional courts is also set out and is guaranteed in various ways. One is the appointment of judges for a fixed term of office (10 years in the Czech Republic, nine years in Bulgaria and Romania, seven years in Slovakia). Another is that judges cannot, in principle, be removed from office before the end of their terms and the causes of resignation are listed in some constitutions (Bulgaria, Art 148). Furthermore, judges enjoy immunity similar to that of members of parliament. Finally, a set of strict incompatibilities ensures that judges cannot take part in the political life or leadership of their country while in office, although the new constitutions usually accept that judges can keep or develop 'scientific, educational, literal [*sic*] and artistic activities' (Slovakia, Art 137(2)).

The general function of constitutional courts is to protect the constitution and to control the constitutionality of laws, and their competences are wide-ranging. They generally encompass the control of the legality of elections (Slovakia, Bulgaria, Romania). In some cases courts can even ban political parties (Slovakia, Art 129(4), Romania, Art 144i), or check their constitutionality (Bulgaria, Art149(5), Czech Republic, Art 87(1)j). In addition, constitutional courts can settle disputes arising between state organs about the delimitation of their respective competences (Slovakia, Art 126, Bulgaria, Art 149(3), Czech Republic Arts 87(1)c, 87(2)b. More rarely, courts can decide on individual complaints about rights (Czech Republic, Art 87(1)d), or resulting from decisions taken by central or local administrative bodies (Slovakia, Art 127). Petitions to the constitutional courts can be lodged by political bodies, such as a qualified number of national representatives, the president, the government and higher courts. When individuals have access to the court, this is generally easy because there is often no requirement to have exhausted the remedies available in ordinary courts first. Constitutional courts' rulings are, in most cases, binding and cannot be appealed, although they can be overruled by an Act of parliament.[23] Constitutional courts in post-communist states are the perfect window into the workings and developments of transitions.

3. HUNGARY

This section aims to underline that, while Hungary followed its own path to liberal democracy, it shared a number of features with other post-communist states in transition. As the Hungarian transition has attracted quite a lot of academic attention and is now well documented and studied,[24] the purpose of this section is not to give an exhaustive account of the course of events, nor does it propose an original analysis of the Hungarian transformation. Its aim is to highlight the four main aspects of the constitutional developments necessary to understand the setting of law importation.

3.1. A Gradual Transformation

In Hungary, the change of regime is generally presented as being a gradual and peaceful process.[25] In 1988, the leadership of Kádár, who was then 76, was contested by a group of younger communists within the party. They soon became aware, from repeated street demonstrations, that the reforms that they were trying to implement did not meet the expectations of most Hungarians. At the same time, opposition movements were starting to emerge with the founding conference of the Hungarian Democratic Forum in 1987. In 1988 the League of Young Democrats (Fidesz) held its first congress in October and the Alliance of Free Democrats was established in November. Early in 1989 the Communist Party accepted the principle of multiparty democracy and agreed to debate

---

[23] On the procedures available before constitutional courts, see H Schwartz, *The Struggle for Constitutional Justice in Post-Communist Europe* (Chicago, University of Chicago Press, 2000), 22–48.

[24] See, eg P Kendé, 'Du réformisme communiste à la démocratie consolidée' in A Smolnar and P Kendé (eds), *La grande secousse en Europe de l'Est, 1989–1990* (Paris, CNRS, 1990), 67; I Pogany, 'Constitutional Reform in Central Eastern Europe' (1993) 42 *International and Comparative Law Quarterly* 333 and G Stokes, *The Walls Came Tumbling Down* (Oxford, Oxford University Press, 1993), 78–101.

[25] R Tökes, *Hungary's Negotiated Revolution, Economic Reforms, Social Change and Political Succession* (Cambridge, Cambridge University Press, 1996). See also N Swain, 'Hungary' in J Batt, P C Lewis and S White (eds), *Developments in Eastern European Politics* (London, Macmillan Press, 1994), 67–82. For Swain, 'Hungary's transition represented the quiet exhaustion of the communist economic system and its political masters' (at 66).

crucial issues with the opposition. Round Tables were then convened in March and started to meet in June 1989.[26] The negotiations were organised with a view to adopting a set of fundamental laws (called 'cardinal laws'), on the creation of a constitutional court, a president for Hungary, a new electoral system and on the introduction of criminal legislation.[27] At the end of the summer of 1989, the negotiators presented the communist parliament with a draft constitutional amendment which abolished most of the typical features of the communist constitution. It was understood that a brand new constitution would be adopted by the next parliament, due to be elected in the following spring. In the meantime, the members of parliament accepted the draft and proclaimed the amended constitution on 23 October 1989, the anniversary of the 1956 revolution.[28]

Hungary had been the first communist country to open its gates to the West and it was also the first state to abolish communism from its constitution.[29] In April 1990, the Hungarian Democratic Forum won the first free legislative elections and József Antall became the Prime Minister. Parliament elected Árpád Göncz, the founder of the Alliance of Free Democrats, a writer and former political prisoner, as the first President of the Republic of Hungary. This was only a starting point and numerous features of the new institutions, of the presidency and of the Constitutional Court in particular, were to be defined by practice, crisis and the personalities of those involved. This first government lasted until 1994 when it was replaced (as in many other post-communist countries) by former communists committed to a programme of economic liberalisation under the leadership of Gyula Horn (1994–98).

3.2. A Revolution under the Rule of Law

Hungary prides itself on being a nation of poets and lawyers. If the role of poetry in the transition remains to be studied, the role of law was primordial in that each step in this process, no matter how unexpected, was controlled and accompanied by a legal response. This probably ensured a particularly smooth process of change in which almost each development has been

---

[26] J Elster (ed), *The Roundtable Talks and the Breakdown of Communism* (Chicago, Chicago University Press, 1996).

[27] The most significant of these laws are presented by F Majoros in 'Ungarns neue Verfassungsordnung: die Genese einer neuen demokratischen Republik nach westlichen Maßstäben' (1990) 2 *OsteuropaRecht* 1

[28] On the 1989 constitutional amendment see G Halmai, 'Von der gelebten Verfassung bis zur Verfassungsstaatlichkeit in Ungarn' (1990) 1 *OsteuropaRecht*, 1 and I Pogany, 'Constitutional Reform in Central and Eastern Europe: Hungary's Transition to Democracy' (1993) 42 *International and Comparative Law Quarterly* 333.

[29] G Kilenyi, 'Ungarn schreitet in Richtung Rechtsstaatlichkeit' [1989] *Europäische Grundrechtszeitschrift* 513; L Kiss, 'Einige Fragen der Rechtsstaatlichleit der Rechtssetzung und des Rechtsquellsystems in der ungarischen Republik' [1989] *Deutsches Verwaltungsblatt* 918; L Kiss, 'Einige Fragen der Rechtsstaatlichkeit und Gesetzgebung in Ungarn' [1990] *OsteuropaRecht* 12.

matched by a legal innovation.[30] The establishment of 'a state under the rule of law' was the declared aim of the transition, as proclaimed by the preamble to the 1989 Constitution:

> In order to facilitate a peaceful political transition to a state under the rule of law, realising a multi-party system, a parliamentary democracy and a social market economy, the Parliament hereby establishes the text of the Constitution of the Republic of Hungary—until the adoption of the new Constitution of our country—as follows.

The 1989 amendment itself was written under the rule of law. This had a very clear procedural implication: the post-communist amendment was adopted in strict compliance with rules set out in the communist constitution. Substantially, however, its content was determined by the Round Table talks held over the summer of 1989. The understanding of the rule of law in the amendment encompasses elements similar to those in other post-communist constitutions and it is enshrined in a prominent position, in Article 2, which reads:

> 1—The Republic of Hungary shall be an independent, democratic state under the rule of law.
> 2—In the Republic of Hungary all power is vested in the people, who exercise their sovereignty through elected representatives and directly.
> 3—No activity of any organisation of society, state organ, or citizen may be directed at the acquisition or exercise by force of public authority, nor at its exclusive possession. Everyone has the right and obligation to resist such activities in a lawful manner.[31]

The first two sentences reflect common features of the rule of law in post-communist constitutions and in liberal democracies. The rule of law is associated with democracy and independence and it represents the law of the people. The third sentence is an explicit prohibition of a monopoly of power. Although the phrasing was general, referring to 'any organisation of society, state organ, or citizen', it was quite clearly designed to prevent the concentration of power in a single party and in its leader, as had been the case under communism. This

---

[30] The Constitutional Court coined the phrase 'revolution under the rule of law': 'The Court thinks that if revolutionary changes have been introduced by strictly keeping all constitutional guarantees then the system change may be considered to be of a morally higher value than the previous, similarly revolutionary changes, for by respecting constitutional limitations, it cannot repeat the crimes and injustices that revolutions usually understand, on the basis of their ideologies, to be justified and permissible': L Sólyom, in L Sólyom and G Brunner (eds), *Constitutional Judiciary in a New Democracy, The Hungarian Constitutional Court* (Ann Arbor, University of Michigan Press, 2000), 38.

[31] In the 1989 version, Art 2—1 read: 'The Republic of Hungary is an independent, democratic state under the rule of law where the values of bourgeois democracy and those of democratic socialism are equally realised.' This phrasing was changed by Act XL/1990 of 25 June. More generally, on the Hungarian transition to the rule of law, see B Schanda, 'Rechtsstaatlichkeit in Ungarn' in R Hofmann, J Marko, F Merli and E Wiederlein (eds), *Rechtsstaatlichkeit in Europa* (Heidelberg, CF Müller Verlag, 1995), 219, and G Kilenyi, 'Ungarn schreitet in Richtung Rechtsstaatlichkeit' [1989] *EuropäischeGrundrechtsZeitschrift* 513.

provision, which does not appear in other post-communist constitutions, perhaps reflected the general uncertainty of 1989, when it was drafted. That is, in the event of a communist victory at the 1990 general elections, this provision ensured that communists would not legally be able to exercise power as they used to (that is if they respected the Constitution). It may well be that this provision was included so as to try to make the return of communist rule impossible. As Article 2 shows, the rule of law was of paramount importance in the revised Hungarian constitution. László Sólyom, the first president of the Constitutional Court, highlighted this point in his introduction to a volume containing a selection of the Court's case law:

> Of all constitutional principles, the rule of law played a special, symbolic role: it represented the essence of the system change, being the watershed between the non-democratic, nonconstitutional, socialist system and the new constitutional democracy. Therefore the rule of law was the constitutional concept in the frame of which the differences in nature and characteristics of the system change could find their expression.[32]

The Hungarian Constitutional Court adopted a formalistic and neutral approach to the rule of law that focused on legal certainty and on the Constitution's coherence.[33] The concept of legal certainty was construed in a series of cases, notably in those on the so-called 'Bokros package', ie the body of statutes introducing substantial modification of the benefits system as part of a vigorous economic rationalisation plan. According to the Court, the very short time existing between the adoption of a statute and its implementation, a couple of weeks in many cases, infringed the principle of legal certainty in that it did not allow people time to adjust to the new situation. The Court therefore ruled that many of these reforms were unconstitutional, not so much because of their content, but because of the process of their implementation. Needless to say, this body of cases on economic reforms provoked numerous controversies and much outrage in political and academic circles.[34]

3.3. The Amended Constitution: an Interim Compromise

At the time of the transition, Hungary's Constitution was an amended version of the Constitution of 1949, which was modelled on the 1936 Soviet Constitution. It had been substantially amended on two occasions: in 1975 (Act I/1975) and in 1983 with the creation of the Council for Constitutional Law (Act II/1983).

---

[32] L Sólyom and G Brunner (eds), *Constitutional Judiciary in a New Democracy: The Hungarian Constitutional Court* (Ann Arbor, University of Michigan Press, 2000), 38.

[33] *Ibid*, 41.

[34] H Küpper, 'Der Sparkurs der Ungarischen Regierung auf dem Prüfstand des Verfassungsgerichts', [1994] *Recht im Ost und West* 101–12; A Sajó, 'How the Rule of Law Killed Hungarian Welfare Reform' [1996] *East European Constitutional Review* 31–42.

Unlike other post-communist countries which opted for the adoption of a completely new constitution to enshrine the change of regime, Hungary heavily amended its existing constitution.[35] The 1989 amendment was distinctive in two ways. First, it was understood that it would be only an interim constitution registering the concessions made by the ruling party during the Round Table negotiations and that it would be replaced by a new constitution to be adopted by the parliament due to be elected in spring 1990. The opposition came into power following the first democratic elections, but the new government, partly because parliament was already under extraordinary pressure to legislate at a great pace on more urgent matters, did not adopt a new constitution. It opted instead to introduce more constitutional amendments and between 1990 and 1994, no fewer than 10 amendments were adopted.[36]

Drafting and adopting a new constitutional text was part of the political programme of the subsequent coalition government elected in 1994 (the Alliance of the Free Democrats and the Hungarian Socialist Party). The process started with a proposal for the constitution drafted by the Alliance of Free Democrats and published in March 1995, soon followed by the Hungarian Socialist Party's proposal. A special parliamentary committee was appointed with a view to drafting a new constitution and parliament issued a moratorium on further constitutional amendments. In March 1996, a set of fundamental principles for the new constitution was published in newspapers and the consultation process began. However, the whole process ground to a halt, due to a failure to agree on the text of the constitution. In December 1996, another project was published by the government but it became clear that there was too little time left to finalise a draft constitution and to organise a referendum before the end of the second government. In July 1997, the government adopted a statute (LIX/1997) in order to introduce some necessary and uncontroversial changes, such as the clarification of the status of ministers and state secretaries and the introduction of a judicial system similar to that existing before the war. This led some commentators to think that Hungary was not going to have a new constitution.[37]

The second distinctive feature of the 1989 Constitution was that, although it incorporated major changes, it contained numerous provisions and, in particular, fundamental rights which were almost directly inherited from the communist constitution. Politically, the 1989 constitutional amendment established the framework in which liberal democracy could develop. The leadership of the Communist Party was abolished and the Constitution explicitly banned the monopolistic exercise of power by one party. In addition, the amendment created two new significant institutions, the president of the Republic and the

---

[35] Poland also opted for a constitutional amendment at first, but then did enact a new constitution in 1997.

[36] See A Masing, *Die Verfassung der Republik Ungarn, Zweisprachige Ausgabe* (Berlin, Arno Spitz, 1995).

[37] K Hiller, 'Neue Verfassung für Ungarn?' [1998] *Recht im Ost und West* 74 and A Arato, 'The Constitution-Making Endgame in Hungary' (1996) 5 *East European Constitutional Review* 31.

prime minister. Lawyers and commentators emphasised these major and significant changes and the amended Constitution was often presented as having left only one provision untouched, that stating that Budapest is the capital city of Hungary.[38] Technically, however, the post-communist Constitution was only an amended version of the previous constitution and its structure, which was itself modelled on the 1936 Soviet Constitution, was maintained. During the debates preparing the 1989 amendment, it was proposed that the importance of the new conception of rights should also be reflected in the structure and that they should appear at the beginning of the text. No agreement was reached on this issue though and the constitutional provisions were presented in the same order as they were in the communist constitution. Fundamental rights therefore remained at the end of the Constitution, in Chapter XII, after a section on 'the Office of the Public Prosecutor' and before a section on 'the Basic Principles of Elections'. Similarly, the provisions creating the new Constitutional Court were inserted in Article 32A, added after Article 32 on impeachment proceedings against the president of the Republic. This single article forms the whole chapter on the Constitutional Court. The same logic applied for other new institutions, such as the Parliamentary Commissioner for Civil Rights and the Parliamentary Commissioner for the Rights of National and Ethnic Minorities created by Article 32B, as well as the State Audit Office and the National Bank of Hungary created by Article 32C.

Significant and symbolic new rights such as human dignity were introduced in a prominent place at the head of the chapter on fundamental rights, in order to indicate clearly the change of values supporting the new legal system. Interestingly, these new rights were generally squeezed into the existing articles so as not to modify the numbering of the articles in the Constitution. This explains the use of letters to extend the existing provisions where needed. More importantly, the phrasing of a number of fundamental rights provisions was in many cases simply a polished version of the communist constitution.

As a result, between 1990 and 1998, the Constitutional Court was left with a Constitution which contained many ambiguities and a number of provisions inherited from the past. Arguably, the amended Constitution was not a very stable and reliable text, as it was always in the process of being amended and no clear political agreement seemed to emerge as to the substance of a new constitution. This uncertainty meant that the Court had to interpret a number of these provisions without having clear guidance from parliament. This was particularly true between January and May 1990, during which time the Court was in the singular position of being the first Western-type institution functioning under a communist government. The importation of the concept of human dignity started during those months with the ruling on trade unions' rights on

---

[38] On the amended Constitution, see G Brunner, 'Die neue Verfassung der ungarischen Republik, Entstehungsgeschichte und Grundprobleme' [1991] *Jahrbuch für Politik* 297; G Halmai, 'Einleitung zur Verfassungsrevision' [1990] *Jahrbuch für Öffentliches Recht* 235–57; G Halmai, 'Von der gelebten Verfassung bis zur Verfassungsstaatlichkeit in Ungarn' [1990] *OsteuropaRecht* 1–11.

23 April 1990 and it continued at a sustained pace until the end of the Court's first term. The Constitutional Court could have shied away from its role and waited for the adoption of a new constitution but instead, it seemed that the interim Constitution encouraged the Court to use its powers to the maximum of its creativity and capacity under Sólyom's presidency.

3.4. A Powerful Constitutional Court

In Hungary, the need for a constitutional court was discussed in academia in the early 1970s and proposals were made to introduce a constitutional law commission, but the 1972 constitutional amendment rejected this idea.[39] The Constitutional Law Council was introduced by a constitutional amendment in 1983.[40] In 1989, the constitutional amendment inserted the chapter on the Constitutional Court in a rather bizarre place within the Constitution, after Article 32 on the impeachment of the president of the Republic. Article 32/A provides that:

> 1—The Constitutional Court shall review the constitutionality of laws and perform the tasks assigned to its jurisdiction by statute.
> 2—The Constitutional Court shall annul the statutes or other legal norms that it finds to be unconstitutional.
> 3—Everyone has the right to initiate proceedings of the Constitutional Court in the cases specified by statute.[41]

This provision introduced two novelties that radically transformed the nature and task of the Council for Constitutional Law: the nullification power and the individual right of petition. The Hungarian Constitutional Court is perhaps the most powerful in the region in that it encompasses all the known powers of Western constitutional courts. Act XXXII 1989 on the Constitutional Court, enacted at the very beginning of the transition, did not quite picture the Court as it developed during its first years of functioning and a number of its features were adjusted subsequently.[42]

---

[39] Generally, on Hungarian socialist law, see S Kurtan (ed), *Vor der Wende: Politisches System, Gesellschaft und Reformen im Ungarn der 80. Jahre* (Wien, Studien zur Politik und Verwaltung, 1993) and I Zajtay, *Introduction à l'étude du droit hongrois* (Paris, Pédone, 1953).

[40] G Rácz, 'Einführung der Verfassungsnormenkontrolle in Ungarn' [1984] *Juristenzeitung* 879; G Rácz, 'L'introduction du contrôle constitutionnel des normes juridiques en Hongrie' [1985] *Revue de Droit Comparé* 136; A Takács, 'Problems of the Protection of the Constitution, with Special Regard to the Constitutional Law Council' (1987) 29 *Acta Juridica Academiae Scientiarum Hungaricae* 177.

[41] The other provisions were amended after 1989.

[42] This Act was among the first fundamental statutes, known as 'cardinal laws', adopted immediately before or after the amended Constitution, which focused on specific and crucial constitutional issues, such as the right of assembly and association, the right to strike, referenda, political parties and electoral reforms. See F Majoros, 'Ungarns neue Verfassungsordnung: die Genese einer neuen demokratischen Republik nach westlichen Maßtäben' [1990] *OsteuropaRecht* 1.

(a) *Constitutional Judges*

Originally, there were supposed to be 15 judges, but in 1994, the parliament brought this number down to 11. The first five judges were elected in 1989 by the then communist parliament and five other judges were elected by the new parliament in 1990. In 1993, Herczegh J left to join the International Court of Justice at the Hague and parliament had to elect two new judges. The election of constitutional judges is a delicate political process. A special parliamentary committee (the nomination committee) in which political parties are represented selects candidates. They are then heard by the legal committee and elected by parliament sitting in plenary session. Political tensions characterised the election of the first judges and it took seven years before all 11 judges were appointed in 1996 and 1997. Between 1990 and 1996, three judges left the Court: two joined other jurisdictions (the International Court of Justice and the Supreme Court of Hungary) and the third because he had reached the age of 70. In 1996, András Holló, who had been the general secretary of the Court since its creation, became a constitutional judge, and has acted since November 1998 as the vice-president of the Court. In 1997, two new judges joined the Court: János Németh, who became its president in November 1998, and István Bagi. The new Court was completed with the departure of the 'first' judges in 1998 and the election of five judges that year to replace them and of three judges in 1999.

Judges are elected for a term of nine years, which can be renewed once. There is a minimum age limit (45 years), and a maximum age limit (70 years). The function of a judge ceases on reaching the age limit, in the event of an incompatibility, death, resignation, expulsion or discharge of their functions. Strict rules of incompatibilities with political offices, together with the requirements of legal qualification (university professorship or a doctorate in legal and political sciences) and experience (at least 20 years of legal practice) created a court composed of a majority of law professors.

(b) *Competences of the Court*

In addition to impeachment of the president of the Republic and review of the constitutionality of local and national referenda, the Constitutional Court has a general function of review of the constitutionality of legal norms, which is broken down into different types of proceedings under article 1 of Act XXXII 1989 on the Constitutional Court.

> The competence of the Constitutional Court shall comprise the following:
> a. the preliminary examination of the unconstitutionality of Bills, of Acts of Parliament, enacted but not yet promulgated, of the Standing Order of Parliament and of international treaties;

b. the examination of the unconstitutionality of legal rules as well as other means of state control;

c. the examination of the conformity of legal rules as well as other legal means of state control with international treaties;

d. the adjudication of constitutional complaints submitted because of alleged violations of constitutional rights;

e. the elimination of unconstitutionality manifesting itself in omission;

f. the elimination of a conflict in connection with the sphere of authority arising between several state organs (bodies), or self-governments;

g. the interpretation of the provisions of the Constitution;

h. proceedings in all cases referred to its competence by an Act.

The competence of the Court, as it was exercised during its first term, slightly differed from the above provisions.[43] The Court had to clarify some of them and narrowed down their scope. This was the case on the preventive review of constitutionality. Due to the imprecise phrasing of the Act on the Constitutional Court, judges had to specify that they would consider a Bill only in its final stage, ie just before promulgation (case 16/1991). Similarly, unconstitutional omission was understood by the Court in a fairly restrictive manner and the Court found an omission only if there was a specific statutory requirement to adopt a norm and failure to do so had created an unconstitutional situation. Although anyone, including the Court itself, can lodge a petition of unconstitutional omission, only about 17 cases a year on average were decided on this ground. Finally, the abstract interpretation of the constitution was restricted by the Court to the direct interpretation of a specific constitutional provision, so as to avoid any overlap with legislative power, as well as an overt politicisation of cases heard on this ground. Consequently, only 19 cases were decided on this basis between 1990 and 1996.

Some competences of the Court were hardly used by petitioners. This was due to a combination of the novelty of such proceedings (and the related ignorance of them of most people) and the fact that, in some cases, the same outcome could be achieved by much easier means. For instance, petitioners very rarely made use of judicial referral to the Constitutional Court by which means parties at a trial, or the judge himself, can ask the Court to review the constitutionality of a contested legal provision. The remedy of 'constitutional complaint,' which on paper appeared to be a potentially attractive remedy for violation of constitutional rights, was in practice rarely used (102 times between 1990 and 1996). This was due to the fact that the general posterior review of the constitutionality of norms made it almost redundant.

---

[43] On the Hungarian Court see the study of G Spuller, *Das Verfassungsgericht der Republik Ungarn, Zuständigkeiten, Organisation, Verfahren, Stellung* (Frankfurt/Main, Peter Lang, 1998) and the introduction to L Sólyom and G Brunner (eds), *Verfassungsgerichtsbarkeit in Ungarn, Analysen und Entscheidungssammlungen, 1990–1993* (Baden-Baden, Nomos Verlag, 1995). See also L Sólyom, 'Aufbau und dogmatische Fundierung der ungarischen Verfassungsgerichtsbarkeit' [2000] *Osteuroparecht*, 231. In English, see L Sólyom and G Brunner (eds), *Constitutional Judiciary in a New Democracy: The Hungarian Constitutional Court* (Ann Arbor, University of Michigan Press, 2000).

The posterior review of norms was by far the most significant remedy before the Court. It is designed in extremely broad terms with no particular procedural requirement, with the result that anyone can lodge a petition on any question. It was thought that this procedure, known as *'actio popularis'*, would play an important role in the transition process, even though the predictably high number of cases brought on this ground could have clogged up the Court. Herman Schwartz aptly summarised why:

> According to one observer, the *actio popularis* was adopted because the opposition was afraid that all high state offices would be filled by former Communists, so they wanted to open up the possibility that ordinary citizens can get to the Court easily. Others suggest that it was to enable the Court to review the entire legal system, because the more people had access, the more issues would get to the Court. According to president Sólyom and other justices, it proved immensely important in the Court's first years.[44]

The posterior review of norms led to the majority of cases decided by the Court: 3,170 between 1990 and 1996. This, however, represented only part of the total number of claims submitted to the Court, which filtered most of the others out, thus managing to avoid a counter-productive caseload. Almost all cases decided on human dignity issues (which will be considered in Part II) were brought under the posterior review of constitutionality. Georg Brunner, a long-time observer of socialist and then post-socialist systems, perceptively described the first Constitutional Court in the following terms:

> It is no exaggeration to state that at present the Hungarian Constitutional Court (*Alkótmánybíróság*) is the most powerful and perhaps even the most active specimen of its kind in the world. . . . This is especially true in the formative period of constitutionalism and the rule of law. Therefore, it is not surprising that the Constitutional Court has in no time become one of the key actors on the stage of Hungarian constitutional life whose performances are thoroughly watched and hotly debated, and both criticised and praised by the general public.[45]

4. CONCLUSION

Writing and adopting new constitutions was only a first step—however fundamental—in the process of elaborating new legal systems. The mere task of drafting new constitutions in such difficult circumstances and within less than a year of initial governmental change in most cases was gigantic. This was even more remarkable, considering that the changes and their scope were not predicted and that, despite a nascent opposition during the 1980s, no alternative project for a constitution was available.

---

[44] H Schwartz, *The Struggle for Constitutional Justice in Post-communist Europe* (Chicago, University of Chicago Press, 2000), 80.

[45] G Brunner, 'Development of a Constitutional Judiciary in Eastern Europe' (1992) 6 *Review of Central and East European Law* 539–40.

The full meaning of the post-communist constitutions took longer to develop. In some cases, as in Poland, Slovakia and to a lesser extent Hungary, further constitutional amendments were needed. In other cases, especially as far as presidents and prime ministers were concerned, personalities and political crises further shaped the constitutions. The difficulty facing post-communist constitutions was twofold. They introduced novel rules, rights and institutions for which a new meaning had to be developed. At the same time, these constitutions were not enacted in a *tabula rasa* situation: they had to deal with the legacy of 40 years (that is more than a generation) of imposed communism. As a result, the main challenge of post-communist transitions was to elaborate a meaning for all these new constitutional words and concepts; more precisely, the challenge was to give these words (which were often similar, eg parliament) a different meaning (and corresponding practice) from that which had prevailed under communism. Law importation was largely used to develop such new constitutional significations.

2

The Importation of Law

————⋙◦⋘————

THE COLLAPSE OF the communist system triggered an unprecedented movement of law between Western democracies and the nascent liberal democracies in Central and Eastern Europe. Although the movement of law beyond
the borders of national legal systems is not a new phenomenon, over the past
decade it has considerably increased, provoking debate about the possible emergence of a *ius commune* in Europe. In post-communist countries, the influence
of foreign law on the design of new constitutions, as well as ordinary legislation,
is a well-known fact, but in its nature and its scope it seems to differ from the
circulation of norms beyond national borders observed before the collapse
of communism. The existing models and explanations of this movement of
law cannot, therefore, be satisfactorily applied to legal developments in post-
communist transitions.

This chapter proposes a novel approach to the movement of law, considering
it in terms of export/import. It focuses specifically on law importation, as a
means to understand and analyse the influence of foreign law on the elaboration
of new legal systems in post-communist countries. In contrast with other perspectives proposed to explain the movement of law beyond national borders,
the perspective of law importation takes the specific context of transition into
account and emphasises the role of the importers of law.

1. MOVEMENT OF LAW BEYOND NATIONAL BORDERS

Legal systems have never developed in complete isolation from each other. In
particular, law-makers have generally considered solutions adopted in other
countries before drafting their own legislation. Although the process of borrowing norms to develop a new law is ancient, its study is comparatively recent.
A Watson, who coined the phrase 'legal transplant' in 1974, opened the way
and, more recently, a younger generation of scholars has observed the process
at various levels and proposed explanations for the circulation of norms which,
it seems, is increasing.

1.1. 'Legal Transplants'

'Legal transplants', since the publication of Alan Watson's book in 1974, seems to have become the preferred term of art to refer to the influences of foreign law on a specific legal system. The content of this seminal book is (too) often reduced to these two words that have been widely used by Watson's successors, without clearly articulating their signification.

Watson himself gave a short and simple definition of legal transplants, as 'the moving of a rule or a system of law from one country to another, or from one people to another'.[1] The author did not seem to grant particular importance to the phrase he chose for the title of his book. Instead, he often used alternative words, such as 'influences', 'movement of law' or even 'reception'. Concerning more specific terminology, Watson made it clear that it was probably too early to use different words and he concluded his fourth chapter, entitled 'Introduction to Legal Transplants', by noting that:

> Actually, receptions and transplants come in all shapes and sizes. One might think also of an imposed reception, solicited imposition, penetration, infiltration, crypto-reception, inoculation and so on, and it would be perfectly possible to distinguish these and classify them systematically. Again we are faced with a choice. There is, I suggest, no point in elaborating a detailed classification of borrowing until individual instances have been examined to see what they reveal.[2]

Watson's main concern in this book was to propose an approach to comparative law, as the introductory and concluding chapters show.[3] He defined comparative law as 'the study of relations of one legal system and its rules with another legal system'. These, he claimed 'are only discoverable by a study of History'. Comparative law is legal history or, more accurately 'the study of historical relationships' or influences.[4] It is in order to illustrate and make these historical relationships visible that Watson coined the famous phrase 'legal transplants'.

Watson's definition of legal transplants is both narrow and loose. It is narrow because he is mainly concerned with legal history and his examples are mainly inspired by the various influences exercised by Roman law on different peoples. In addition to this historical perspective, Watson only considered the area of private law. Implicitly, he seemed to endorse SFC Milsom's opinion, expressed in 1969, which he quoted at the beginning of his book:

---

[1] A Watson, *Legal Transplants* (Edinburgh, Scottish Academic Press, 1974), 21. This book was reedited in 1993. Watson's more recent publications on this topic include 'From Legal Transplants to Legal Formants' [1995] *American Journal of International and Comparative Law* 469 and 'Aspects of Reception of Law' [1996] *American Journal of Comparative Law* 333.

[2] Watson, *Legal Transplants*, above n 1, at 30.

[3] For a more detailed explanation of Watson's theory on comparative law, see the clear article by W Ewald, 'Comparative Jurisprudence (II): The Logic of Legal Transplants' [1995] *American Journal of International and Comparative Law* 489.

[4] Watson, *Legal Transplants*, above n 1, at 6.

Societies largely invent their constitutions, their political and administrative systems, even in these days their economies; but their private law is always taken from others.[5]

Furthermore, Watson only considered *voluntary* legal transplants. In his view, legal transplants take place in connection with a substantial movement of population. Here Watson distinguished three categories, which he did not illustrate directly with examples:

> First, when a people moves into a different territory where there is no comparable civilisation, and takes its law with it. Secondly, when a people moves into a different territory where there is a comparable civilisation and takes its law with it. Thirdly, when a people voluntarily accepts a large part of another people or peoples.[6]

This quotation underlines a crucial aspect of Watson's definition, which is too often forgotten, namely that legal transplants are associated with *large movements of population* or more precisely people, taking their law with them. These elements considerably reduce the scope of legal transplants to voluntary and historical influences in the area of private law only and in connection with population movements.

At the same time, however, Watson put forward a set of 12 propositions in order to refine the notion of legal transplants, most of which are phrased in very loose terms.[7] Today, the first three propositions are easy to understand and difficult to disagree with: transplanting is extremely common, it is in fact the 'most fertile source of development' and 'to a truly astounding degree, law is rooted in the past'.[8] The fourth proposition is that transplanting rules, even from a different kind of system, is 'socially easy'. Fifth, transplants almost always involve a change in the law mainly due to factors such as climate, economic conditions and religious outlook. Sixth, private law is particularly prone to legal transplants. Seventh, the time of transplanting usually coincides with the reform of the particular transplanted rule. Eighth, transplanting is possible even when the receiving society is 'much less advanced materially and culturally'. Ninth, even when totally misunderstood, foreign law does exercise an influence. Tenth, the more authoritative a particular foreign model, the more likely it is that it will be transplanted. Eleventh, reliance on legal transplants depends on the inventiveness of a nation, that is, the more inventive it is, the less it needs to rely on foreign influences to develop its law. Twelfth, Watson compared law to technology, in that inventions in both have benefits for more people than just those who introduced them.

---

[5] SFC Milsom, *Historical Foundations of the Common Law*, (London, 1969), ix, as quoted by Watson, *Legal Transplants*, above n 1, at 8.

[6] *Ibid* at 29–30.

[7] Here, I am largely following Watson's ch. 16 on 'Some General Reflections'.

[8] W Ewald underlined the originality of Watson's groundbreaking approach: 'For Watson's theory flies in the face of some of the most treasured preconceptions of modern legal thought. Since the time of Montesquieu it has frequently been assumed, sometimes explicitly, more often tacitly, that the law changes in response to forces *external* to law': 'Comparative Jurisprudence (II): The Logic of Legal Transplants' [1995] *American Journal of International and Comparative Law* 490.

However interesting and novel at the time of its publication, Watson's definition of legal transplants is arguably not very helpful for understanding the elaboration of post-communist legal systems, for three main reasons. First, the elaboration of post-communist legal systems largely modelled on Western law did not follow from a large movement of a population or a people. It is true that numerous Western 'experts' travelled to Eastern Europe, but for most of them these were short trips and they soon returned to their home countries. Western populations did not massively go to post-communist countries and did not settle down there *en masse*. As a result and strictly speaking, the influence exercised by the West on the elaboration of new legal systems does not fit with Watson's definition of legal transplants. Secondly, the long-term approach, ie the historical perspective that he adopts, despite having its advantages, does not help much with understanding post-communist transitions, which have happened too recently to allow a long-term perspective to be taken yet. Furthermore, because of this perspective, Watson's approach does not aid understanding of the detailed mechanism of transition; in particular, it disregards the role played by individual actors who transplant foreign rules into their own legal systems. Thirdly, post-communist constitutions were largely drafted following Western models. This quite clearly contradicts a (then) common assumption that public law and, in particular constitutional rules, can only be the result of national inventiveness and that, as a result, they are not subject to foreign influences, or are subject to them to a lesser extent than private law.

These points, however, do not tarnish the attractiveness of Watson's analysis, which can be considered as a starting point for understanding post-communist transitions. In fact, 'legal transplants' has now become a generic phrase to refer broadly to the influence of foreign law on the drafting of new legislation and to the movement of law beyond national borders.[9] Authors who employ this popular phrase, however, seem to prefer using it as a convenient expression rather than in the strict context developed by Watson.[10] Gianmaria Ajani has studied the elaboration of post-communist legislation, especially in the field of civil and commercial law and he has largely endorsed Watson's phrase.[11] In an article published in English,[12] Ajani dealt with terminological considerations in his first footnote. Although he made it clear that he did

---

[9] P Legrand expressed the view that legal transplants did not take place in the context of post-communist legal systems, in 'The Impossibility of Legal Transplants' [1997] *Maastricht Journal of European and Comparative Law* 111. This opinion, however, seems to be based on Legrand's concept of law contrasting with that of Watson, rather than on empirical observation of post-communist legislation and constitutions.

[10] See for instance TW Waelde and J Gunderson, 'Legislative Reforms in Transition Economies: Western Transplants, a Short-Cut to Market Economic Status' [1994] *International and Comparative Law Quarterly* 345.

[11] See his book *Diritto dell'Europa Centrale* (Torino, Utet, 1996) which offers a substantial survey of the new *legislation* in this region, as well as of the legal systems as they were before the fall of communism.

[12] G Ajani, 'By Chance and Prestige: Legal Transplants in Russia and Eastern Europe' [1995] *American Journal of International and Comparative Law* 93.

not intend to 'enter the terminological debate,' he differentiated between two aspects:

> This is not to say that I do not consider the differences between a set of more general terms (such as borrowing or influence) that indicate the *process* of legal change, and narrower concepts (such as legal transplants or reception), that refer to the *result* of a circulation.[13]

He reminded the reader that Watson himself was careful not to be too rigid in his terminology and also accepted a variety of words. Ajani, despite following this general approach, was more specific in relation to the elaboration of post-communist legislation. He noted that Russia and other countries in Central Europe elaborated their law in connection with legal developments in Western Europe and that, as a result, most of them had been categorised together with the Germanic legal systems. Ajani also complemented the notion of legal transplants by adding another metaphor, namely that of supply and demand of institutional models. However, he did not elaborate on this potentially interesting idea. Rather, he seemed to use it in order to structure his description by identifying a 'demand of new models of civil and commercial law' which was met by 'the supply of new models' emanating essentially from international organisations and the European Union (EU) through the European Agreements. Sadly, the most interesting element in this metaphorical description is not explored: Ajani did not indicate the price to be paid for the new institutional models. Moreover, he provided only a limited explanation of the reason for choosing a model, stating that it depends both on prestige and on chance. Although these criteria also apply to most commercial transactions, they do not seem to provide a sufficient explanation for the specific process taking place in Central Europe.

1.2. 'Transjudicial Communication'

This phrase is borrowed from the title of an article published by Anne-Marie Slaughter in 1994 in which she noted that 'courts are talking to one another all over the world'. She proceeded to try to elaborate a typology of what she calls 'transjudicial communication'.[14] According to her typology, communication between courts can be horizontal, vertical or mixed (horizontal and vertical). Horizontal communication takes place between courts having the same status, ie between national courts or between supranational courts. Vertical communication takes place between supranational courts and national courts. The example given here is that of the European Court of Justice and national courts, or of the European Court of Human Rights and national courts. This is completed by three types of conversation reflecting the 'degree of reciprocal

---

[13] *Ibid.*
[14] A-M Slaughter, 'A Typology of Transjudicial Communication' [1994] *University of Richmond Law Review* 99–137.

engagement': monologue, direct dialogue and intermediated dialogue. 'Direct dialogue' represents 'communication between two courts, that is effectively initiated by one and responded to by the other'.[15] Such dialogue takes place, for instance, between national courts and the European Court of Justice. 'Monologue' often corresponds to horizontal communication in which a court mainly speaks to the litigants and is not engaged in an exchange with foreign courts, here the example provided is that of the American Supreme Court. Finally, 'intermediated dialogue' refers to national courts whose communication is encouraged by a supranational court, such as the European Court of Human Rights, which is 'self-consciously undertaking this dissemination, with a specific audience of national courts . . . in mind'.[16] Within the EU, this phenomenon has also been observed by other scholars, of which the best known is probably J Weiler.[17]

Arguably, however, the enthusiasm of these authors is inversely proportional to the frequency of judicial communication. Remarkably, very few examples of such communication are provided in scholarly studies which seem to be elaborated on the basis of (so far) exceptional rulings. American scholars, like Mary A Glendon, have noted the lack of such communication on the part of the Supreme Court, whose case law seems to develop in complete isolation from other national courts.[18]

In civil law countries, national courts make very scarce use of comparative law in support of their reasoning. In other words, national courts rarely make specific references to legal situations or cases decided abroad in order to solve a given problem.[19] This does not necessarily mean that courts do not consider the comparative dimension of a particular issue. However, comparative references are seldom made explicit in cases. The use of comparative law which might have inspired judges for a particular ruling can often only be revealed by reading between the lines.[20] Sometimes, the source of inspiration can become apparent in the course of (often confidential) interviews with judges. So far, national judges have not decided cases mainly on the basis of solutions or reasoning developed abroad by other domestic courts.

---

[15] A-M Slaughter, 'A Typology of Transjudicial Communication' [1994] *University of Richmond Law Review*, 112.

[16] *Ibid*, 113.

[17] J Weiler, 'A Quiet Revolution: The European Court of Justice and its Interlocutors' [1994] *Comparative Political Studies* 510. See also P Pescatore, 'Le Recours dans la Jurisprudence de la Cour de Justice des Communautés Européennes à des Normes Déduites de la Comparaison des Droits des Etats Membres' [1980] *Revue Internationale de Droit Comparé* 337; J Polakiewicz, 'The European Human Rights Convention in Domestic Law' [1991] *Human Rights Law Review* 125.

[18] MA Glendon, *Rights Talk: The Empoverishment of Political Discourse* (New York, The Free Press, 1991). In particular, see her ch. 6 on 'The Insularity of Rights'.

[19] The situation is different for courts in common law countries, which tend to refer to each other more often, for inspiration or enlightenment in some circumstances, due to their belonging to the same 'family'.

[20] This is another point of contrast with common law courts, where judges in the higher courts generally provide lengthy and detailed explanations for their reasoning. Civil law judgments are much shorter and, at their worst, cryptic.

Constitutional courts are no exception and do not commonly import foreign law into their case law. This follows from two well-established principles. One is that the constitution is the supreme law of the land to which no other body of law is superior. Some constitutions grant international law a status that is sometimes higher than the constitution, but no constitution provides that the law of other countries shall have an equal or higher ranking than the constitution itself. This is combined with the principle of separation of powers, according to which constitutional courts are strictly prohibited from acting as legislators. A consequence of this principle is that whereas legislators are free to use any arguments, including foreign and comparative law, constitutional courts are meant to refer only to provisions of positive constitutional law.[21] In practice, most constitutional courts go beyond this strict framework and rely on general principles. These principles are, however, usually connected to historical traditions, doctrinal writings or even case law which developed within national boundaries. In so doing, courts are often suspected of and heavily criticised for usurping the role of the law-maker.

This is not to say that some constitutional judges are not curious about legal developments taking place in other countries and well informed about them. Although this is quite difficult to assess and even more difficult to generalise, some evidence of comparative reflection can be seen in the preparatory work for judicial decisions of which academics might catch a glimpse in the occasional references made by former judges, advisers, or lawyers (when they are involved in the process of constitutional adjudication). Generally, the influences that foreign law can potentially exercise on judicial reasoning in a particular case are not visible.

When courts do refer to foreign law and relevant case law, it is generally when the resolution of the problem before them requires them to consider specific aspects of foreign law. Such instances have increased with the trend towards the internationalisation of economics and related law. As RJ Miner, an American judge at the Court of Appeals, recently observed:

> The global economy has brought an increasing variety of foreign law issues to the federal courts. Indeed, one international commercial transaction may implicate the law of several nations. Aside from foreign law issues relating to foreign trade, federal courts are faced daily with immigration matters, tort claims, public law disputes, arbitration enforcement proceedings, domestic relation suits and even criminal cases that call for the determination and application of foreign law. These cases are beginning to form a significant part of the business of the federal courts.[22]

In this context, it would seem normal that judges consider foreign law and mention it in the course of their reasoning. Indeed, most examples given to

[21] The Constitutional Court of South Africa is a famous exception to this general trend. This is explained by the fact that the Constitution itself explicitly encourages the Court to rely on comparative law for the purpose of interpreting the Constitution.

[22] RJ Miner, 'The Reception of Foreign Law in the U.S. Federal Courts' [1995] *American Journal of International and Comparative Law* 581.

illustrate the nascent 'transjudicial communication' are cases involving foreign law because of the nature of the dispute. However, even in these cases, (American) judges seem reluctant to apply foreign law and usually find a way to set it aside and only apply domestic (American) law. RJ Miner, speaking at the Annual Meeting of the American Foreign Law Association, expressed his regrets about this approach. He pointed out that, despite the existence of specific rules of interpretation of foreign law laid down in the Rules of Civil Procedure and the assistance of experts and lawyers to the court, American judges have a 'tendency to duck and run when presented with issues of foreign law.'[23]

'Judicial communication' reflects the fact that courts are increasingly aware of other courts. However, this seems to be taking place essentially in a very precise institutional framework. Very little communication has so far been observed between domestic courts. Most of the communication goes on between a supranational court, such as the European Court of Justice or the European Court of Human Rights, and the domestic courts of states which are members of these supranational institutions. In other words, the norms enacted by these institutions are binding on the member states and, ultimately, on their courts. This is one aspect of the movement of law in post-communist countries. Yet what we are also witnessing in these countries is the incorporation of law which is foreign but, significantly, not binding on the importing court, even in an indirect way, such as the case law of the European Court of Justice might be. Imported law is the law of another national system with which there is no legal connection, so the reasons for law importation have to be sought outside the mechanism of binding effect. Unlike 'judicial communication', where some dialogue begins to emerge between domestic courts and supranational courts, law importation reflects a one-way process between the constitutional courts of two countries. While the Hungarian Court abundantly imported law from German constitutional case law, the German Constitutional Court in Karlsruhe did not respond by importing law from Hungarian case law. Finally, 'judicial communication' does not explain why the Hungarian Court relied on German constitutional case law in such a systematic way. Both 'judicial communication' and 'legal transplants' leave too many questions unanswered.

2. EXPORTING WESTERN LAW

Juan J Linz and Alfred Stepan noted the unprecedented weight of what they call 'international influences' in post-communist transitions:

> When we place in comparative perspective the transitions in the Soviet Union and the ex-Warsaw Pact countries of East Central Europe (Poland, Hungary, Czechoslovakia,

---

[23] RJ Miner, 'The Reception of Foreign Law in the U.S. Federal Courts' [1995] *American Journal of International and Comparative Law* 581.

the German Democratic Republic, Romania and Bulgaria), one of their most distinctive qualities concerns the variable we call *international influence*. One of the editors of the classic four-volume study of the transitions in southern Europe and South America, Laurence Whitehead, argued that 'in all the peacetime cases considered here internal forces were of primary importance in determining the course and outcome of the transition attempt, and international factors only play a secondary role.' Clearly, such a judgement would be obviously unwarranted for East Central Europe, given the speed with which Communism collapsed in 1989 and the fact that Czechoslovakia, Romania and Bulgaria began their transitions almost *before* any significant domestic changes had occurred.[24]

By 'international influences', the authors understand a combination of foreign policy, *zeitgeist* and diffusion. In the case of post-communist transitions they highlight the role of the Soviet Union, which undoubtedly accelerated the process of liberalisation. The West also played a considerable role in post-communist transitions. However, the term 'international influences' is both too weak and too general to cover the West's massive and direct involvement in the reconstruction of post-communist legal systems. Yet the difficulty lies in finding a suitable label for this involvement (which is more than mere influence) that would help to analyse and understand the role of foreign law in the process of writing constitutions after the collapse of communism.

2.1. An Inflation of Metaphors

The phrases that have so far been used to describe the massive Western influence exercised on post-communist systems are metaphorical and are attractive because of the image they convey. For instance, 'legal transplants' conjures up the image of a botanical operation and the idea of moving a plant to a different location, or maybe the transplanting of an organ from one person to another. In a similar vein, the Western influences have been referred to as the grafting of a new institution or a new rule onto a different legal system. The academic can observe the process in much the same way as a gardener or a surgeon and be happy if the graft is successful, or sad if it is rejected. This approach, however, does not provide much explanation of the process involved. At best, the metaphors offer some graphic description of Western influences on post-communist legislation. At worst, they can be criticised for not corresponding to the most basic reality: that is, one could argue, that there is in fact no actual graft or transplant. This is because the Western rule is not cut away from its original environment; instead, it continues to exist there at the same time as it is reproduced as part of a new legal system elsewhere.

---

[24] JJ Linz and A Stepan, *Problems of Democratic Transition and Consolidation: Southern Europe, South America and Post-communist Europe* (Baltimore, Johns Hopkins University Press, 1996), 235–36.

Interestingly, this diversity of vocabulary does not correspond to a diversity of phenomena observed by academics who, despite the range of terms used, all seem to concur on one point: namely, post-communist law and constitutions in particular were drafted on the basis of extensive borrowing from the existing law of Western democracies. The denominations might differ (borrowing, reception, influences, transplants or imitation), but they all address the same process.

The diversity of vocabulary is perhaps just a reflection of academic individualism, as well as the creative imagination of scholars, whereby they are keen to propose their own word which, they think, is an improvement in comparison to their colleagues' terminological choice. It is possible that there is also a national preference for some words and metaphors. Terms such as 'legal transplants' or 'cross-fertilisation' may be considered to be more Anglo-Saxon. Watson's work and, in particular *Legal Transplants*, is so far only available in English and this might explain why this phrase has mainly been influential in Anglo-American academia. If there is such a thing as a national academic approach, then French academia, often oblivious to English bibliography, has followed a different path. One of the recurring French metaphors is that of 'mimetic institution building' or 'institutional mimicry'.[25] This approach suggests that in a manner not unlike that of chameleons, post-communist law developed in imitation of Western legal systems. The underlying logic is easy to understand. In order to become Western liberal democracies, post-communist countries endeavoured to look like them and massively copied Western law. Just as the chameleon changes colour to blend into the surrounding environment, so the post-communist institutional mimics hoped to be considered equal to liberal democracies and integrated into their reassuring family, and thence into the EU. Although there is a lot of truth in this representation, the term 'institutional mimicry' focuses on one outcome of the transitions and in so doing does not take account of the processes and actors involved in reaching that outcome.

All of these metaphors make a welcome but limited contribution to the study of what is a complex and emerging field. However, it must be acknowledged of course that any attempt to find a suitable and generally acceptable label for the processes and outcomes of transitions inevitably comes up against the boundaries of the limits of language and the signification of words. Nevertheless, like other scholars involved in the study of this area, I have also chosen a metaphor, but my selection of the term 'law importation' is intended to focus on the way and the context in which foreign law was used in the elaboration of post-communist law.

[25] The idea of institutional mimicry was proposed by one of the few books published in French on this issue, ie a collection of essays, Y Mény (ed), *Les Politiques du Mimétisme* (Paris, l'Harmattan, 1993). This metaphor seems to have been inspired by earlier work done on the impact of French (administrative) law on post-colonial countries in the 1970s. On this topic, see in particular J Bugnicourt, 'Du Mimétisme Administratif en Afrique' [1973] *Revue Française de Sciences Politiques* 1239–67 and G Langrod, 'Genèse et Conséquences du Mimétisme en Afrique' [1973] *Revue Internationale des Sciences Administratives* 119.

2.2. Many Channels of Exportation

The West's involvement is best understood in terms of law exportation, which went through different channels. This process was characterised by the involvement of a large number of international institutions as well as individual experts; states, although playing an important role, were not the main actors.

(a) *International Institutions and Non-Governmental Organisations*

Institutions were probably the most visible exporters of law to post-communist countries in transitions. Adrian GV Hyde-Price considered some of them in what he called 'the impact of external factors on the democratisation process.' While he was mainly concerned with specifying 'how external factors can facilitate this process of domestic political reform,'[26] he also referred to institutions that actually played a significant role in it. Hyde-Price singled out the European Community, the Conference for Security and Cooperation in Europe (CSCE) and the Council of Europe. These institutions created bodies or forums for the specific purpose of assisting the states of the former Soviet bloc. For instance, following the joint declaration signed in Luxembourg in 1988, the European Community developed a specific form of bilateral agreement on economic and commercial cooperation to match the needs of these countries. In 1991, in response to the aspirations of an increasing number of post-communist countries to join it, the EU created the famous 'Association Agreements' (also called 'European Agreements'). In the meantime the decision was taken to support the reforms in Eastern Europe, with the result that the PHARE (Poland/Hungary: Aid for Restructuring of Economies) system was born. This programme supported six broad categories of projects: improving parliamentary practice, promoting and monitoring human rights, supporting independent media, developing NGOs and representative structures, encouraging local democracy and participation, and finally promoting education and analysis. The CSCE, which Hyde-Price described as 'one of the great and unexpected success stories of modern European diplomacy,'[27] was also influential. In this respect Hyde-Price underlined the important role played by the CSCE in establishing a bridge between East and West and, more particularly after the Paris Summit in 1990, in creating specific institutions, such as the Office of Free Elections based in Warsaw.

The Council of Europe is probably the European institution which reacted the most quickly to the collapse of communist regimes, in that it admitted most of the post-communist countries very soon after new governments were elected.

---

[26] AGV Hyde-Price, 'Democratization in Eastern Europe, the External Dimension' in G Pridham and T Vanhaven (eds), *Democratization in Eastern Europe, Domestic and International Perspectives* (London, Routledge, 1994), 224.

[27] *Ibid*, 236.

Again, a specific forum, called the Venice Commission (also called 'the Commission of Democracy through Law') was created within the Council of Europe with a view to providing support for the reforms. It has been building up a substantial database on constitutional adjudication and constitutional rights in Europe and it edits a Bulletin of Constitutional Case Law. Perhaps more interestingly, the Venice Commission has organised frequent seminars where Eastern and Western lawyers have met and debated selected issues.[28] Financial and economic institutions, such as the World Bank, the International Monetary Fund and the European Bank for Development and Reconstruction can also be added to this list. Although they operated differently from the institutions named above, they did have a very strong impact on drafting legislation in former Soviet states, in particular on the development of new economic policies.

Another channel of exportation went through the countless non-governmental organisations, foundations, charities and professional bodies that involved themselves in Central and Eastern Europe after 1989. Training and education programmes also played a role, although probably not immediately in 1989, but very soon after. The most prominent of the education bodies created after the collapse of the communist regimes is probably the Central European University based in Budapest and in Prague. It is the most visible part of a huge body of institutions providing education and training for post-communist lawyers in the arcane sciences of liberal democracy and the market economy.

(b) Individual Experts

Countless experts, individually or grouped under an ad hoc project, provided specific advice in response to specific needs and problems.[29] Experts, mainly scholars, flooded Eastern Europe at the end of the 1980s. Some authors have compared their zealous efforts to those of pilgrims.[30] A religious metaphor was also used by Andras Sajó, a Hungarian professor teaching at the Central European University, to describe the Western experts landing in Central Europe as 'missionaries.' In relation to this process, Sajó noted wryly that:

---

[28] Some of the themes debated are 'Constitution-Making as an Instrument of Democratic Transition' (Istanbul, 1992), 'Constitutional Aspects of the Transition to a Market Economy' (Moscow and Sofia 1993), 'The Role of the Constitutional Court in the Consolidation of the Rule of Law' (Bucharest, 1994), 'The Protection of Fundamental Rights by the Constitutional Courts' (Brioni, Croatia, 1995) and 'The Principle of Respect for Human Dignity' (Montpellier, 1998).

[29] Frédérique Dahan and Janet Dine took part in a Technical Assistance to the Commonwealth of Independent States project in the framework of the European Union. They related their experience on giving advice on commercial and industrial activities to Russians at the Conference on Comparative Law in the 21st Century organised by the Institute of Advanced Legal Studies and held in London in July 2000.

[30] R Dorandeu, 'Les Pélerins Constitutionnels', in Y Mény (ed), Les Politiques du Mimétisme Institutionnel (Paris, l'Harmattan, 1993), 83.

Allegedly, planeloads of frustrated Western law professors brought to Eastern Europe their pet private draft codes that had been ridiculed back home. These were sold to the new democratic regimes as inevitable.[31]

In other cases, it would be more appropriate to speak of salesmen trying to sell ready-made or 'flat pack constitutions', as was reported to Renaud Dorandeu about an American 'expert'. In this account, the person in question was touring Central Europe with a catalogue of constitutions for the price of $250,000. It was reported that the American's constitutions were turned down and that he was horrified to be told that the French provided free constitutional assistance.[32] This anecdote is interesting at several levels. First, it illustrates the different strategies and manners in which the West provided its assistance. Secondly, it reveals that some of the expertise on offer was not free. Although this issue is not pursued here, it is important to remember that there was often a price of one form or another attached to Western advice. This is certainly a fascinating aspect of Western involvement in post-communist reform, but it is one for which exact details will probably never be available. Thirdly, Dorandeu's anecdote illustrates the competition between various exporters. Beyond the almost stereotypical opposition between American and French approaches to most issues, this account reveals the existence of a 'market of institutions' with a wide range of competing models on offer.[33]

(c) Mixed Motives

The involvement of the West (the countries and institutions on the liberal and capitalist side of the Iron Curtain) in the reconstruction of post-communist legal systems has had different motivations. These have ranged from a genuine and generous desire to assist the post-communist countries, to an attempt to control the outcome of events that shook the foundations of Europe (and of the world), in order to satisfy a need to maintain some stability and security in this area. A statement by the US Deputy Secretary of State, Lawrence S Eagleburger, at the annual conference of the US Export-Import Bank in 1991, summed up the spirit of Western involvement in 'democratic institution-building':

> One thing we in the West should not do is sit in judgement on our East European friends, or attempt to dictate choices which are theirs to make. . . . However, there are certain things which the West, particularly we in the United States, can do to help ensure that the difficult economic transition on the way does not destabilise either the fragile new democratic institutions or peace in the region as a whole. . . . we must continue to provide advice and technical assistance in the field of democratic institution-building.

---

[31] A Sajó, 'Universal Rights, Missionaries, Converts and "Local Savages"' (1997) 6 *East European Constitutional Review* 45.

[32] Dorandeu, above n 30, at 83.

[33] The phrase is borrowed from S Pejovitch, 'Der Markt der Institutionen, Osteuropa zwischen Nationalismus und Liberalismus' [1995] *Transit* 44.

Our friends in the region tell us that such help to date has been absolutely critical to the success achieved thus far—the elections held, the constitutions written and the like. Henceforth we must concentrate on strengthening democracy at the grass-root level, namely the institutions of local government plus those bodies which safeguard and mediate a healthy pluralist society—such as unions, press organs and the judiciary.[34]

The American assistance referred to by the deputy secretary of state appeared to be disinterested, as the speaker insisted that no judgement should be made and that East European countries should ultimately be free to make their own decisions. The main reason that he gave for American support was maintaining peace in the whole region and protecting the new and fragile institutions. However, the context of this speech, namely the annual conference of the US Export-Import Bank, sheds a slightly different light on the motivations for assistance: they were not solely about developing democratic institutions but also (and primarily?) about establishing market economies and new trading relationships with them. Considered in this light, Eagleburger's reference to the 'difficult economic transition' is not coincidental.

Western export, however generously motivated in the first place, developed into a set of standards that post-communist countries could not ignore. Hyde-Price pointed out that the particular situation of transition in Eastern Europe provided the West with a 'powerful set of policy tools for shaping political developments in the region.'[35] Specifically, some criteria set out by the West, mainly by organisations such as the EU or the Council of Europe, were a prerequisite for being admitted to these institutions. This is particularly clear in relation to the EU, which set out at the Copenhagen summit in 1993 the conditions for admitting new member states from Central and Eastern Europe. Remarkably, because EU membership was, at first, a much desired aim throughout the region, many post-communist states drafted most of their legislation in compliance with particular EU regulations or directives, long before their membership was officially considered.[36] The Council of Europe operated in a similar way, although admission was granted more quickly. Central and Eastern European countries were first granted a 'special guest' status in the Parliamentary Assembly. Full membership was possible once they held free elections and accepted the ECHR, together with its additional protocols.[37]

---

[34] Quoted by AGV Hyde-Price, 'Democratization in Eastern Europe, the External Dimension' in G Pridham and T Vanhaven (eds), *Democratization in Eastern Europe: Domestic and International Perspectives* (London, Routledge, 1994), 245.

[35] *Ibid*, 227.

[36] AVG Hyde-Price sums this attitude up in saying that: 'Indeed, for nearly all of them [Eastern European Countries], the Community became a central focus for their post-communist foreign policies, with the goal of achieving full membership high on the agenda of East-Central Europeans' *ibid*, 230. See also A Evans, 'Voluntary Harmonisation in Integration between the European Community and Eastern Europe' (1997) 22 *European Law Review* 201.

[37] Remarkably all these criteria were much more stringent and demanding on post-communist countries than they originally were for the first members of the EEC or the Council of Europe.

As seen in the previous chapter, post-communist constitutions are generally characterised by the adoption of Western legal terminology and the incorporation of institutions and rights similar to those existing in liberal democracies. This importation of law was not only a response to the exportation of law, but arguably it was also deliberately sought by post-communist countries as part of a strategy for rebuilding their legal systems and their constitutions in particular.

3. DEFINING LAW IMPORTATION

Law importation refers to an active process of creation and development of a new law on the basis of elements extracted from chosen foreign legal orders and subsequently incorporated into the new body of law.[38] Law importation has four essential characteristics.

First, law importation differs completely from the logic of compliance with legally binding international law, often referred to as the reception of law.[39] The law that is imported does not have its origin in an international convention, but instead comes from the law of foreign states from which the importing state is independent. In other words, post-communist countries were not under the legal obligation to draft their constitutions in compliance with Western constitutions. In the example chosen here, Hungary imported significant aspects of its law from Germany. Legally speaking, however, Hungary had no obligation to import German law into the constitutional amendment of 1989, nor was the Hungarian Constitutional Court obliged to import some elements from German constitutional case law in order to develop its own constitutional reasoning. It did so by its own choice. In the context of post-communist transitions, law importation and compliance with international requirements, however, do not exclude each other. Numerous post-communist states have adopted legislation in compliance with international law before it became binding on them, ie before they joined a particular international organisation. This is particularly striking in relation to the law of the EU, which many post-communist states hoped to join. When areas of law that had to be rewritten fell within the scope of EU law, it was often easier for post-communist legislators to follow the existing EU rules rather than start from scratch. Convenience was not the only

---

[38] I gratefully acknowledge the impact of the stimulating workshop on Comparative Law in the 21st Century held at the Institute of Advanced Legal Studies in London in July 2000. The quality of the debates confirmed the crucial role of law importation in the development of legal systems. I am grateful to the organisers, Professor Andrew Harding and Professor Esin Örücü, as well as to the participants. See A Harding and E Örücü (eds), *Comparative Law in the 21st Century* (The Hague, Kluwer Law International, 2002).

[39] See in general E Stein, 'International Law in Internal Law: Toward Internationalization of Central-Eastern Constitutions?' [1994] *American Journal of International Law* 427, and D Feldman, 'Monism, Dualism and Constitutional Legitimacy' [1999] *Australian Yearbook of International Law* 105–26.

reason for adopting 'EU compatible' legislation, however. Although EU law is not binding on non-members, it has had a sort of 'pre-binding effect' on post-communist states. Legislators anticipated its binding effect by enacting legislation in harmony with EU requirements, in order to demonstrate that their legal systems met EU standards and that they were worthy of EU membership.

Secondly, law importation also differs from a simple use of comparative law as a source of inspiration in judicial reasoning. Although like comparative law it involves an element of foreignness, looking outside the importers' legal system, law importation goes beyond merely referring to the law of other countries. In some decisions, the importing court might list a number of foreign legal systems and clearly identify the sources it has considered, whereas in others the foreign legal system is not named. Law importation differs from the comparison of law in the way the elements of foreign law are used by the importing court. After a comparative survey but more often without an explicit comparison, the importing court extracts a chosen element of foreign law from its original context and incorporates it into its reasoning, with no explanation of the reasons for its choice.

Thirdly, law importation is initiated by a deliberate choice on the part of the importers in favour of a particular foreign model and it has to be distinguished from the general influences that one legal system might exercise on another. The choice in favour of a particular model may be guided by the wider context in which the importation takes place and there is little doubt that the massive export of Western law influenced the importing of Western law by post-communist countries. However, there was no automatic correspondence between the law that was exported and the law that was imported. Law exportation did encourage post-communist law-makers to consider foreign solutions, but importers had the last word when it came to choosing a particular model. The reasons for the importers' choice depend on the actual characteristics of a particular model as well as, crucially, on how it is perceived by the importers. The subjective appreciation of a particular body of foreign law is linked to the importers' own personalities and background, their perception of their own legal system and the particular aim they want to achieve through law importation.

Fourthly, law importation is part of a strategy to develop the law. In the example of the right to human dignity and the Hungarian Constitutional Court, importing the law from German constitutional case law enabled the Hungarian Court to introduce a new concept of fundamental rights after the collapse of communism, as will be explained in the next four chapters. It is this element of strategy that is the overarching characteristic of law importation. It reveals the importance of the rational choice made by importers to develop their legal system in a particular way in response to specific needs.

3.1. Who Imports Foreign Law?

The importers of law are part of an intellectual and professional élite.[40] In the context of post-communist transitions, they have often been educated in the West, either through post-graduate and even doctoral training in a Western university, or shorter specialised courses. From their time abroad they have gained not only specialised knowledge in their own area of expertise, but have also established links with Western colleagues. Since the collapse of communism, knowledge of Western law (as well as of other disciplines) has been invaluable and importers have drawn their strength and legitimacy from their knowledge of Western politics and law, which they share with a small section of the population only. This Western knowledge-based élite overlaps with a professional élite, including for example constitutional judges, advisors to the government, senior academics and members of parliament involved in the dynamics of change at the highest level of state power.

When law importation is used by legislators to reform parts of their legal systems, it is a phenomenon worthy of scholarly consideration and curiosity even though from a legal perspective it does not raise major questions. This is of course because legislators are free to seek inspiration wherever they think it appropriate. Similarly, academics are equally entitled to consider foreign law in order to support an argument involving a domestic issue.[41] However, when undertaken by judges, law importation is a rare occurrence and even, as suggested earlier, paradoxical. Consequently, when the judicial members of this importing élite use foreign law in a way that does not seem to meet our expectations of their function, it begs the question why.

3.2. Why Import Western Law?

Like other forms of reliance on foreign models, law importation corresponds to a time of substantial law reform, which in the case of post-communist transitions affected the entire legal system. Throughout the former communist bloc there was a general consensus on the need to abolish communist law and to replace it with law based on liberal principles.

---

[40] B Badie, *L'Etat Importé, Essai sur l'Occidentalisation de l'Ordre Politique* (Paris, Fayard, 1992).

[41] In post-communist transition, academics and university teachers suffered from the change of system, ie the fact that overnight their teaching (and presumably research activities) had to develop on a different ideological basis. In addition, they suffered from the lack of resources which forced many of them to take up legal practice to make ends meet (the average monthly salary for a Hungarian university teacher is £300). B Pätzold reports on their difficulties in 'Stratégies de Survie des Intellectuels Hongrois' [2001] *Le Monde Diplomatique* (July) 7. In those circumstances, the academics' impact, social status, and perhaps as well their credibility were damaged.

An additional reason for law importation is the fact that domestic resources are not readily available. In the early years of post-communist transitions, the pace of the changes was such that it was almost impossible for the reformers to devise and implement entirely home-grown reforms in the time available. This was reinforced by further pressure in terms of the quality of the reform which had to be achieved. In other words, post-communist countries were expected to achieve within a couple of years a level of law comparable to that of well-established liberal democracies in the West. Post-communist constitutions were supposed to meet the standards of their Western counterparts and Bills of Rights, or the equivalent set of constitutional provisions, were expected to guarantee the same degree of protection to individuals from the beginning of the transition. Almost no time was available to experiment with constitutional drafting in order to find the most suitable provisions. In addition to the time constraint, two sets of circumstances characteristic of post-communist transitions greatly encouraged law importation: the failure of communist law and the phenomenon of institutional optimism.

(a) The Failure of Communist Law

The perception of the failure of communism was particularly acute in the immediate aftermath of the Cold War, the end of which can arguably be dated to the demise of communist regimes in Eastern Europe. This was essentially a war between two rival ideologies, communism and liberalism. Continuing the bellicose metaphor, the collapse of one of them meant the triumphant victory of the other, which was celebrated in the West and in the East. 'Communism is dead, long live liberalism' encapsulates the spirit of the years 1990–91.

At the time of its fall, it was clear that nothing could be expected from communism. Communist parties fell from power throughout the region. Their survival instinct led them to rechristen themselves as 'socialist parties' and with membership being no longer compulsory, they were deserted at great speed. In the meantime, opposition movements came into existence and several political parties were created, some of them brand new, others resuming a pre-war existence. Consequently communist parties, even in their renovated forms, spectacularly lost the first free elections.[42] Due to the tight link between communist ideology and law, the perception of the former's failure was extended to the latter. Suddenly, communist law became inadequate: it was the wrong sort of law. As a result, it soon became obvious that yet another reform of communist law would not meet the expectations of the people demonstrating on the streets, nor those of opposition movements. Communist law had to go.

---

[42] For instance: in Czechoslovakia (8–9 June 1990) the Communist Party won only 13.5 % of the seats; in Hungary (25 March–8 April 1990) the Hungarian Socialist Workers' Party won 3.7 % of the seats. Source: J Elster, UK Preuß and C Offe, *Institutional Design in Post-communist Societies: Rebuilding the Ship at Sea* (Cambridge, Cambridge University Press, 1998), 149–51.

The perception of failure was reinforced by the sudden collapse of commun-ism and its replacement, at least on paper in new constitutions and legislation, by liberal principles and law. Whereas at the economic level the propriety of shock therapies was widely debated (and eventually administered, with various degrees of success),[43] at the constitutional level this does not seem to have been an issue and 'constitutional shock therapies' were administered throughout the region. One exception to this is perhaps Poland, which made some amendments to its existing constitution and waited until 1997 to enact a new one. Hungary too proceeded with an amended constitution, but even this interim measure abolished the most striking features of the communist understanding of law.[44] On paper and in political discourse, the switch from communist to liberal con-stitutions was almost instantaneous.[45]

The perception that communist law had failed was reinforced by a glorified and idealised vision of the West and of liberal law. This was arguably a result of the limited (and at first impossible) access to the West available to people in the Eastern bloc. Gradually, mainly through the media (the radio in particular) and through some rare and dear trips abroad, a cultural image of the West developed which did not correspond much to the reality.[46] This selective representation of the West had more to do with a longing for a better life than accurate observa-tion. Often, this idealised vision did not stem from direct knowledge or experi-ence, but corresponded to the way in which people of communist countries imagined life to be in the West.

In addition, when Western exporters flooded Central and Eastern Europe with advice on writing constitutions, they arguably did not try very hard to pro-pose an alternative or, possibly more accurate picture of the West. This was not necessarily done deliberately in order to deceive. Rather, it was linked to the way in which the expertise was delivered and this for several reasons. First, because advice was given on very specific and limited areas of law, the repre-sentation of reality was necessarily distorted.[47] Secondly, due to the sudden need for expertise, very few Western experts could claim to have reasonable know-ledge (not to mention an ability to speak the language) of the local situations and issues on which they provided advice. As a result, the underlying theme of any Western expertise is likely to have been 'West is best', with some variations depending on the nationality or the model offered. Knowledge and solutions, in short instant happy democracies, were to come from the West. This belief and

[43] See the entry 'Thérapies de choc' in J-Y Potel, *Les Cent Portes de l'Europe Centrale et Orientale* (Paris, Les Éditions de l'Atelier, 1998), 290.

[44] See ch 1.

[45] However, for all sorts of material and practical considerations some of the new institutions were not put in place for a few years.

[46] See F Feher, 'Imagining the West' [1995] *Thesis Eleven* 52.

[47] *The Guardian* noted with some amusement that MPs behaved in an unusually nice way so that their Mongolian guests, who had come to London to observe parliamentary practice, would form a positive impression: 'MPs Flatter to Deceive on the Mongolian Question', 15 March 2000 and 'Mongolian Guests Learn Lie of the Land', 16 March 2000.

spirit at the very beginning of the transition were very well summarised by an editorial in a German journal: 'Ex Occidente Lux?'.[48] In 1995, the editor who coined this phrase ended it with a question mark. However, back in 1990–91, there was little doubt that it was an assertion that was questioned neither by the West nor by the East. No in-between solution was offered (or if it was, it was not adopted). Typical communist institutions were happily and proudly abolished and substituted by their liberal counterparts.

(b) 'Institutional Optimism'

The early stages of the transition took place in a very euphoric atmosphere both in the West and in the East. The festivities marking the fall of the Berlin Wall on 9 November 1989 are a good illustration of that happiness and joy. The end of communist dictatorships, that most people had stopped hoping would come, had come. The old dreams and unrealistic aspirations for freedom had been realised. No war had been needed to bring European peoples back together in a spirit of rediscovered friendship and liberty. With the peaceful collapse of communist regimes, the unthinkable had happened: from then on, everything seemed possible and all hopes might come true.

This enthusiasm extended to the law-makers and produced in the post-communist countries what the sociologist Pierre Kendé appropriately identified as 'institutional optimism'.[49] This optimism led the post-communist lawyers to believe that creating democratic institutions would automatically lead to the establishment of democracy itself.[50] As a result, institution-building attracted all the attention during the first couple of years and creating new democratic institutions was given priority by post-communist reformers. This 'institutional optimism' was shared by the West and its experts and the first requirements that they set out were phrased in institutional terms. Consequently, the criteria for assessing the progress of democracies were very much institutional criteria.[51]

[48] [1995] *Transit* Editorial. This journal which was created in response to the transition presents a critical and informative perspective on this issue.

[49] P Kendé, 'L'Optimisme Institutionnel des Élites Postcommunistes', in Y Mény (ed), *Les Politiques du Mimétisme* (Paris, L'Harmattan, 1993), 237.

[50] '[The new democratic consensus] is characterised by the presupposition that it is sufficient to endow a country with democratic institutions for that country to transform itself immediately or very rapidly into a democracy. This presupposition could be called "institutionalist" and it is in this sense that we refer here to "institutional optimism" ': *ibid*, 238, author's translation from French.

[51] In her introduction to the book she co-authored with B Parrot on *The Consolidation of Democracy in East-Central Europe,* Karen Dawisha gives the following definition of democracy: 'In line with recent research, a procedural and minimalist conception of democracy was employed. Democracy is defined as a political system in which the formal and actual leaders of the government are chosen through regular elections based on multiple candidacies and secret balloting, with the right of all adult citizens to vote. It is assumed that leaders chosen via free and fair elections, using universal adult suffrage, will be induced to modify their behavior to be more responsive to popular wishes and demands than leaders in authoritarian states' (Cambridge, Cambridge University Press, 1997), 40.

The organisation of free and pluralist elections was an imperative condition for Central and Eastern European states to start being considered as post-communist democracies. A responsible government, an independent judiciary and a set of fundamental rights were further examples of institutional requirements.

Furthermore, one could argue that 'institutional optimism' was induced and encouraged by the nature of Western expertise. This expertise was largely based upon a particular conception of democracy, namely that of formal or procedural democracy. In other words, it essentially rested upon a set of institutions and formal requirements. Being born and educated in this model, Western experts (unconsciously?) promoted it in post-communist Europe. As the recipe for democracy is extremely complex and ultimately a bit mysterious, opting for the institutional perspective was probably the easiest and quickest way to teach its basic ingredients—that is to say that it was easier to sketch out a set of institutions and indicate ways to establish them, than to explain the other conditions that are needed for democracy to flourish. From the perspective of meeting criteria, ie measuring the 'progress' of post-communist democracies, the institutional approach had the great advantage of being relatively easy to implement and to assess. For instance, it was easier to call for elections and make sure that they were reasonably free and fair (a group of Western observers would do) than to make sure that those elections made sense to the voters, ie a democratic sense as opposed to the sense they used to have under communism.

It is true though that democracy cannot exist without democratic institutions. Hence, eliminating the 'bad', ie undemocratic and communist institutions and creating new ones on the model of those existing in liberal democracies was a logical step in the process of transition from communist regimes. However, as Kendé rightly pointed out, institutional optimism implies that reality is only perceived in terms of institutions.[52] As a result, other important aspects for the elaboration of democracy were given less attention. They include the development of informed and critical public opinion, the importance of civil society,[53] a certain sense of belonging and participating in democratic government, a certain education and shared belief in democratic values and principles.[54] Finally, and more importantly perhaps, post-communist countries lacked the time to experience democracy. It has taken over 200 years for the West to elaborate democratic governments, which in many ways are still far from perfection, but

[52] P Kendé, above n 49, at 242. According to Kendé, this assumption was the source of several illusions and resulting errors.

[53] In 1997, the sociologist Bill Lomax wondered about 'The Strange Death of Civil Society in Post-communist Hungary' [1997] *Journal of Communist Studies and Transition Politics* 41.

[54] Post-apartheid South Africa, interestingly, made a lot of efforts to educate people in new values, to make them aware of their rights, to promote the constitution to the public, to involve them in the day-to-day process of democratisation. As far as I know, this is a quite unique effort to develop an education in democracy. Although, arguably, it was just as needed, a similar attempt was not made in post-communist Europe.

post-communist countries were expected to achieve a comparable level of democracy within less than 10 years.

3.3. Measuring the Success of Law Importation

In the early years of transition, law importation was perceived as a safe method for post-communist countries to become liberal democracies. Western law provided a much needed source of stability in the turmoil of transition and it can be said that law importation was a relatively easy way to introduce drastic legal reforms.

However, it is more difficult to assess whether law importation works in terms of whether it has been 'socially easy', to borrow Watson's phrase. It can be safely asserted that the vast majority of people in Central and Eastern Europe no longer wanted to live under communist regimes and suffer the censorship and economic hardship that this implied. Similarly, there is little doubt that they wanted to be freer, happier and wealthier. There is also little doubt that the Western life-style and consumerism appealed to a large majority of people. However, whether society as a whole understood and endorsed law importation as a remedy to the crisis situation is a different question. People had initiated and supported the fall of communist regimes, but they were on the whole far less involved in the process of choosing and building up the new institutions and laws. At the same time the abolition of socialist rights, namely the system of social benefits and support, in the name of economic rationalisation caused great distress for populations who suddenly lost their safety net. In this sense perhaps, the imported liberal rights which took priority in constitutions, as well as in state budgets, left a lot of people dissatisfied and bitter with the imported solutions. So perhaps, in order to appreciate the social ease (or, as may be the case, the difficulty) of law importation, distinctions have to be made—that is, law importation is perceived differently by different people. Whereas the minority of importers and all the professionals directly involved in this process may have found that law importation was easy, the lay people, the vast majority who have to live with the imported law, may have found this more difficult.

When attempting to answer the question whether law importation works, it has to be borne in mind that its perceived success will vary according to the expectations that may be associated with it. In a very simplistic way, three types of expectations may be identified. First, low expectations would rest on the belief that law importation, no matter how perfectly undertaken, could not turn any legal system into an ideal one. As a result, law importation would not be expected to introduce the full range of necessary reforms, but only to trigger a reaction which would eventually have some impact on the importing system. In this sense, law importation would almost always be considered as successful because something new would always come out of it, be it negative or positive.

A second type of expectations could be both higher and more cautious. Here, law importation as a method of reforming the law could be seen to work only if the cultural gap between exporter and importer were considered and bridged. The success of law importation would be linked to the requirement for some sort of cultural translation or adaptation of the imported law to its new environment. This 'mind the cultural gap' warning derives from observing failed law importation to (mainly) colonies and the resulting difficult emancipation of their legal systems. It also derives from the idea that law is not universal and must always be adjusted to culturally different environments. Thirdly, if the expectations were that an entire legal system would be imported then, because this is not possible, law importation would inevitably be considered a failure in all cases.

Moreover, to appreciate the success of law importation, the choice of perspective for observation arguably matters a great deal. If the process is observed from the exporter's point of view, the mere exportation of their law might be enough to be deemed successful. Whether and how the exported law works within the imported system then becomes almost irrelevant. In this context, any major transformation of the imported law might be understood as a failure to import the law, or more precisely, as a failure to import the law as it was in its original context. By contrast and for less self-centred exporters, modification of the original law can be considered as a positive effort to adjust the law to the new environment in order to make it work.

If the importer's perspective is adopted to assess the success of the operation, that is if we look at law importation from the insider's point of view, the picture becomes instantly more complex. Again, the perceived success of importation very much depends on expectations. For instance, if the expectation is to show on paper that post-communist constitutions have rejected communist principles and adopted liberal ones, then at this minimal level law importation will almost always be considered successful. If law importation is expected to create new rules to fill in the gap left by abolished socialist norms, then importing relevant foreign law might be perceived as a quick, easy and successful way of creating new rules. A caricatural representation of this might be 'a copy and paste job' whereby a foreign norm is copied from its environment and then pasted onto its new one. However, if law importation is expected to be understood and appropriated by the majority of those who deal with it and if law importation is to provide actual and effective solutions to a given situation, then its success is more difficult to ensure.

An answer to the more ambitious question as to whether law importation can turn or has turned the post-communist countries into functioning liberal democracies will not be suggested here. This is mainly for two reasons. First, the exact aim of the transition is not clear enough to know if it has been achieved. In fact, the aim of the transition, aside from the abolition of the most unbearable features of communism and of the typical features of its law, has arguably not been clearly set out. Secondly, this issue can not be debated at such a level of generality. Arguably, insight into whether law importation is successful can only be gained from the limited and narrow approach of a case study, which will be conducted in the next four chapters.

4. CONCLUSION

The particular nature of post-communist transitions raises new questions and, possibly, delivers new answers on the birth of new legal systems. For the first time, history has provided us with a unique field of experimentation and of reflection. The existing approaches to understanding the elaboration of law are no longer able to propose satisfactory tools for understanding the development of post-communist constitutions.

Law importation is a response to these new challenges. The perspective of law importation proposes to observe the transitions and the elaboration of a new law from the insider's perspective and it highlights the role of individual actors in this process. The importers of law were politicians, advisors, legislators and, most intriguingly, they were judges and especially judges of the newly created constitutional courts. Their role in the development of new legal systems was essential: they brought the newly adopted constitutions to life and gave those new principles and rights a real dimension. The study of one particular imported right, the right to human dignity as elaborated by the Hungarian Constitutional Court, is used here to explore the strategy of law importation.

PART II

THE STRATEGY OF IMPORTATION: THE RIGHT TO HUMAN DIGNITY IN HUNGARIAN CASE LAW, 1990–98

The period 1990 to 1998, which corresponds to the first term of the Hungarian Constitutional Court, was characterised by an abundant use of foreign law in judicial reasoning. Analysis of the numerous references to foreign constitutions reveals a real strategy of importation. Among the various sources used for importation, German constitutional law occupied a privileged position, in that it was the primary body of law on the basis of which the Hungarian Court developed its conception of fundamental rights.

This importation strategy is particularly well illustrated by the interpretation of the right to human dignity (*az emberi méltósághoz való jog*) under Article 54(1) of the 1989 Hungarian Constitution. Human dignity is the most important of the fundamental rights enshrined in the post-communist constitution and this is highlighted by the fact that it is set out in the first provision of the chapter on fundamental rights and duties. The Hungarian Constitutional Court interpreted human dignity as being the source of other fundamental rights which are not specifically listed in the Constitution. The numerous rights discovered by the Court in the wake of human dignity were used as key arguments in a number of prominent and controversial cases, which paved the way to the elaboration of a new legal system. Some of these cases involved issues that one would expect to be connected with human dignity, such as abortion or the death penalty. The majority of cases, however, were less obviously related to human dignity and they involved issues such as the power of trade unions to represent employees, the right of sportsmen to take part in competitions, the powers of public prosecutors, the right to marry freely and the right of access to higher education. The link between human dignity as it is phrased under Article 54(1) and its construction by the Hungarian Court is the general personality right (*az általános személyiségi jog*), which the Court imported from German law.

REVEALING IMPORTATION THROUGH COMPARISON WITH GERMAN CASE LAW

The Hungarian Court's importation strategy is not explicit. Making it visible and exploring its scope is only possible through a careful analysis of Hungarian constitutional case law with comparative references to German case law. Due to the novelty of Hungarian case law, it is presented here in a fairly comprehensive manner. Relevant extracts of cases are translated into English and tables illustrating significant aspects of the case law are included where appropriate.[1] German case law is presented here in a deliberately selective manner and specific aspects of German law are only explained when they are relevant for understanding the Hungarian interpretation of human dignity. The presentation of German constitutional case law is, however, complemented by references to edited collections of cases, commentaries on the German Basic Law and original case reports published in German.[2]

IMPORTATION STRATEGY

The comparison between Hungarian case law and key German cases reveals numerous striking similarities. Further analysis of judicial reasoning in the Hungarian cases shows that almost the entire interpretation of human dignity developed by the Hungarian Court is imported from German case law. Chapter 3 therefore presents the Hungarian interpretation of human dignity under Article 54(1) of the 1989 Constitution and shows that numerous aspects of this right were imported from German constitutional case law.

The first step in this strategy is the choice of the right model and chapter 4 explores the various elements involved in choosing German law. The comparison with German case law is taken further in chapter 5 and reveals a number of differences, which are perhaps less visible at first. The nature of these differences is such that they amount to instrumentalising the German model, which was used by the Hungarian Court in order to develop its own understanding of human dignity. This transformation forms part of the importation process and, as explained in chapter 6, it enabled the Court to lay the foundations of a new concept of constitutional rights after the collapse of communist law.

---

[1] Unless otherwise indicated, the translations presented here are my own. A selection of Hungarian constitutional case law is presented in English in L Sólyom and G Brunner (eds), *Constitutional Judiciary in a New Democracy: The Hungarian Constitutional Court* (Ann Arbor, University of Michigan Press, 2000).

[2] German Federal Constitutional Court (ed), *Nachschlagewerk der Rechtsprechung des Bundesverfassungsgerichts* (R v Decker and CF Müller Verlag, 1978), looseleaf edition regularly updated; I Richter and GF Schuppert (eds), *Casebook Verfassungsrecht* (München, CH Beck Verlagbuchhandlung, 1996). Commentaries on the German Basic Law are useful: R Wassermann (ed), *Kommentar zum Grundgesetz für die Bundesrepublik Deutschland* (Darmstadt, Luchterhand, 1984); I v Münch (ed), *Grundgesetzkommentar* (München, CH Beck Verlag, 1985); F Klein, H v Mangoldt and C Starck (eds), *Das Bonner Grundgesetz* (München, Vahlen, 1999); and textbooks: T Maunz and R Zippelius (eds), *Deutsches Staatsrecht* (München, CH Beck Verlag, 1998); K Hesse *Grundzüge des Verfassungsrechts der Bundesrepublik Deutschland* (Heidelberg, CF Müller Juristischer Verlag, 1988). In English, see D Kommers, *The Constitutional Jurisprudence of the Federal Republic of Germany* (Durham and London, Duke University Press, 1997).

3

Importing Human Dignity from German Law

———⇒·◦·⇐———

HUNGARIAN CONSTITUTIONAL CASE law on human dignity is diverse and innovative, but little known. A close reading of its terms shows that it has largely been imported from German constitutional law. This chapter presents the Hungarian law and explores its links with the German equivalent, in order to demonstrate this importation.[3] At the root of Hungarian law is the right to human dignity as enshrined in the 1989 constitution under Article 54 which reads:

1—In the Republic of Hungary everyone has the inherent right to life and human dignity, of which no one can be arbitrarily deprived.

2—No one shall be subjected to torture or to cruel, inhuman or degrading treatment or punishment; it is particularly prohibited to conduct medical or scientific experiments on human beings without their consent.[4]

The Hungarian interpretation of the right to human dignity was imported from German constitutional case law in one of the very first cases decided by the Court in 1990 (case 8/1990). In that case, which was about the representation powers of trade unions, the Hungarian Court imported, at the stroke of a pen, the most characteristic aspects of the right to human dignity as it had been interpreted by the German Constitutional Court. Far from being an isolated importation, case 8/1990 inaugurated a long series of cases that were based on the imported right to human dignity. Each right imported further aspects of human dignity from German case law and thus elaborated a complex and rich signification for this right.

---

[3] C Dupré, 'Importing German Case Law: the Right to Human Dignity in Hungarian Constitutional Case Law' in G Halmai (ed), *The Constitution Found? The First Nine Years of Hungarian Constitutional Review on Fundamental Rights* (Budapest, INDOK, 2000), 215; C Dupré, 'The Right to Human Dignity in Hungarian Constitutional Case Law', in *The Principle of Respect for Human Dignity* (Strasbourg, Council of Europe Publishing, 1999), 68 and C Dupré, 'Importing German Law: the Interpretation of the Right to Human Dignity by the Hungarian Constitutional Court' [2000] *OsteuropaRecht* 144.

[4] This translation is that available on the Constitutional Court's website. I prefer the term 'innate' to 'inherent' to qualify the nature of the right because it is a closer translation of the Hungarian term (*veleszületett*) and the image it evokes (the right with which we are born) played a role in the reasoning of some cases, notably the first case on abortion (64/1991).

1. IMPORTING A GENERAL DEFINITION: CASE 8/1990

At first glance, case 8/1990 involved an issue which was not directly related to the right to human dignity, namely the powers that trade unions had to represent their members, as set out in the 1967 Labour Code. According to this provision, trade unions had a general power to represent workers and this allowed them to represent even those workers who had not consented to being represented. The applicants challenged this provision on the basis that, since the change of regime, the representation of employees' interests was exercised on a pluralist basis. As a result, they argued, the former communist regulations no longer complied with the new constitutional requirements.

The Court examined the constitutional provisions which were directly related to trade union power and organisation. The first one, Article 4 of the 1989 Constitution reads:

> Trade unions and other representative organisations shall protect and represent the interests of employees, members of co-operatives and entrepreneurs.

The second provision on trade unions, Article 70C(1), is listed at the end of the chapter on fundamental rights and duties and reads:

> Everyone has the right to establish or join organisations together with others in order to protect his economic and social interests.

The Court did not elaborate on the specific provisions on trade unions, nor did it find that they were breached by the challenged provisions.[5] The Court then turned to Article 54(1) which enshrines the right to life and human dignity. Following a strict reading of the Constitution, the right to human dignity seemed remote from the issue at stake in the case. However, the Court linked it to the merits of the case by construing the right to human dignity as a right to self-determination—that is, in the Court's reasoning, this right was violated by trade unions when they represented the workers without their authorisation. Such logic enabled the Court to rule that the challenged provisions were unconstitutional and to nullify them on this ground. It is at the end of the case, after the Court reached its conclusions, that it clarified its interpretation of human dignity by declaring:

> The ruling of the Constitutional Court is based on the interpretation of the right to human dignity. The provisions of art. 54(1) of the constitution define this right as

---

[5] The Court held: 'The Constitutional Court did not find the disputed provision unconstitutional either under Art 4 or Art 70C(1) of the Constitution: Art 4 extends the trade unions' right to engage in the protection of interest and representation, which appears also in the former Constitution, to other organisations formed for the protection of interests. Neither this rule, nor the provision of Art 70C(1) pertaining to the freedom of forming trade unions and other organisations for the representation of interests prescribe what interest protection and representation activities include': L Sólyom and G Brunner (eds), *Constitutional Judiciary in a New Democracy, The Hungarian Constitutional Court* (Ann Arbor, University of Michigan Press, 2000), 106.

everyone's innate right at the beginning of the chapter entitled 'fundamental rights and duties'. The Constitutional Court considers the right to human dignity as one of the formulations of the general personality right. Modern constitutions and constitutional case law name the general personality right in terms of several of its aspects, such as the right to free fulfilment of personality, the right to self-determination, the general freedom of action or the right to a private sphere. The general personality right is a 'mother-right,' that is a fundamental subsidiary right on which the Constitutional Court as well as other courts can rely in order to protect individual autonomy in instances where no specific named fundamental rights can apply to the facts of the case.

What is immediately striking about this passage is the way the Court refers to non-specific constitutional sources as the basis of its interpretation, which has been derived from outside the Hungarian constitutional order. The Hungarian Court did not name the origin of this importation, which was disguised under the phrase 'modern constitutions and their case law.' However, almost every single word of this definition points to German case law as being its origin. More precisely, this understanding of human dignity as associated to the 'general personality right' (*az általános személyiségi jog*) corresponds to the interpretation of Articles 1 and 2 of the German Basic Law (*allgemeines Persönlichkeitsrecht*). Moreover, all the rights mentioned above by the Hungarian Court have been developed in German constitutional case law. The right to free fulfilment of one's personality (*a személyiség szabad kibontakozásához való jog*) is enshrined in Article 2(1) of the Basic Law (*freie Entfaltung der Persönlichkeit*). The general freedom of action (*az általános cselekvési szabadság—allgemeine Handlungsfreiheit*), the right to free self-determination (*az önrendelkezés szabadságához való jog—Recht auf freie Selbstbestimmung*) and the right to a private sphere (*a magánszférához való jog—Recht auf eine Privatsphäre*) were developed by the German Court under Articles 1(1) and 2(1) of the Basic Law.

The notion of 'mother-right' (*anyajog*) is also of German origin (*Muttergrundrecht*) and the name indicates its function. The image is clear: human dignity is a right which gives birth to other rights. In other words human dignity, in its association with the general personality right, is a right from which the Court can derive more specific rights which are not contained in the Hungarian Constitution. The Hungarian Court relied on human dignity in this case where no specific right could be found to protect the autonomy of the individuals involved. However, the phrase 'mother-right' was not directly coined by the German Constitutional Court; its origin is to be found instead in doctrinal writings, mainly in the work of HC Nipperdey.[6] Although the German Constitutional Court has not developed this metaphor, it has made the same use of human dignity, ie in connection with the general personality right and in the absence of another specific fundamental right. Following German terminology,

---

[6] HC Nipperdey, 'Freie Entfaltung der Persönlichkeit', in KA Bettermann, FI Neumann and HC Nipperdey (eds), *Die Grundrechte. Handbuch der Theorie und Praxis der Grundrechte* (Berlin, Duncker und Humblot, 1962), 759.

human dignity associated to the general personality right is a general provision that the Court can use in instances where a need for protection arises but the Basic Law lacks the relevant provision.

2. IMPORTING THE VARIOUS COMPONENTS OF THE RIGHT TO HUMAN DIGNITY

The importation of human dignity was made possible by two operations, which were implicitly carried out by the Court in case 8/1990 and which the Court had to elaborate and clarify in subsequent case law. Although they were simultaneous in that case, the two operations are distinguished here for the sake of analytical clarity. First, the Court separated human dignity from its twin right contained in Article 54(1), the right to life. This provision associates the two rights: 'everyone has the innate right to life and to human dignity.' In case 8/1990, however, the Court did not consider the latter option and ignored the right to life. It is true that this case, involving the power of representation vested in trade unions, was clearly not about the right to life. Yet the Court did not even refer to the exact wording of Article 54(1), nor did it discuss the link between life and dignity under this provision. This arguably can be explained by the fact that the Court had to separate the rights to life and human dignity if it wanted to import the general personality right.

The second operation consisted of associating the right to human dignity with the general personality right, as it is in German case law. This both created a link with German case law and extended the understanding of human dignity to encompass the general personality right, which in German law has led to the discovery of several sub-rights. This made it possible for the Hungarian Court to import these other sub-rights from German law. Table 1 presents a synopsis of the various aspects of the right to human dignity in Hungarian constitutional case law and lists the variety of rights imported in the wake of the general personality right from German case law.[7] Table 1 further illustrates the variety of situations to which the right to human dignity, in its various aspects, has been applied. Only in rare instances, in the cases on the death penalty and on abortion, did the Court apply the right to life and human dignity together in a strict interpretation of Article 54(1). Finally, Table 1 shows that a number of cases on similar issues arose during the period considered, thus enabling the Court to confirm and to refine its construction of the right to human dignity.

---

[7] This study does not include cases where human dignity is interpreted in relation to the equality provision of Art 70A: '1—The Republic of Hungary shall ensure the human and civil rights for all persons on its territory without any kind of discrimination, such as on the basis of race, colour, gender, language, religion, political or other opinion, national or social origins, financial situation, birth or on any other grounds whatsoever. 2—Any kind of discrimination described in paragraph (1) shall be strictly penalised by the law. 3—The Republic of Hungary shall promote the equality of rights for everyone through measures aimed at eliminating the inequality in opportunity.'

Table 1: Human dignity—a multi-faceted right

Cases	Issue(s) raised leading to use of human dignity	Rights derived from human dignity
8/1990	power of representation vested in trade unions	workers' right to self-determination
23/1990	unconstitutionality of capital punishment	right to life and human dignity
27/1990	right to take part in sports competitions	free fulfilment of personality and general freedom of action
15/1991	creation of a personal identity number and processing of personal data	right to a private sphere
46/1991	enforced payment of a debt	right to honour and good reputation
57/1991	filiation, ie questioning and ascertaining identity of one's biological father	right to self-determination and right to self-identification
64/1991	abortion, protection of the foetus and rights of the pregnant woman	right to self-determination, right to life and right to private sphere
9/1992	power of the public prosecutor to initiate a 'protest of illegality'	right to self-determination in civil judicial proceedings
22/1992	requirement for the military and firemen to receive the authorisation of their superior officer before marrying	right to self-determination in relation to the right to marry freely
4/1993	clarification of the meaning of freedom of religion in relation to the issue of restitution of some real estate to churches who owned them before the communist nationalisation	freedom of action, freedom of conscience and freedom of religion
23/1993	requirement for policemen to receive the authorisation of their superior officer before marrying	right to self-determination in relation to the right to marry freely
1/1994	public prosecutors' powers to intervene in judicial proceedings in the name of 'important state or social interests'	right to self-determination in judicial proceedings
28/1994	rules on redistribution (as part of the process of compensation and privatisation) of land and on regulations on the protection of nature	right to a healthy environment (Art 18 Constitution) in connection with the right to life
36/1994	freedom of expression, ie the right to criticise official persons	right to honour for official persons, ie those involved in public life

Table 1: Human dignity—a multi-faceted right *cont.*

Cases	Issue(s) raised leading to use of human dignity	Rights derived from human dignity
56/1994	power to take disciplinary action against civil servants because of their behaviour outside work	right to a private sphere for civil servants
35/1995	exclusion from higher education of persons subject to a prohibition on participation in public affairs	right to free fulfilment of one's personality in relation to access to higher education and the right to study
43/1995	reform of the social security system as part of a programme of economic austerity resulting in the abolition of a number of benefits/ allowances for mothers and children	protection of the right to life in relation to a number of child and maternity benefits/allowances
75/1995	rules concerning the 'witness' in proceedings to determine the paternity of a child when the 'witness' might turn out to be the father, power of the court to order certain medical tests	right to self-determination of the 'witness' in civil judicial proceedings versus right to self-identification of the child
12/1996	requirement to produce a certificate of good morals issued by the Ministry of Interior to be admitted to some institutions of higher education	right to self-determination and fulfilment of one's personality in relation to admission to higher education
24/1996	restriction of freedom of action for associations dealing with works of art, in particular requirement to receive the authorisation from a panel composed of experts appointed by the Ministry of Culture	the right to general freedom of action for certain moral persons
20/1997	powers of public prosecutors to ban the publication of any printed matter when 'it infringes the rights of others' or it incites crime	right to self-determination in relation to deciding on the publication of certain printed matter

2.1. The Right to Life and Human Dignity

In a minority of cases, ie those on abortion and the death penalty, the Hungarian Court developed a literal approach to Article 54(1). The construction of the right to human dignity was influenced, as in German constitutional case law, by the Kantian principle that the essential quality of humanity is dignity. Dignity defines human beings as subjects and makes it impossible to reduce them to mere objects. In German case law, this idea is often summarised and expressed in terms of the distinction between subject and object, the assertion being that human beings cannot be considered as mere objects. This underlying Kantian conception of human dignity was first announced in a concurring opinion by the president of the Court, L Sólyom, in case 23/1990, decided in October 1990. In this case the Court nullified the rules in the Penal Code providing for the death penalty for a number of serious crimes. In a short ruling, whose core reasoning rested on the right to life and human dignity, the Court held that the death penalty was unconstitutional, essentially because it breached Article 54(1). The judges joined many separate opinions to the case and in his, the president of the Court clarified his understanding of human dignity:

> The right to human dignity is not merely a declaration of a moral value. The concept that human dignity is a value a priori and beyond law, and is inaccessible by law in its entirety does not preclude this value from being regarded as the source of rights—as many international conventions and constitutions do by following natural law—or the law from requiring the respect of dignity or the transformation of some of its aspects into a real right. . . . We shall see that the right to human dignity will fulfil its function *only if it is interpreted in unity with the individual person's right to life; if we leave this out of consideration, abstract dignity will allow treatment of a concrete individual as an object.*[8] (emphasis added)

In this passage, L Sólyom proposes a very strong interpretation of human dignity. In his view, human dignity is not only a fundamental value, which positive law cannot harm or negate, but also a 'super right' in that it is a right from which other rights can be derived. While clarifying here the notion of 'mother-right' mentioned in case 8/1990, Sólyom explains how this is possible. Further, he insists on the importance of the link between the right to life and human dignity, on the basis of which the Court as a whole ruled that the death penalty was unconstitutional. According to Sólyom, separating the two would lead to negating the human quality of individuals, thus making it possible for the law—and this is the Kantian reference—to treat them as mere objects.

This interpretation of human dignity was confirmed a year later in the first case on abortion, the rules on which were fairly liberal in communist Hungary. In this case (64/1991) the Court ruled that the existing rules on abortion were unconstitutional. The Court examined many grounds, but the heart of the case was based on its understanding of the right to life and human dignity, in which the Court emphasised the 'untouchable essence of humanity':

> The right to human dignity means that there exists within the individual's autonomy, within his free self-determination a core which cannot be subjected to the disposition of others, *according to which—following the classic phrase—human beings remain a subject and cannot be transformed into an object or a tool.* This understanding of the

---

[8] Concurring opinion by L Sólyom, case 23/1990, in L Sólyom and G Brunner (eds), *Constitutional Judiciary in a New Democracy: The Hungarian Constitutional Court* (Ann Arbor, University of Michigan Press, 2000), 130–31.

right to human dignity distinguishes human beings from legal persons that can be totally subjected to legal regulations and that do not possess an untouchable essence. (emphasis added)

The definition of human beings as subjects with dignity led the Court to emphasise the importance of autonomy and self-determination of individuals. In particular, this idea was embodied by the creation through importation of a right to self-determination, derived from human dignity. More generally, as shown below, the Court used human dignity to protect individual autonomy. However, human dignity is not only a value, but also a fundamental constitutional right whose definition is most clearly formulated by L Sólyom in his concurring opinion in the Court's ruling banning capital punishment:

> The right to equal dignity, in union with the right to life, must ensure that bare lives of different value are not to be treated differently by the law. No one is more or less worthy of life. Because of equal dignity, the life and human dignity of a disabled person and a moral monster are equally untouchable. Human dignity is shared by every human being, no matter to what extent he/she has achieved the inherent possibilities of human beings and the reason therefor.[9]

The Hungarian Court's reasoning in this passage directly echoed German case law[10] and subsequently put the Court in an uncomfortable position when it had to rule on the constitutionality of abortion. This is because if strictly applied,[11] this logic might have led the Court to recognise that the foetus had a right to life and to human dignity, ie a right to be born and that abortion was therefore not constitutional. In case 64/1991 on abortion, the Hungarian Court pointed out that:

> Human life and dignity of all those who are human beings is untouchable independently of their stage of development and of their physical and intellectual situation, as well as of the degree of achievement of their human potential, and for whatever reason.

---

[9] Concurring opinion by L Sólyom, case 23/1990, in L Sólyom and G Brunner (eds), *Constitutional Judiciary in a New Democracy: The Hungarian Constitutional Court* (Ann Arbor, University of Michigan Press, 2000), 131. See also T Horváth, 'Abolition of Capital Punishment in Hungary' [1991] *Acta Juridica Hungarica* 153–66.

[10] German case law recognises that criminals, no matter how horrendous the crime, should not be deprived of their dignity through the punishment process. BVerfGE 28, 389, [391] of 9 June 1970: 'In the fight against criminality, the criminal should not be considered as a mere object by infringing his social value and his right to be respected which are constitutionally protected.'

[11] Indeed this was part of the reasoning of the German constitutional ruling on abortion. BVerfGE 39, 1, [41] of 25 February 1975: 'Life in the sense of a developmental existence of an individual begins, according to established biological-physiological findings, on the fourteenth day after conception (implantation, individuation). The developmental process thus begun is a continuous one which manifests no sharp demarcation and does not permit any precise delimitation of various developmental stages of the human life, nor does it end with birth. . . . Therefore [we] may not limit the protection of Article 2(2)[1] of the Basic Law either to the 'completed' human being after birth, or to the independently viable nasciturus. [Article 2(2)[1]] guarantees the right to life to everyone who "lives"; no distinction can be made between individual stages of the developing life before birth or between prenatal and postnatal life.', as translated and quoted by D Kommers, *The Constitutional Jurisprudence of the Federal Republic of Germany* (Durham and London, Duke University Press, 1997), 337.

However, in this case, the Hungarian Court was not prepared to answer the thorny question of the legal status of the foetus. Instead, the Court developed the notion of an institutional, or objective, protection of the right to life under Article 8(1) which imposed on the state a duty to protect fundamental rights.[12] This duty extends to lives which are in formation and it further means that the state 'has a duty to secure the conditions of life for the future generations.'[13] In addition, the Court based its reasoning on the specific formal requirements, as set out in Article 8(2) of the Constitution.[14] Following these provisions, issues involving fundamental rights and duties have to be regulated by statutes and not by norms of an inferior ranking (which were numerous under the communist regime), such as the ministerial decrees on abortion which petitioners challenged before the Court. Finally, the constitutional judges ruled that, since abortion involved fundamental rights in relation to the issues of the legal status of the foetus and of the pregnant woman's protection, it had to be regulated by an Act of parliament under Article 8(2) of the Constitution. Consequently, the Court nullified the ministerial decrees on abortion and called for parliament to enact a statute to respond to this issue.

In 1998, the Court delivered a second ruling on abortion following the enactment of Act LXXIX/1992 on the protection of the life of the embryo (48/1998). In this case, the Court did not depart from its previous position, that is it did not recognise a legal capacity for the foetus and insisted on the duty of objective protection of life and dignity. The core of the 48/1998 ruling focused on the constitutionality of abortion during the first 12 weeks of pregnancy that may be requested by a woman who finds herself in a 'situation of serious crisis'. The Court accepted that parliament might allow abortions in such cases, but it held that Parliament must also provide measures to ensure the protection of the foetus's life. In the absence of such measures, the Court ruled that this particular provision was unconstitutional.[15]

The right to life was interpreted in two other instances by the Constitutional Court, which led it to explain further its notion of objective (or institutional) protection of fundamental rights. In case 28/1994, the Court was asked to decide on the constitutionality of statutes providing for the redistribution of land, in

---

[12] Article 8(1): 'The Republic of Hungary recognizes the inviolable and inalienable fundamental rights of man; *to respect and to protect them is the primary obligation of the State*' (emphasis added).

[13] L Sólyom and G Brunner (eds), *Constitutional Judiciary in a New Democracy: The Hungarian Constitutional Court* (Ann Arbor, University of Michigan Press, 2000), 183.

[14] Article 8: '2—In the Republic of Hungary rules pertaining to fundamental rights and duties shall be determined by statute, which, however, may not limit the essential contents of any fundamental right. 3—[*repealed*] 4—During a state of national crisis, state of emergency or state of danger, the exercise of fundamental rights may be suspended or restricted, with the exception of fundamental rights enshrined in Articles 54–56, Article 57(2)–(4), Article 60, Articles 66–69 and Article 70E.'

[15] See H Küpper, 'Das Zweite Abtreibungsurteil des Ungarischen Verfassungsgerichts' [1999] *OsteuropaRecht* 155–69.

the context of compensation for and privatisation of land that had been nation-alised under communism. Some of this land was to be transferred to the envir-onmental protection authorities and this led the Court to consider the constitutional nature of the right to a healthy environment under Article 18 of the 1989 Constitution.[16] According to the Court, this right was not an individ-ual fundamental right, nor merely a state objective that the state was free to pursue as it pleased. The Court gave a very strong interpretation, analysing it as part of the institutional protection of the right to life:

> The right to environmental protection is most closely related to the right to life, for the right to a healthy environment is, in fact, a part of the objective, institutional aspect of the right to life. The responsibility of the State to maintain the natural basis of human life is isolated and named as a separate constitutional 'right.' If Art. 18 of the Constitution were absent, the State duties in the area of environmental protection could also be deduced from a broad interpretation of Art. 54(1) of the Constitution.
>
> The express declaration of the right to a healthy environment bestows a special con-stitutional weight upon the consequences which necessarily follow from the State's objective responsibility to protect life. These objective State duties are broader than the sum total of the individual rights to life.[17]

Case 43/1995 clarified further the notion of 'objective protection' of fundamen-tal rights in that it held that the state could not abolish the system of maternity and child benefits existing under communism, without giving sufficient notice to the individuals concerned so that they might prepare themselves for the change in the social security system. This case was part of a group of cases prompted by the introduction of drastic austerity measures in June 1995, known as the 'Bokros package' named after the Minister for the Economy. The argument at the heart of these cases was the rule of law under Article 2 of the Constitution.[18] In its inter-pretation, the Court emphasised the requirement of legal certainty which was infringed by the law-maker, because of the lack of time given to people to adjust to the new system. In order to reinforce its point, the Court emphasised the import-ance of the state duty to protect mothers and children under the Constitution. In particular, the Court linked the provision of maternity benefits, pregnancy allowances and other benefits threatened by the austerity package to the right to life under Article 54(1)—that is, as interpreted in case 64/1991 and repeated in case 43/1995 'the guarantee of living conditions of future generations.'[19]

Although the reasoning on the specific issues of environmental protection and child and maternity benefits cannot be traced back to particular German constitutional cases, the concept of objective protection of fundamental rights is

---

[16] Article 18: 'The Republic of Hungary recognises and shall implement everyone's right to a healthy environment.'

[17] L Sólyom and G Brunner (eds), *Constitutional Judiciary in a New Democracy: The Hungarian Constitutional Court* (Ann Arbor, University of Michigan Press, 2000), 303.

[18] Article 2(1): 'The Republic of Hungary shall be an independent, democratic state under the rule of law.' See also ch 1.

[19] L Sólyom and G Brunner (eds), *Constitutional Judiciary in a New Democracy: The Hungarian Constitutional Court* (Ann Arbor, University of Michigan Press, 2000), 331.

to be found in German constitutional case law. It can be understood by saying that fundamental rights have two aspects: a subjective aspect and an objective aspect. The subjective aspect is centred on the individual's needs and it emphasises the need for protection against state actions or interferences with his life. The objective aspect highlights the protection that the state has to provide, not so much to individuals in particular, but rather to legal institutions such as marriage or ownership within which fundamental rights can blossom. One of the leading academics who has developed this notion is Klaus Stern.[20] The influence of his work on the development of the concept of constitutional rights in Hungary is no secret and the president of the Court, L Sólyom, acknowledged it in an article published in a special issue of *OsteuropaRecht* celebrating Hungary's millennium:

> Positive law was not the only one to be appropriated. Those who are familiar with the theory discover easily the influence of famous theoreticians or textbooks. The '*Stern*' was very often used at the Court in Budapest.[21]

German constitutional case law was an obvious source of direct importation, but as seen above the Hungarian Court also imported ideas from influential academic writings to develop its own understanding of human dignity. This is completed by the importation of several constitutional rights, which themselves have been construed by the German Court under Articles 1(1) and 2(1) of the Basic Law on the right to free fulfilment of one's personality.

2.2. Human Dignity and the General Personality Right

The association of human dignity and the general personality right is crucial in that it enabled the Court to develop numerous other rights, which were not originally contained in the Hungarian Constitution of 1989. The Court remained vague on the exact nature of the link between the two rights, but it seems that the two rights have an equivalent meaning and scope when they are interpreted together.

The general personality right which the Court claimed to see in 'modern constitutions' is in fact again to be found in German case law. Interestingly, this right is not contained in the German Basic Law itself, but was construed by the German Constitutional Court.[22] The general personality right has been an

---

[20] K Stern, *Das Staatrecht der Bundesrepublik Deutschland*, vol III/1 (München, Beck, 1988), § 65.

[21] L Sólyom, 'Aufbau und dogmatische Fundierung der Verfassungsgerichtsbarkeit in Ungarn' [2000] *OsteuropaRecht* 233.

[22] The German Court implicitly recognised this right in BVerfGE 6, 32, *Elfes* case, 16 January 1957. It was explicitly developed in a famous case involving the private life of Princess Soraya in 1972 (BVerfGE 34, 269, *Princess Soraya*, 14 February 1972). The facts at the origin of the case were simple and involved a conflict between Princess Soraya and a weekly magazine which had published information concerning her private life. The Princess, however, contrary to what the magazine claimed, had not given any interview. She sued the magazine for breach of her personality right and her right to honour. Both the first instance court and the appeal court accepted the claim and ordered the magazine to pay the applicant damages of DM 15,000. However, at that time, the general

important element of German constitutional case law and the German Court has used it mainly in connection with Article 2(1) of the Basic Law. Similarly, most of the other rights (the general freedom of action, the right to a private sphere and the right to free self-determination) were elaborated by the German Constitutional Court on the basis of Article 2(1) on the right to free fulfilment of one's personality. The table below shows that most aspects of the Hungarian interpretation of human dignity can be traced back, very precisely in some cases, to rulings of the German Constitutional Court.

Table 2: **The importation of human dignity from German constitutional case law—synopsis**

Aspects of human dignity	*Hungarian law*	*German law*
Const. articles	**Art 54(1)**: 'In the Republic of Hungary, everyone has the innate right to life and human dignity. No one shall be deprived of it in an arbitrary manner.'	**Art 1(1)**: 'The dignity of the human being is inviolable. It is the duty of all state authority to have regard to it and to protect it.'
Object/ subject	—Definition of human being (23/1990) —Abortion (64/1991, 48/1998) —Procedural rights (9/1992, 1/1994, 75/1995)	—BVerfGE 27, 1, [6], *Microcensus* (16 June 1969) —BVerfGE 9, 89, [95], *Hearing after an arrest* (8 January 1959), in relation to art. 103(1) of the Basic Law ('In court everybody is entitled to a hearing in accordance with the law.')
Self-determination	—Self-identification (57/1991, 75/1995) —Freedom to marry (22/1992 and 23/1993) —Procedural self-determination in civil matters (9/1992, 1/1994 and 75/1995	—BVerfGE 79, 256, [268], *The right to ascertain one's parentage* (31 January 1989) —Requirement of procedure under the rule of law: arts 1 and 2 in connection with art. 103 Basic Law, BVerfGE 7, 53, [57] (18 June 1957)

personality right was only based on case law and no German statute provided for the allocation of damages for the compensation of immaterial harm. Following a constitutional complaint filed by the magazine, the Constitutional Court was then asked to decide on the constitutionality of the lower courts' decisions and it confirmed the ruling of the Court of Appeal.

Aspects of human dignity	Hungarian law	German law
	—Pregnant women/abortion (64/1991, 48/1998)	—Abortion cases I, BVerfGE 39, 1, [41] (25 February 1975) and II 88, 203, [253] (28 May 1993)
	—Informational self-determination (15/1991)	—BVerfGE 65, 1, [42], *Census Act* (15 December 1983)
	—Workers/trade unions (8/1990)	
Private sphere	—Data collection and processing, ie personality profile (15/1991)	—BVerfGE 65, 1 [42], *Census Act* (15 December 1983) also and generally: BVerfGE 34, 205, *Divorce Records* (18 January 1973) and BVerfGE 32, 373, *Medical Confidentiality* (8 March 1972)
	—Good reputation and honour (46/1991, 36/1994 and 56/1994)	—Protection of personal honour: BVerfGE 34, 269, *Princess Soraya* (14 February 1972) and BVerfGE 54, 208, [217], *Böll/Walden* (3 June 1980)
	—Pregnant women/abortion (64/1991, 48/1998)	—Abortion cases I, BVerfGE 39, 1, [41] (25 February 1975) and II, 88, 203, [253] (28 May 1993)
Free fulfilment of one's personality	—Generally mentioned in most cases —Specifically in case 27/1990 on amateur sportsmen —Right to admission to higher education institutions (35/1995 and 12/1996)	—Art 2(1) Basic Law: 'Everyone has the right to a free fulfilment of his personality, in so far as he does not injure the rights of others or violate the constitutional order or the moral law.'
General freedom of action	—Sportsmen taking part in competitions (27/1990)	—Art 2(1) of the Basic Law —Very broad understanding developed in the *Elfes* case, BVerfGE 2, 32 (16 January 1957).

Table 2: The importation of human dignity from German constitutional case law—
synopsis *cont.*

Aspects of human dignity	Hungarian law	German law
General Freedom of Action *cont.*		Other cases include: *Feeding pigeons* BVerfGE 55, 159 (5 November 1980) and *Horse riding in the woods*, BVerfGE 80, 137 (6 June 1989)
	—In judicial proceedings (9/1992, 1/1994, 75/1995 and 20/1997)	—In judicial proceedings, together with the rule of law principle, BVerfGE 7, 53, [57] (18 June 1957); 7, 275, [279] (13 February 1958); 9, 89, [95] (8 January 1959)
	—Of moral persons, ie associations (24/1996)	—Of moral persons, such as limited partnership and trading company generally recognised under Art 2(1), BVerfGE 10, 89, [99], *Erft Public Corporation* 29 July 1959); 42, 212, *Quick* (26 May 1976)
	—Freedom of religion, (4/1993)	—Specific constitutional provision: Art 4 Basic Law on freedom of faith, conscience and creed

Sources: Hungarian case law: case reports and website of the Constitutional Court (www.mkab.hu). German constitutional case law: case reports and summaries presented in German Federal Constitutional Court (ed), *Nachschlagewerk der Rechtsprechung des Bundesverfassungsgerichts* (Heidelberg, R v Decker and CF Müller Verlag, looseleaf edition regularly updated); I Richter and GF Schuppert (eds), *Casebook Verfassungsrecht* (München, CH Beck Verlagbuchhandlung, 1996), and D Kommers, *The Constitutional Jurisprudence of the Federal Republic of Germany* (Durham and London, Duke University Press, 1997).

Table 2 presents Hungarian case law on human dignity and the general personality right, together with a selection of relevant German cases, which were chosen for their similar terminology, reasoning and sometimes facts (particularly on the right to self-identification in case 57/1991). The German cases mentioned are also those that are most often quoted to illustrate a particular interpretation of human dignity and the general personality right.

Table 2 highlights the fact that for each particular aspect of human dignity in Hungarian case law there is a corresponding case (more often a line of case law) in German law. It further highlights that the use of particular aspects of human dignity in Hungarian case law is strikingly similar to German case law. For instance, the right to self-determination protects individuals in the course of judicial proceedings in both sets of case law. The synopsis in Table 2 can be complemented by a brief presentation of each aspect of human dignity in Hungarian constitutional case law.

(a) The Right to Free Fulfilment of the Personality

The right to free fulfilment of one's personality is explicitly enshrined in Article 2(1) of the Basic Law and has been the starting point for the development of many other rights in German case law.[23] In Hungary, however, the right to free fulfilment of one's personality was perhaps the least used by the Hungarian Court. It appeared only in three cases between 1990 and 1998. In case 27/1990, the Court used it together with the general freedom of action to grant amateur sportsmen the right to leave their associations and to participate freely in sports competitions. The free fulfilment of one's personality was used by the Hungarian Court in two later cases involving access to higher education. In case 35/1995, the Court held that the blanket exclusion from higher education institutions of all persons subject to a prohibition on participation in public affairs was unconstitutional, because it was an unproportional restriction of their right to higher education derived from human dignity and free fulfilment of their personality. The second case, 12/1996, repeated this reasoning and applied it in relation to the requirement to present a certificate of good morals issued by the Ministry of the Interior to establish that the applicant to an institution of higher education has no previous criminal conviction. The Court ruled that this amounted to an unconstitutional processing of personal data and emphasised the importance of higher education for the fulfilment of one's personality.

(b) The General Freedom of Action

The German Constitutional Court construed the general freedom of action for the first time in a landmark ruling from 1957, applying it to the leader of a political party (named Elfes) who protested against the German rearmament policy and who had been denied the renewal of his passport.[24] In Hungary, the general

---

[23] E Benda, 'Privatsphäre und "Persönlichkeitsprofile"' in *Festschrift f. W Geiger* (Tübingen, JC Mohr, 1974), 23–44; HD Jarass, 'Das allgemeine Persönlichkeitsrecht im Grundgesetz' [1989] *Neue Juristische Wochenschrift* 857–62; R Scholz, 'Das Grundrecht auf freie Entfaltung der Persönlichkeit in der Rechtsprechung des Bundesverfassungsgerichts' [1975] *Archiv für Öffentliches Recht* 80.

[24] BVerfGE 6, 32, (41, 42), *Elfes* case, 16 January 1957: 'Even if the freedom to travel abroad is not part of the freedom to travel within Germany, it can still be guaranteed by deriving it from the general freedom of action within the limits of the constitutional order under art. 2(1).' In this case, the applicant claimed that the refusal to renew his passport violated his freedom to travel abroad. The German Basic Law, however, does not contain a specific fundamental right to travel abroad, but only guarantees the freedom of movement within the boundaries of the national territory (Art 11). The German Court excluded this provision from its reasoning because it did not encompass the

freedom of action was not very frequently used by the Constitutional Court. Although it seems to be implicit in most cases, the Court highlighted it only in some cases where it was particularly important. For instance, as seen above, the Court used it in connection with the free fulfilment of one's personality to guarantee amateur sportsmen a right to leave their association freely (case 27/1990). In case 1/1994, the Court referred to the general freedom of action using its negative form, that is the general freedom not to act. In that case, the Court ruled that individuals had the right *not to start* judicial proceedings if such was their decision. As a result, the Court ruled that the general powers of the state prosecutor, in particular the power to initiate proceedings for the protection of 'important state or social interests' without the concerned individual's authorisation, were unconstitutional.[25]

In case 24/1996, the Hungarian Court extended the general freedom of action to moral persons, such as associations. This case involved the infamous system of controls over cultural life that existed under communism. One aspect of this system was that associations dealing with works of art had to seek permission from a panel composed of experts from the Ministry of Culture. The Hungarian Court declared that this rule was unconstitutional because it breached the general freedom of action of these associations. As the Court had so far consistently applied human dignity and the general personality right to human persons and, moreover, because it tightly linked the notion of dignity to the definition of humanity (in cases 23/1990 and 64/1991), case 24/1996 seemed to contradict this well-established line of case law. However, this inconsistency is explained when the case is compared to the general freedom of action as construed on the basis of Article 2(1) by the German Court. Significantly, the German Court has used the general freedom of action in relation to moral persons, as well as in relation to individuals.[26] Arguably, the logic of the Hungarian reasoning in case 24/1996 can be explained by the importation of this extended interpretation of the general freedom of action from German case law.

---

freedom to leave the territory of the German Federal Republic. It then went on to link this freedom with the right to free fulfilment of one's personality (under Art 2(1)) and derived from it the general freedom of action. On this basis, the court concluded that the applicant had a right to travel abroad.

[25] On the procuracy, see I Szikinger, 'The Procuracy and its Problems: Hungary' (1999) 8 *East European Constitutional Review* 85.

[26] In its case law, the German Constitutional Court has read into the general personality right a right to economic freedom of action, which also applies to moral persons. See the cases referred to in Table 2 and I Richter and GF Schuppert (eds), *Casebook Verfassungsrecht* (München, CH Beck Verlagbuchhandlung, 1996), 99–100. In German case law, this particular interpretation of the general freedom of action in relation to moral persons is supported by Art 19 of the Basic Law which does not exclude persons other than human beings from enjoying fundamental rights. Chapter 5 will come back to this issue in more detail.

(c) The Right to a Private Sphere

As in German law, the Hungarian Court read the right to a private sphere into the human dignity provision of the Constitution. The German Basic Law does not provide for the general protection of privacy,[27] so the German Constitutional Court developed it under Articles 1(1) and 2(1). For example, the right to a private sphere has included the protection of individuals against the disclosure of divorce records in disciplinary proceedings and the disclosure of the medical file of a patient facing a criminal trial.[28] The right to a private sphere has led to abundant case law in Germany and it also protects the right to honour and reputation, particularly the right not to have statements falsely attributed (by a magazine) to oneself as established in the *Princess Soraya* case.[29]

In contrast, the Hungarian Constitution does contain a provision that generally protects privacy (Art 59)[30], but rather than relying on it, the Hungarian Court imported the notion of the private sphere from German case law and incorporated it into its own case law under Article 54(1). The Hungarian Court first used the right to a private sphere in case 46/1991 in relation to enforced debt payment procedures according to which, after a period of 30 days, a debtor may be forced by a public official to pay what he owes. The Court ruled that in so doing the administration might target the wrong person due to the lack of a guarantee that he would be identified in an accurate manner. As a result, the Court ruled that this violated the right to a private sphere and to a good reputation derived from human dignity:

> Hence, in the absence of sufficient guarantees, the authorisation of an executory clause breaches the provisions contained in art. 54(1) and art. 59(1) of the Constitution which protect the inviolability of the domicile and human dignity.
>
> Indeed, by taking into account its character, the executory clause presents the debtor to the other parties (for instance his/her employer or his/her house mates) in an unfavourable light, that is as a person on whom administrative force has to be imposed in order to force him/her to fulfil his/her obligations. *In this context, the Constitutional Court insists on the fact that the right to human dignity contains not only the right to a good reputation, but also among others the right to the protection of the private sphere.* In consideration of this, the application of administrative force without justification encroaches upon the fundamental right to human dignity; *in so doing the State interferes without justification in the relationships belonging to the private sphere.* (emphasis added)

---

[27] The Basic Law enshrines the right to privacy of correspondence, post and telecommunications in Art 10, as well as the inviolability of the home in Art 13.

[28] Respectively: BVerfGE 34, 205, *Divorce Records*, 18 January 1973 and BVerfGE 32, 373, *Medical Confidentiality*, 8 March 1972.

[29] BVerfGE 34, 269, 14 February 1972, see above n 22.

[30] Article 59: '1—In the Republic of Hungary everyone has the right to the good standing of his/her reputation, the inviolability of his/her private home and the protection of his/her personal secrets and data. 2—A majority of two-thirds of the votes of the Members of Parliament present is required to pass a statute on the protection of personal data.'

Three months later, in the abortion case (64/1991), the Court reaffirmed the existence of an expectant mother's right to a private sphere, but it did not elaborate on it and in particular it did not venture into determining its scope. The Court further used the right to a private sphere and a good reputation in case 36/1994, in which the petitioner claimed that the penalty of two years' imprisonment for injuring the honour of an official person, under the Criminal Code of 1978 as modified in 1993, was unconstitutional. The Court accepted this claim and found those provisions to be unconstitutional, basing its reasoning on the broad interpretation of freedom of expression, combined with a more restrictive understanding of the private sphere of public persons, as opposed to that of private individuals. In case 56/1994, the Court had to examine the constitutionality of the obligation imposed on civil servants to behave in a certain way even outside work. In this case the Court ruled that the disciplinary sanctions imposed on civil servants for not behaving appropriately outside work was a restriction of their right to a private sphere, as derived from the right to human dignity and that restriction did not meet the constitutional requirements. Although the range of cases is much more limited than in Germany, the interpretation of privacy as encompassing the protection of a private sphere and the protection of honour and reputation generally followed German case law.

(d) The Right to Self-Determination

The right to self-determination is the most developed of the aspects of human dignity and it is also the most versatile. It can be understood as the ability of individuals to take decisions that influence their lives without interference from the state, or related state bodies. The right to self-determination was at the heart of the first case on human dignity (8/1990). In this case, it meant that trade unions could no longer automatically represent employees, that is without being authorised by them to do so. The right of employees to self-determination meant that they could decide not to be represented by trade unions if they so wished. In the abortion case (64/1991), the Court briefly mentioned the pregnant woman's right to self-determination (together with her right to a private sphere). Although the Court did not expand on this right, it clearly meant the right to choose to have an abortion. However, in that case the reasoning did not focus on the scope of the rights involved (including the foetus's right to life) and the Court focused instead on the formal requirements (namely a statute) to regulate these rights.

In case 57/1991, the Court further 'discovered' a right to self-identification: a right to question and ascertain one's biological origins. This case was brought before the Court under the procedure of repressive concrete norm control. This was an unusual way to challenge a legal provision before the Constitutional Court, which enables it to intervene during proceedings before an ordinary court, or as in this case, after a judicial decision. In this case the petitioner was the father of a child whom he had raised on his own for several years. Following the final judicial decision reversing the presumption of his paternity of the child, the child had been taken away from him. The petitioner challenged the constitutionality of the provisions of the Family Act of 1952, which regulated the process of reversing the presumption of paternity in Hungarian law. Under this Act there are two routes available to challenge the presumption of paternity. The first is open to the legal guardian of the child and can be initiated within one year after the notification of the child's birth, if the child has not reached the legal age of majority. After her majority, the child herself can initiate the proceedings within one year after her nineteenth birthday. However, in both cases, a judicial ruling on the presumption of paternity is final, that is it cannot be challenged, nor appealed against. It is this situation that the petitioner in case 57/1991 claimed was unconstitutional. In his case, following the judicial ruling reversing the presumption of paternity of his son, the petitioner had no possibility to appeal the ruling, nor could the child himself challenge the court's ruling after reaching the age of majority. In this case the Hungarian Constitutional Court held that:

> At the same time, the Constitutional Court points out that the right to ascertain one's biological origins together with questioning and challenging the legal presumption of paternity is everyone's most personal right and it falls within the scope of the 'general personality right' contained in art. 54(1) of the constitution. Under art. 54(1) of the constitution, everyone has an innate right to human dignity and shall not be deprived of it in an arbitrary manner.
>
> The Constitutional Court explained in its ruling 8/1990 (23 April) that it considered the right to human dignity as being one of the names for the 'general personality right.' It asserted that modern constitutions and constitutional case law have referred to this right by several of its aspects, for instance: the right to free fulfilment of one's personality, the right to free self-determination, the general freedom of action or the right to a private sphere. The general personality right is a 'mother-right', that is a subsidiary fundamental right which is used to protect individual autonomy when none of the named fundamental rights can apply to the given situation.
>
> According to the Constitutional Court, the right to self-determination and the right to self-identification form part of the 'general personality right.' The right to self-determination and the right to self-identification mean that it is everyone's most personal right to question his/her biological origin, to discover and to ascertain his/her parentage, further, that beyond the direct biological relatives, no one can question biological ascendance. The deprivation of this right resulting from a judicial procedure initiated by third parties and of which the outcome is unquestionable and cannot be appealed nor reviewed, breaches the child's right to identity and in so doing violates the general personality right which is constitutionally protected.

This extract illustrates a typical use of human dignity: the Hungarian Court referred to the founding case 8/1990 and repeated its understanding of human dignity and the personality right. It then singled out a particular aspect of human dignity and related it to the facts of the case. In addition here, the Court went on to derive a new right from human dignity: the right to self-identification. In fact, this right was imported from German case law and the following extract from a case decided on 31 January 1989 on a similar issue reveals how closely the Hungarian Court mirrored the German reasoning on the right to self-identification:

> The right to free fulfilment of the personality together with human dignity guarantee individuals an autonomous domain for the organisation of their lives, in which they can develop and protect their own individuality (Cf. BVerfGE 35, 202, [220]). However, the comprehension and the fulfilment of individuality are tightly connected with the knowledge of its constitutive elements. They encompass, among other things, one's origin. One's ascendance determines one's genetic heritage and thus also influences one's personality. . . . The determination of one's own individuality and the comprehension of oneself has more to do with a multiple process in which the knowledge made available by biological means is in no way determining on its own. *Origin, as a characteristic of individuality, forms part of the personality; the knowledge of one's own origin, independently of scientific results, offers the individual important points of reference to understand and fulfil one's individuality. Consequently, the right to personality also encompasses the knowledge of one's own origin.* It cannot be questioned that there are cases in which it is impossible to clarify an individual's origin and in which the fulfilment of the personality has to take place without this knowledge. Art. 2(1) in connection with art. 1(1) does not grant any right to access the knowledge of one's origin, but it can only protect against the denial of accessible information.[31] (emphasis added)

This case was brought before the German Court by a woman who wished to challenge the presumption that her mother's husband was her father. However, under German law the procedure for reversing the legal presumption of paternity was not available to those whose parents are married and have no intention to divorce, as in the case of the petitioner. The case was first heard before an ordinary court where the judge, following the process of concrete constitutional review, referred the matter to the Constitutional Court. The constitutional judges were asked to decide whether the Civil Code provisions breached the German Basic Law and in particular the child's right to free fulfilment of her personality.

This case was decided in the context of academic and political debates about the relevance of a right to ascertain one's genetic origin, particularly in relation to those born as a result of medically assisted procreation technology. This ruling of the German Constitutional Court, in which the judges acknowledged the existence of a right to know one's biological origins, was supported by these debates. Moreover, this case was part of a substantial body of case law in which the German Court had associated the notion of identity with the fulfilment of the personality under Article 2(1) of the Basic Law.[32] The German Court further developed this line of case law in acknowledging a right to know one's origin. Finally, in this case the German Court is cautious not to phrase this right in absolute terms. That is, the court guarantees a right to have access to information which exists, but which for some reason—as in this case—is not available to the individual.

---

[31] BVerfGE 79, 256, (268), 31 January 1989.
[32] A Schmidt-Didczuhn, '(Verfassungs)Recht auf Kenntnis der eigenen Abstammung?' [1989] *Juristische Rundschau* 228–32.

In comparison, the link made by the Hungarian Court in case 57/1991 between Article 54(1) and the right to question one's biological origin was less clearly explained. However, it may be better understood when read in the light of the German case. In the extract from case 57/1991, which is quoted at the beginning of this section, the Hungarian Court mirrored the German reasoning in a somewhat less articulate style. First, it associated the general personality right and human dignity with the importance of knowing one's origins. While this was explicit in the German case, it was implicit in the Hungarian case in that the Court directly linked the general personality right under Article 54(1) and the need to be able to reverse the legal presumption of paternity. The right to self-identification was reaffirmed by the Hungarian Court in case 75/1995, which also involved the legal presumption of paternity and in particular the judicial proceedings with a view to reversing it.

Interestingly, in this case, this aspect of self-determination conflicted with another aspect developed by the Court: the right to self-determination in judicial proceedings. The latter was first used by the Court in case 9/1992 relating to the constitutionality of the chief public prosecutor's power to appeal against ordinary courts' rulings in some cases. This sort of appeal, called the 'protest of illegality,' was inherited from the socialist system of 'supervision of legality' in which the chief public prosecutor and the president of the Supreme Court played a central role. It enabled them to lodge a protest against any final judgment of a civil or criminal court if they deemed that that judgment was in violation of the law. The Court found this power to be unconstitutional because it breached the self-determination right of the parties:

> In civil matters, the protest of illegality further violates the parties' self-determination right because it makes it possible to raise a protest in all cases, without considering the merits of the case, and thus, through the protest of illegality, it is possible to alter the final judgment and to affect the parties independently of their will. The breach of this fundamental principle, as well as of civil procedure, also breaches the constitutional right to self-determination (case 8/1990 of 23 April). According to well-established case law, the right to self-determination is a component of the right to human dignity and consequently the protest of illegality conflicts with art. 54(1) of the constitution.

In this case, the Hungarian Court also relied on the requirement of the rule of law under Article 2 of the Constitution and in particular it referred to Article 57(1), which is more specifically related to equality before the law.[33] The right to self-determination was subsequently used by the Court in all cases involving public prosecutors' powers: case 1/1994 concerned their power to intervene in judicial proceedings to protect 'important state and social interests' and case 20/1997 concerned their power to ban the publication of certain printed matter.

---

[33] Article 57(1): 'In the Republic of Hungary everyone is equal before the law and, in the determination of any criminal charge against him/her or in the litigation of his/her rights and duties, everyone is entitled to a fair and public hearing by an independent and impartial court established by statute.'

In these cases, the interpretation of the right to self-determination led the Court to rule that those powers were unconstitutional and it ensured that individuals who are involved in judicial proceedings have some control over the course of the proceedings.

3. CONCLUSION

The scope of law importation from Germany between 1990–98 was wide-ranging and it included various legal elements, such as aspects of constitutional case law, academic debates and specific fundamental rights. The Hungarian Court also imported techniques of interpretation, such as the concept of 'mother-right,' which involves deriving 'sub-rights' from a main right, ie the right to human dignity and, very importantly, the association between dignity and the general personality right. Law importation also extended to entire judicial arguments, as shown by the case on self-identification, which is a striking mirror image of a case decided by the German Constitutional Court. Indeed, the Hungarian Court was such an enthusiastic importer of law that in early cases, involving privacy issues, it apparently ignored the Hungarian Constitution, which contains a provision generally protecting private life (Art 59). Rather than relying on the domestic provision, the Hungarian Court developed its own general approach to privacy by importing into its interpretation of Article 54(1) the notion of a private sphere, construed in German case law on the basis of human dignity and the general personality right.

The question which arises now is why did the Hungarian Court choose German law as its privileged source of importation? The beginning of an answer can be suggested: German case law on human dignity and the general personality right is highly developed and abundant. This made it an attractive source from which the Hungarian Court could draw in order to find a solution for almost all questions arising in Hungary. However, the German Court is not the only court to have produced abundant case law since the Second World War and the reasons for choosing Germany as a source of importation appear to be more complex. They will be considered in the following chapter.

4

Choosing the Right Model

I N ITS REASONING on human dignity and the general personality right, as
shown in the previous chapter, the Hungarian Constitutional Court kept
referring to 'modern constitutions and their practice' (*'modern alkotmányok,
illetve alkotmánybírósági gyakorlat'*) as the source of its inspiration. The choice
of 'modern constitutions' cannot be explained by the fact that they are legally
binding on the Hungarian Court, since Hungary is an independent and sovereign state. In fact, the phrase 'modern constitutions' only refers to constitutions
and does not include binding international conventions on human rights, such
as the International Covenant of Civil and Political Rights or the European
Convention on Human Rights, to which the Hungarian Constitutional Court
refers explicitly and separately. Furthermore, the choice of 'modern constitutions' as a source of importation to rebuild the Hungarian legal system cannot
be explained in terms of a relationship of political subordination, as was the
case when colonies adopted the law of the colonial power, or the losers of a war
had to comply with the winners' instructions for reconstructing their legal systems.

A better explanation of this term can be found when the phrase 'modern constitutions' is understood as being a response to the flood of Western law
exporters, who promoted their constitutions as being the best way to foster
democracy in post-communist countries. This, however, is still only a partial
explanation as not all foreign exportations were equally successful. As importation was derived from a narrow range of foreign systems, this indicates that the
importers of law undertook a further selection from the range of models offered
to them. This selection has often been explained in terms of a particular model's
prestige, which is said to determine the success of that model's spread abroad.
However, prestige on its own does not explain the choice in favour of a particular system for the purpose of importation. A crucial factor that operates
together with prestige in influencing the importers' decision is the knowledge
that importers of law have of a particular legal system. The last criterion affecting the importers' choice perhaps best illustrates that law importation is a deliberate strategy. In addition to prestige and knowledge of a particular foreign
model, importers consider the use that they can make of this model. In other
words, in the Hungarian example, constitutional judges imported the right to
human dignity and the general personality right from German case law because

it was prestigious, they had a good knowledge of it and it suited their needs particularly well, namely to develop quickly a number of fundamental rights.

1. PRESTIGE

Scholars who have studied the reception of law have pointed out that the prestige of a legal system was a decisive factor in this process. Watson, in his seminal book on legal transplants, considered the notion of the authority of legal systems which were transplanted to other countries. In chapter 15 of his book, which focuses on this idea, he reminded us that the very first laws were given by the supreme authority, namely by gods and here Watson referred to Yahveh, Apollo and Zeus.[1] Later, when the divine explanation of the origins of law waned, legal systems still originated in an authoritative figure and Watson referred to the impact of Frederick the Great and Napoleon in the elaboration of legal systems. Referring to similar examples, the Italian comparatist Rodolfo Sacco emphasised the prestige factor in the diffusion of Roman law and later the Napoleonic Code throughout Europe and of English and French models in Africa:

> Prestige assisted the *ius commune* in its conquest of Europe; prestige lay behind the Napoleonic Code and it pushed the German scientific and scholastic legal models beyond the frontiers of the sphere of Roman law; prestige made the penetration of English and French legal models into Africa irreversible; and the prestige of the Sharia has caused the erosion of numerous African customs.[2]

In relation to the development of post-communist legal systems, scholars have also noted that the prestige of a particular model was influential in its choice by post-communist law-makers. This was observed for instance by Ajani in his work on post-communist law and it was reflected in the title of one of his publications 'By Chance and Prestige: Legal Transplants in Russia and Eastern Europe'.[3] However, this notion is never clearly explained, although its general meaning is easy to grasp, ie it is the perception that a particular constitution is good, reputable, reliable, and admirable.

A dictionary definition of prestige refers to 'widespread respect and admiration felt for someone or something on the basis of the perception of their

---

[1] 'It would, I supposed, be unreasonable to regard as transplants laws given by gods to men. But Yahweh directly gave the Ten Commandments to Moses on Mount Sinai, Apollo, through the Delphic oracle, gave Lygurcus the laws of Sparta, Zeus gave the Cretans their laws and Hermes gave the Egyptians theirs through Mneves': A Watson, *Legal Transplants: An Approach to Comparative Law* (Edinburgh, Scottish Academic Press, 1974), 88.

[2] *La Comparaison au Service de la Connaissance Juridique* (Paris, Economica, 1991), 124. However, in this account the role of prestige is slightly overestimated compared to other factors, such as war, military conquest and colonisation.

[3] G Ajani, 'By Chance and Prestige: Legal Transplants in Russia and Eastern Europe' [1995], *American Journal of International and Comparative Law* 93.

achievements or quality.'[4] On this basis the prestige of a particular legal system can be said to be linked to the country in which it applies and it derives from a combination of elements, such as the country's role on the international and the European stages, its political and economic power, its capacity to exercise leadership in the world and to portray itself as the protector of a number of democratic values. In addition, in the context of post-communist transitions, the prestige of a particular country was related to its ability to embody an ideal representation of the West. The United States of America and Germany were perhaps the two countries most obviously associated with this image of 'the West.' This was reinforced by the very active role of both Americans and Germans in the process of post-communist transitions in Eastern and Central Europe at the political, economic and financial levels. They were not, however, the only exporters of law, as most European countries also took part, in one way or another, in the exportation of law to post-communist countries.

1.1. Modern Constitutions

In Hungarian constitutional case law, the prestige of foreign models is reflected in the phrase 'modern constitutions' (*modern alkotmányok*). This phrase, which identifies the source of importation of human dignity, may be understood as an indication that the Court carefully chose its model and that it did not consider just any type of constitution. The Hungarian Court did not refer to 'prestigious constitutions,' but the idea of modernity arguably reflects the prestige of these constitutions. In this context, modernity has at least two aspects. The first is purely temporal: modern means recent and the German case law on human dignity, which has been elaborated since 1949, is clearly modern in this sense. More importantly the second aspect of modernity is linked to the perception of a certain quality, with which the Hungarian Court wants to be identified. In the same way that the German Basic Law and, in particular, its catalogue of fundamental rights (as its first chapter has come to be known) were one of the first modern attempts to protect fundamental rights in Western Europe, the Hungarian Court aimed to be one of the first courts to protect fundamental rights in Central Europe.

This is very clear in relation to human dignity, which has a particularly prominent status in the German Basic Law. Its status is reinforced by the fact that the German Constitutional Court has developed a sophisticated and rich interpretation of human dignity, turning it into a powerful tool for protecting fundamental rights. By importing the right to human dignity and the general personality right from German case law, the Hungarian Court signalled its determination to construe the Hungarian constitution in a similarly elaborate

---

[4] *New Oxford Dictionary of English* (Oxford, Clarendon Press, 1998). Interestingly the origin of the word goes back to late Latin meaning 'illusion' and 'conjuring tricks.'

and modern way. Moreover, in referring to modernity as its source of inspiration, the Hungarian Court sought to bridge the gap existing between the newly created post-communist courts and courts of well-established liberal democracies. In other words, the Hungarian Court itself wished its case law to be identified with 'modern constitutions.'

In the context of post-communist transition, the elaboration of a 'modern' interpretation of fundamental rights also meant the rejection of the outdated communist conception of rights and the introduction of a new standard of protection, in line with that existing in 'modern constitutions.'[5] By importing the law from 'modern constitutions,' the Hungarian Court aimed to be the most up to date (some would say activist) court for the protection of fundamental rights. In fact, the Hungarian Court pushed the idea of modernity to its limits and some of the Hungarian cases are extremely progressive and could also be described as *avant-garde*. Such cases include, for example, case 28/1994 on the right to a healthy environment, which the Court interpreted as being linked to the right to life, or case 15/1991 on personal data protection, in which the Court specifically referred to a number of constitutions and ruled that:

> In the absence of a definite purpose and for arbitrary future use, the collection and processing of personal data were unconstitutional. The right to the protection of personal data, the so-called right to informational self-determination, as guaranteed under art. 59, permitted everyone the freedom to decide about the disclosure and use of their personal data to the extent that the approval of the person concerned was generally required to register and use it. In addition, art. 59 ensured that *such person could monitor the entire route of data processing thereby guaranteeing the right to know who used the data and when, where and for what purpose it was used*.[6] (emphasis added)

It is difficult to think of a constitutional court in Europe which makes it a constitutional requirement that individuals have the 'possibility to monitor the entire route of [their personal] data processing.' Even the German Constitutional Court, which also required respect for the right to informational self-determination in the processing of personal data for the population census, did not require that individuals have such a tight control over their personal data.[7] Furthermore, the Hungarian case can be contrasted with a recent case

---

[5] Ch 6 will consider this issue in more detail.

[6] Case 15/1991, L Sólyom and G Brunner (eds), *Constitutional Judiciary in a New Democracy: the Hungarian Constitutional Court* (Ann Arbor, University of Michigan Press, 2000), 140.

[7] In 1983, the German Constitutional Court ruled that: 'However, the right to "informational self-determination" is not unlimited. The individual does not possess any absolute, unlimited mastery over "his" data; rather, he is a personality . . . developing within the social community. Even personal information is a reflection of social reality and cannot be associated purely with the individual concerned. The Basic Law has resolved the tension between the individual and society by postulating a community-related and community-bound individual, as the decisions of the Federal Constitutional Court have repeatedly stressed. The individual must in principle accept certain limits on his right to informational self-determination for reasons of compelling public interest'. BVerfGE, 65, 1, *Census Act* as quoted and translated by D Kommers, *The Constitutional Jurisprudence of the Federal Republic of Germany* (Durham and London, Duke University Press, 1997), 325.

decided by the French Constitutional Council, which did not find that it was unconstitutional for the state to cross-reference personal data on different databases for the purpose of double-checking tax declarations submitted by citizens without informing them.[8]

Finally, in the context of Hungarian constitutional adjudication, modernity refers to the latest developments in the field of constitutional rights, that is even when they are still at a theoretical stage. For instance, the Hungarian Court imported Ronald Dworkin's conception of equal treatment and equal dignity. In so doing, the Court demonstrated its awareness of the latest theoretical developments and its endeavour to follow the path opened by one of the leading theoreticians (or at least the most popular) in this field. The president of the Court, Sólyom acknowledged this source of inspiration in an article published in the *Yale Journal of International Law* in 1994:

> The Court has applied several of Ronald Dworkin's theories, first as a statement of basic principles, then as a detailed test for the constitutionality of discriminatory legislation.[9]

Sólyom referred in footnotes to two of the American author's works, namely *Law's Empire* and *Taking Rights Seriously* and to two cases delivered by the Hungarian Court on the notion of discrimination, that is cases 9/1990 and 21/1990. Strikingly, the first case in which the Court introduced the argument on discrimination directly echoed Dworkin's reflections on the notion of equal treatment developed in chapter 7 of *Taking Rights Seriously*. In particular, the following paragraph seems to have been inspirational:

> There are two different sorts of rights which [citizens] may be said to have. The first is the right to *equal treatment*, which is the right to an equal distribution of some opportunity or resource or burden. . . . The second is the right to *treatment as an equal*, which is the right not to receive the same distribution of some burden or benefit, but to be treated with the same respect and concern as anyone else. . . . In some circumstances the right to treatment as an equal will entail the right to equal treatment, but not, by any means, in all circumstances.[10]

In case 9/1990 the Hungarian Constitutional Court held that:

> The prohibition of discrimination [under Art 70A of the Hungarian Constitution] means that everyone has to be treated as an equal in law (as a person with equal dignity), namely that it is impossible not to respect the fundamental right to human dignity, and that aspects of the distribution of entitlements and benefits have to be determined by considering in an equal manner the individual circumstances with the same respect and circumspection.[11]

---

[8] French Constitutional Council ruling on the Budget Bill for 1999, 29 December 1998.

[9] L Sólyom, 'The Hungarian Constitutional Court and Social Change' [1994], *Yale Journal of International Law* 228.

[10] R Dworkin, *Taking Rights Seriously* (London, Duckworth, 1981), 227.

[11] Article 70A reads: '1—The Republic of Hungary shall ensure the human rights and civil rights for all persons on its territory without any kind of discrimination, such as on the basis of race,

In this case, which was delivered two days after the first human dignity case, the petitioner questioned the constitutionality of the tax law for 1989 on the ground that it breached the prohibition of discrimination under Article 70A of the Constitution. The tax law provided that families with more than three children and single parents with more than two children should pay a reduced amount of income tax. The Court held, mainly on the basis of its understanding of equality as outlined above, that the taxation law did respect the principle of equality, on which this case was the first of a long series of complex and controversial decisions.[12]

1.2. Western Constitutions

According to the Hungarian Constitutional Court, prestigious constitutions are only those of Western democracies. In some cases, particularly those decided on highly sensitive issues, the range of modern constitutions referred to by the Court is impressive. Two cases are remarkable in this respect: case 15/1991 on the constitutionality of the personal identification number and the processing of personal data and case 16/1991 on the timing of the referral of a Bill to the Constitutional Court for review.

In case 15/1991, the Hungarian Court had to determine the constitutionality of a Law Decree from 1986 on the state population register which contained unified personal data records. Under the Law Decree, the aim of the register was to 'promote the enforcement of citizens' rights and the fulfilment of their duties to provide assistance for the activity of state and private organisations.' Each citizen was to be identified in the register by a personal identification number (PIN) and the register could supply individuals' personal data to state and private organisations, which were to be specified by a decree issued by the Council of Ministers. In addition the register could, in some instances, supply the data of one private person to another. The Court held that these provisions violated the right of personal data protection under Article 59 of the Constitution. In particular, it found that the aim of the register was phrased too broadly to be constitutional, because it potentially made possible any kind of use of the personal data contained in it. In the course of its reasoning, the Court referred to numerous Western jurisdictions, including that of Germany:

colour, gender, language, religion, political or other opinion, national or social origins, financial situation, birth or on any other grounds whatsoever. 2—Any kind of discrimination described in paragraph (1) shall be strictly penalised by the law. 3—The Republic of Hungary shall promote the equality of rights for everyone through measures aimed at eliminating the inequality in opportunity.'

[12] Some of these cases appeared in an English translation in L Sólyom and G Brunner (eds), *Constitutional Judiciary in a New Democracy: the Hungarian Constitutional Court* (Ann Arbor, University of Michigan Press, 2000). The early cases however, ie 9/1990 and 21/1990, have not been translated so far. For a selection of relevant extracts, see the case book edited by the Constitutional and Legislative Policy Institute (COLPI), *Alkotmányos Elvek és Esetek* (Budapest, COLPI, 1996).

The use of PIN varies widely from country to country. In a number of countries there are de facto universal PINs as a result of the unhindered introduction and application of an identification code originally adopted for definite purposes. The number itself was originally introduced for the purposes of the population register or as a social security number. Examples for the former one are Belgium, Denmark, Iceland, the Netherlands and Norway, while for the latter Finland or Switzerland. The Swedish personal number, considered as a copybook example of the universal personal number, was originally a registration number in the birth certificate records.

In other countries, personal numbers are forbidden or even considered unconstitutional. In Portugal, a 1973 Act of Parliament ordered the introduction of the universal PIN starting in 1975. On the other hand, Art. 35(2) of the 1976 Constitution, issued after the downfall of the fascist regime, forbids the linkup of personal data storage systems, and according to para. (5): 'It is forbidden to assign nationally uniform personal numbers to citizens.' In France and in the Federal Republic of Germany, public opposition to the idea of a population register using PINs led in 1978 to the promulgation of the Law Decrees on Data Protection and to the abandonment of integrated data storage systems and PINs.

The German Federal Constitutional Court declared as early as in 1969 that the 'registration and catalogue listing of citizens which affect the entire person of those citizens' are incompatible with the fundamental right to human dignity to which the State has no right even under the anonymity of statistical data acquisition (BVerfGE 27, 1, 6); the so-called population census decision, which in 1983 formulated the right to informational self-determination, considers PIN as a 'decisive step' leading to personality profiles the avoidance of which shall be accepted even by other means of limitation on informational self-determination (BVerfGE 65, 1, 27, 53, 57)....

The dangers of electronic data processing to the autonomy of personality became widely recognised in the 1970s. From this time on, the PIN became a symbol for the total control of citizens, for an approach to efficiency alone and for the treatment of persons as objects.[13]

The Hungarian Court closed this comparative survey by briefly mentioning a report issued by the Data Protection Expert Committee of the Council of Europe on 15 December 1989. It is thus clear that here the Court accumulated evidence in support of treating PINs with extreme caution. The range of countries mentioned in this case is impressive, as it encompasses most European countries, including Iceland which rarely features in comparative surveys. With these examples, the Court constructed the argument that in all those countries, PINs were created and used for a very specific purpose: the registration of births, the administration of social security and general population registration. The Court did not consider the detailed regulation of PINs in each country and the strength of its comparative survey lies in the number of examples, rather than in the detail of its analysis. Significantly, all of the countries mentioned here are Western democracies, while former communist countries, which presumably

---

[13] L Sólyom and G Brunner (eds), *Constitutional Judiciary in a New Democracy: the Hungarian Constitutional Court* (Ann Arbor, University of Michigan Press, 2000), 147.

also have PIN legislation, are excluded from the list. A similar pattern can be observed in the case decided immediately afterwards.

Case 16/1991 was triggered by the vague phrasing of the Constitutional Court Act, which did not specify the exact timing for the referral of a Bill to the Court for a review of its constitutionality.[14] In addition, this case concerned the review of a Bill involving the sensitive issue of compensation 'for damages unjustly caused by the State to the properties of Citizens after 8 June 1949,' which had not yet been voted on by parliament.[15] In its decision, the Court developed its abstract views on the constitutionality of compensation but ultimately it rejected the petition altogether because of the wrong timing of the referral. It was the first time that the preventive norm control procedure had been used before the Court and in order to clarify its exact nature, the judges mentioned a wide selection of foreign constitutional provisions on this matter:

> The preventive norm control is exercised in this way in any system which has adopted the procedure of preventive norm control of legal texts (art. 61 of the French consti-tution, art. 278 of the Portuguese constitution, art. 26 of the Irish constitution before promulgation, art. 127 of the Italian constitution contains similar provisions for the control in case of violation of legislative power. For the preventive control of inter-national treaties, art. 78 of the Spanish act on the constitutional court requires that the text of the international treaty be first finalised; similar requirements and rules were applied to the preventive norm control of statutes until 1985 when this particular power of the constitutional court was abolished because of its interference with the legislative process.)

The constitutions mentioned by the Court complete the range of 'modern constitutions' considered in the previous case and illustrate the Hungarian Court's effort not to follow one specific national model only. As highlighted by the president of the Court, judges consciously took great care to balance the German influence. In fact, Péter Paczolay, the then advisor to the president of the Hungarian Court, explained this clearly in his contribution to *Constitution-Making in Eastern Europe* and stated that the Hungarian Court intended to develop its case law in a 'framework of Europeanism':

> The constitutions of several different Western democracies have had an indelible impact on the current text of the Hungarian constitution. The objective of the Constitution was to create a document in conformity with European constitutional standards, in order to establish a framework for 'Europeanism'. . . .

---

[14] Art 1(a) of Act XXXII/1989 on the Constitutional Court: 'The competence of the Constitutional Court shall comprise . . . the preliminary examination of the unconstitutionality of bills, of Acts of Parliament, enacted but not yet promulgated, of the Standing Order of Parliament and of international treaties.'

[15] L Sólyom and G Brunner (eds), *Constitutional Judiciary in a New Democracy: the Hungarian Constitutional Court* (Ann Arbor, University of Michigan Press, 2000), 151–58. More generally, on compensation issues, see I Pogany, *Righting Wrongs in Eastern Europe* (Manchester, Manchester University Press, 1997).

For example, the influence of the German *Grundgesetz* (Basic Law) and of the Italian constitution was very strong, and from among the constitutions of more recent democracies those of Spain and Portugal had a clear impact. The U.S. Constitution, because of its unique character, had no direct influence on particular Hungarian provisions, only a more general effect on the basic constitutional principles (for example, constitutional government, separation of powers, guarantees against majority tyranny, judicial review, supremacy of the constitution, and limited government).[16]

Within the 'framework of Europeanism' that Paczolay refers to, the Hungarian Court operated a further selection and it overwhelmingly imported German law, as seen with human dignity in the previous chapter. The PIN case (15/1991) is particularly revealing of this further selection. In this case, as quoted above, the Court presented a very wide range of constitutional solutions for dealing with PINs. Strikingly, although the Hungarian Court referred to no fewer than 11 foreign systems, German constitutional cases were the only specific references on this issue, and the Hungarian Court mentioned the two leading German cases using the German way of referencing. Furthermore, it quoted significant sentences from both cases and briefly outlined the essence of the German Court's reasoning.

In addition, the Hungarian Court largely imported from German cases the key concepts of the German approach to personal data, such as the right to informational self-determination, the 'personality profile' and the 'adherence to the purpose to be achieved' (known in Germany as '*Zielbindung*'). This very precise importation shows that the Hungarian Court knew the German system better than those also mentioned in its comparative survey and therefore that the choice of German case law as a privileged source of importation was determined by the judges' knowledge of this legal system.

2. KNOWLEDGE

The influence of German law on Hungarian law after the collapse of communism is not surprising. After all, before the First World War, Hungary was part of German-speaking Mittel Europa and despite two wars and 40 years of communism, it remained broadly within the Germanic sphere of influence. This meant that knowledge of German was widespread in Hungary, especially among lawyers, who were generally familiar with German law, as Sólyom recalled in the issue of *OsteuropaRecht* celebrating the Hungarian Millennium in 2000:

Hungary belonged to the traditional sphere of influence of the German language and culture. Accordingly, German law and jurisprudence were well known. I myself own textbooks by *Windscheid* and by *von Gierke*, which come from the library of a

---

[16] P Paczolay, 'The New Hungarian Constitutional State', in AED Howard (ed), *Constitution-Making in Eastern Europe* (Washington, Woodrow Wilson Press Center, 1993), 36.

Hungarian county court judge. In the course of the past two centuries, German sources have been drawn upon whenever the need to modernise arose. This can be seen in relation to the old commercial law for instance and, a hundred years later, in relation to legislation reforming economic law during the eighties, the foundations of which were worked out by my colleagues thanks to fellowships at the Max Planck Institutes. Soon afterwards, at the Round Table talks, I myself proposed adopting the model of the German voting system.[17]

The German influence is reflected in the drafting of the 1989 Constitution, in particular as far as the fundamental rights and their protection are concerned. The design of the Hungarian Constitutional Court itself is also largely modelled on the German Court: except of course for federal issues, both courts have a similar range of competences. The Hungarian Court has a number of additional powers, such as the preventive review of the constitutionality of Bills and the posterior review of norms which is open to everyone (known as the 'popular action'). However, the importation of specific elements from a foreign legal system, such as the particular interpretation of a right or particular techniques of legal reasoning, cannot be solely explained by the broad influence of that foreign country in the importing state. Speaking the language of this legal system is crucial if the importers are to be able to identify the aspects of it that they wish to incorporate or use in their domestic law.

2.1. A Matter of Language

As Watson noted in relation to the work of the Law Commission for Scotland, languages, or rather the ignorance of certain languages, operate as a sort of negative selection criteria:

> Thus in this case (and in others), a body set up to suggest law reforms begins normally not by trying to think its way through to its own solution based on local conditions and character but by examining external solutions. . . . But the process is not entirely free from chance. Non-legal factors—library and linguistic deficiencies—reduce the rôle which might be played by certain systems. It should be noted that neither the Commissioners nor the Commission's legal staff are selected primarily because of their experience in Comparative Law or their linguistic skills.
>
> It is obvious that if books are not available in libraries or if they are written in a language which is not understood, the law in them will not be directly influential. Further, books in a language which is not commonly known tend not to be bought by libraries, hence cannot be used even by those few persons capable of reading them, and so their potential influence is even more diminished.[18]

---

[17] L Sólyom, 'Aufbau und dogmatische Fundierung der ungarischen Verfassungsgerichtsbarkeit' [2000] *OsteuropaRecht* 230.
[18] A Watson, *Legal Transplants: An Approach to Comparative Law* (Edinburgh, Scottish University Press, 1974), 92–93.

In Hungary for historical reasons, German has long been a sort of second language, in particular for lawyers.[19] It replaced Latin as the legal language under the Habsburg Empire in 1784. At that time, governmental business was conducted in German, as were probably most administrative matters until 1867, when Hungarian eventually became the official language after the 'Compromise' regulating the relationship between Hungary and Austria.[20] These political and cultural links survived the wars and Soviet domination, as well as the imposition of Russian as a second language.[21] As a result, German was learnt and spoken by many Hungarians under the communist regime and seemed to have remained the language of (most) lawyers in Hungary.

This probably reflects in part the attitude of the speakers of a language which is so difficult to learn for foreigners. This linguistic peculiarity might have made it clear to Hungarians that they could not expect foreigners to learn their language.[22] As some of the constitutional judges pointed out to me, under communism comparative law materials were usually not translated since it was assumed that comparatists could read the original. It appears from reading the constitutional cases, that German was not only the lawyers' language but also, and possibly primarily, the language of the law. In other words, many grammatical constructions, in particular those used to demonstrate and to argue a point of law seemed to me to be direct translations from the German. In cases on human dignity, this is reinforced by the importation and direct translation of German phrases and words, as seen in the previous chapter.

The criteria for selecting constitutional judges in Hungary do not include any linguistic requirement, but the rules' insistence on legal expertise and knowledge has led to the selection of a significant proportion of German-speaking judges. The Act on the Constitutional Court specified two alternative requirements: members of the Court must have been either practising lawyers with at least 25 years professional experience, or academics, ie doctors in law or political science.[23] At

---

[19] For a more precise account of the long-standing links between German law and Hungarian law, see K Göczi, 'Die deutsch-ungarische Rechtsverbindungen von der frühen Neuzeit bis in die Gegenwart: Wissenstransfer, Kodifikationen und Liaisonen' [2000] *OsteuropaRecht* 216–29.

[20] G Balázs, *The Story of Hungarian: A Guide to the Language* (Budapest, Corvina, 1997): 'For a long period of time, Latin was the language of official communications and served as a lingua franca among the various polyglot groups. Latin was the language used in every-day communication among the higher classes. Hungarian was spoken only in the smaller Hungarian rural towns and villages and within the families' (at 133).

[21] This raises the question of the actual impact of Soviet law on Hungarian law during 40 years of communist rule. I would argue that the influence of Soviet law was concentrated on the most visible communist features, such as state institutions or socialist rights. To a large extent, however, Hungarian law, or more precisely the structures in which law was thought about and developed, were perhaps less seriously questioned or altered by Soviet law than one might think.

[22] Hungarian is not an Indo-European language, but one of the Finno-Ugric languages.

[23] Art 5 of Act XXXII 1989 on the Constitutional Court: '(1) Any Hungarian citizen with a law degree who has no prior conviction, and is over 45 may be elected as a member of the Constitutional Court. (2) The members of the Constitutional Court shall be elected by Parliament from among the outstanding theoretical legal experts (university professors or doctors of political sciences or law), or lawyers with at least twenty five years of practice in the field. Practice in the field

the same time, Article 32A(5) of the Constitution provides for a strict political incompatibility:

> Members of the Constitutional Court may not be members of a political party and may not engage in any political activities beyond the duties arising from the competences of the Constitutional Court.

A significant majority of the first constitutional judges were senior academics.[24] The president László Sólyom (born 1942, graduated 1965) had been a professor at the University of ELTE in Budapest since 1982. The vice-president, Tamás Lábady (born 1944, graduated 1968) had been a civil court judge, as well as a lecturer since 1973. Antal Ádám (born 1930, graduated 1953) was a professor of constitutional law at the University of Pécs. Péter Schmidt (born 1926, graduated 1951) was a professor of constitutional law at the University of Budapest. András Szabó (born 1928, graduated 1953) taught law at the School of Law in Szeged. János Zlinszky (born 1928, graduated 1956) lectured in Roman law at the School of Law in Miskolc. Only three judges, Géza Kilényi (born 1936, graduated 1958), Ödön Tersztyánszky (born 1929, graduated 1957) and Imre Vörös (born 1944, graduated 1968) came from legal practice.[25]

Among the first constitutional judges, this legal experience went together with a remarkable knowledge of foreign languages.[26] The majority of the first Hungarian judges had an excellent command of at least two Western languages, a frequent combination being either German and French or German and English. Most judges could read legal literature in these three languages and they were fluent in at least one of them (as I found out when I interviewed them). Their advisors, slightly or markedly younger than judges themselves, also spoke several languages. Linguistic skills were probably, at least implicitly, criteria for selecting advisors to the Court and those who could not speak a Western language at the time of their appointment were encouraged to make some

shall be in a field which requires a degree in political sciences and law. (3) No person who, in the four years preceding the election, has been a member of the Government, or employee of a Party, or an executive in state administration shall be a member of the Constitutional Court.'

[24] F Majoros, 'Zur Entwicklung der Verfassungsgerichtsbarkeit in Ungarn' [1993] *OsteuropaRecht* 106 and H Schwartz, 'The New East European Constitutional Courts', in AED Howard (ed), *Constitution-Making in Eastern Europe* (Washington, Woodrow Wilson Press Center, 1993), 209.

[25] There were two other judges but they left the Court soon after their election. Géza Herczegh became a judge at the International Tribunal at The Hague in 1993 and Pál Solt became the Chief Justice of the Hungarian Supreme Court in June 1990. All information provided by the brochure on the Hungarian Constitutional Court, *The Constitutional Court of Hungary*, edited by the Court itself.

[26] I do not include Russian because its teaching was compulsory. In Hungary, anecdotal evidence indicates that most school children were proud of deliberately achieving the bare pass mark in Russian tests. Ten years after the collapse of communism, the *lingua franca* of the former Soviet Empire seems to have become English.

progress.[27] The librarian of the Court spoke very good English too and her library contained a number of books in German, English and French.[28] In addition, this was the only library in Hungary with a complete collection of the case reports of the American Supreme Court. As Watson pointed out, the knowledge of a foreign language (Latin in his example) can greatly contribute to the expansion of the related legal system.[29] Beyond the well-stocked library, the main source of legal information on foreign 'modern constitutions' was the personal network of friends or colleagues that each judge (and their advisors) were intensively developing in the years of the transition.

2.2. Personal Connections: the Availability of Knowledge

Knowing a language made it possible for judges and their advisors to read legal materials directly and hence to develop a very precise understanding of the particular element that the Court aimed to import. I suggest that the time when importers acquired this knowledge and its ongoing availability to them were crucial in choosing the German model.

Importers needed to have knowledge of a foreign system acquired before the transition and before they became constitutional judges if they were going to import from it during the early stages of the transition. Even some superficial knowledge might have been enough, although some Hungarian constitutional judges clearly had solid knowledge of German constitutional law. Without prior knowledge, importers could not know where to look for inspiration. Prior knowledge was also crucial considering the workload of Hungarian judges who delivered about 500 cases on average each year between 1990 and 1993. With so much work on their hands, little time was left for learning about a new system from scratch. Judges and their assistants nevertheless endeavoured to broaden their knowledge, so as to include other systems, such as Italian, Portuguese or Spanish. These models were far less influential than German law and this is arguably because of linguistic difficulties, as well as because judges had no or little prior knowledge of these systems when they delivered their first cases.

---

[27] Interestingly, over the four-year period in which I conducted this research (1994–98) I observed a change from German to English as being the most widely spoken foreign language at the Court, in that towards the end of this period I found myself speaking English with people with whom at first I spoke German. I must acknowledge that this linguistic evolution was at the same time parallel to my own, due to the English-speaking environment of the European University Institute where I was based. I could observe the efforts made by the younger generation of advisors at the Court to improve or to learn English, as well as the courageous decision of a judge in his late 60s to improve his knowledge of English.

[28] This does not include the books owned personally by judges and kept in their offices.

[29] A Watson, *Legal Transplants: An Approach to Comparative Law* (Edinburgh, Scottish Academic Press, 1974), 93: 'Clearly, one factor in the widespread reception of Roman law was that what later came to be called the *Corpus Juris Civilis* was written in Latin, a language understood by all educated men in Europe for many centuries.'

Nevertheless, importers also needed to develop their understanding and knowledge of the legal system from which they started importing law. Well-stocked libraries provided day-to-day resources and as seen above, quite a selection of textbooks and case reports of foreign courts, including the American Supreme Court, were available at the Hungarian Constitutional Court, either in the library or on judges' own bookshelves. The ongoing availability of detailed knowledge of foreign legal systems was extremely important. It was ensured thanks to the support that judges could expect from broadly two groups of people.

The first group included the judges' personal assistants. The president of the Court had three assistants, whereas his colleagues had one (sometimes more) assistant each. In addition to their linguistic abilities, these assistants all had some knowledge of comparative law. In fact, some of them were sent abroad to complete their legal training or, for shorter periods of time, to develop their comparative knowledge in a particular area, such as that of human rights. Max Planck Institutes in Germany welcomed a number of staff from the Hungarian Constitutional Court at one time or another during their careers.

The second group of persons included foreign lawyers who had been in contact with judges before the collapse of communism. These personal connections were revived and enlarged with the need to reform Hungarian law in 1989 and included contacts with academics, as well as constitutional judges abroad. As Sólyom indicated, these personal connections were important resources and could be activated by telephone and by fax:

> At the time, I was in constant contact with the [German] Federal Constitutional Court. Both sides knew that the other side was working on a compensation case. I was pleased that the Hungarian Court delivered its judgement two weeks before [the German Court] and I nevertheless read with the greatest interest the German case, which arrived immediately by fax.[30]

This account relates to compensation cases, but it is safe to assume that the same exchanges went on for most other Hungarian cases, in particular when they involved issues which also arose before the German Constitutional Court. Arguably, the older the contact was with particular foreign lawyers, the more Hungarian judges were likely to turn to them to discuss particular issues. The relationships with foreign lawyers that had started before the change of regime were, I think, particularly crucial in the choice of a foreign model. They were instantly available, and the existing relationships meant that foreign lawyers could be contacted in a fairly informal way in the circumstances of the change of regime. Constitutional judges, however, did not restrict themselves to those contacts. In fact, they kept developing new connections by attending conferences abroad, giving lectures to academic circles, visiting colleagues abroad and inviting them to Budapest.

---

[30] L Sólyom, 'Aufbau und dogmatische Fundierung der ungarischen Verfassungsgerichtsbarkeit' [2000] *OsteuropaRecht* 231.

The role of the exporters of law such as the experts invited to Budapest, as seen in chapter 2, was essential in the promotion of the rule of law and fundamental rights. Although they clearly brought with them a great deal of legal knowledge, their ability to influence directly the importation of their own legal system is, however, less straightforward. When they did influence the drafting of new legislation, this seems to be due to a particular set of circumstances, as Esin Örücü and Jan Smits observed in relation to the Dutch Civil Code in Russia:

> We know that the new Dutch Civil Code has won the competition as one of the competing models in Russia in the preparation of the Russian Civil Code. However, Smits makes additional and revealing observations. Today, according to him, smaller countries such as the Netherlands are in a much better position to export their law than countries who play the 'politics of power.' Smits says that the Russian drafting team were well aware that the Dutch experts had no other goal but to improve the quality of law reform in Russia. He suggests that the superpowers are more readily accused of legal chauvinism. Secondly, Smits makes the point that Dutch law is able to fulfil its exporting task because in her past the Netherlands was itself an importing country. Thirdly, the new Dutch Civil Code of 1992 is influenced by German, French and English laws and is the outcome of thorough comparative studies. Added to this is the fact that the Dutch Code offers a mixture of market economy and the idea of a social *Rechtsstaat*. These factors are part of its attraction as an ideal model, especially as a source of inspiration.[31]

These observations show that a number of factors influenced the choice of a foreign model and, as in the Russian example cited above, the personalities of the exporters themselves, as well as their attitude towards the reform of a particular aspect of post-communist law, played a role. The way in which the exporters' legal system developed was also relevant for the drafters of the Russian Civil Code, who appreciated the fact that it had been subject to various foreign influences, thus mirroring their own experience in drafting a code.

Linguistic awareness and prior knowledge of a particular legal system, however, are still only part of the picture and are not enough to explain the ongoing importation process throughout the first nine years of Hungarian constitutional adjudication. The remaining factor to be taken into account here was the suitability of a particular legal system, which was carefully considered by the importers of law, further illustrating their deliberate choice of what law to import.

3. SUITABILITY

Within the range of legal systems to which they had access through language, legal knowledge, personal contacts, as well as exportation, importers of law

---

[31] E Örücü, *Critical Comparative Law: Considering Paradoxes for Legal Systems in Transition* (Deventer, Kluwer Law International, 1999), 124.

opted in favour of the legal system which best suited their interests and their particular need. This notion of suitability comprises various elements.

A first element in assessing the suitability of a legal system for importation is related to the importers' ability to single out a particular aspect which is relatively self-contained and thus easy to extract from its original environment. The obstacle here does not seem to be the cleavage between civil and common law systems which is often invoked as a barrier between these two groups of systems. Instead, the obstacle is the inability of a particular element of law to make sense outside the cultural and historical context where it developed. In this respect, UK law is very difficult to export to an environment different from the common law sphere, such as that prevailing in post-communist countries. For example, the concept of civil liberties, which in the early stage of transition was the only British approach to the protection of fundamental rights, does not make sense outside the specific legal historical context of the United Kingdom. Having a written constitution facilitates the exportation of law, because it is easier to know what the rules are and how they operate. The French system, however, even though it has a written constitution, faced similar problems to the United Kingdom in exporting its law, because of the lack of a clear written Bill of Rights—that is, although the 1789 Declaration of the Rights of Man is considered by the Constitutional Council for the interpretation of the constitution, this Declaration cannot be fully understood if it is not complemented by several decades of constitutional case law. These two systems were thus not very suitable for importation into Hungarian case law, despite the fact that most judges spoke English and some of them French, and were generally familiar with their workings.

In addition, the difficulty of gaining access to these legal systems might have been an obstacle to their importation. The lack of a written constitution requires the study of politics, history, as well as a whole body of case law before the UK system makes sense. This is not an easy process for someone with little time to devote to this task. To put it slightly bluntly, it is not a very foreign user-friendly system. The French system, almost for opposite reasons, is no more user-friendly for foreign lawyers. The written constitution only provides some insight into the system, which also needs to be complemented by case law. French cases, with their condensed and often cryptic style, are not a model of clarity for those not trained in the arcane science of French judicial reasoning. In contrast, the German legal system is comparatively more user-friendly for non-German lawyers. It has a written constitution with a list of fundamental rights that are clearly spelt out and the constitution itself has been abundantly commented on in textbooks, which provide detailed information on each constitutional provision. This makes it relatively easy to catch up on the latest developments in relation to the general personality right, for instance. Similarly, German constitutional case law is analysed and summarised in a number of case books which greatly facilitate understanding a whole line of case law.

A second element in assessing the suitability of a foreign legal system for importation is that legal systems need to be generally compatible. Compatibility benefits from long cultural and legal links between two countries. The importation of a particular aspect from a legal system, such as a right, will be facilitated if the importers' system was inspired by the foreign system. The importation of human dignity was not an exception in Hungarian post-communist law; it is only one small aspect of the wider German influence on the Hungarian post-communist constitution. To remain with the above mentioned counter-examples, the UK and the French systems were not compatible with nascent constitutional adjudication in Hungary; the former especially because it does not have a distinct constitutional adjudication body and constitutional issues arise and are settled together with other issues without distinction. Moreover the fact that the UK, at the time, did not have positive rights, which was one of the most important aspects in the reconstruction of post-communist legal systems, meant that it was not going to be influential in this area of law. The French system is arguably not more compatible in that its system of constitutional adjudication has a very restrictive scope and, although it has led to the protection of fundamental rights, there is no specific remedy to that effect. In contrast, the German system has many advantages for Hungarian importers. It has a central constitutional court that is well-established and well-integrated into the wider institutional framework and that is well-respected. It is a powerful court before which numerous remedies are available and a large part of its work is dedicated to the protection of fundamental rights.

This was, I would suggest, decisive for the Hungarian Court, because in the early years of the transition, its general agenda was twofold: protecting fundamental rights and finding its place within the general institutional framework, in particular in relation to the law-maker. German case law in relation to the protection of fundamental rights is sophisticated and copious. The meaning of a particular constitutional right, such as human dignity, has been developed at length and analysed in academic writing exploring most of its aspects. This provided substantial and detailed information on the actual and potential uses of a particular constitutional provision or principle. In addition, German case law on human dignity and the general personality right covers a very broad range of situations. This means that Hungarian judges could rely on German case law, at least for inspiration, and in many cases for actual importation as German cases considered a number of issues which were likely to arise before the Hungarian Court. At the same time, human dignity and the general personality right could have a very versatile use when imported into Hungarian case law. Indeed, they were developed by the Court for the protection of individuals in a dazzling variety of circumstances, ranging from an employee's right not to be represented by trade unions, to issues such as abortion and the death penalty and even, as explained in the previous chapter, the right of certain associations dealing with works of art to engage freely in financial transactions (see Table 1). In fact, the imported notion of human dignity was such that it could be used in almost all situations of violation of fundamental rights. From the point of view of judicial reasoning, one of the most interesting characteristics of human dignity was, arguably, its open-ended nature. Human dignity could be used by the Hungarian Court to develop quickly a system of fundamental rights protection and therefore to assert itself in its task of constitutional adjudication.

4. CONCLUSION

Law importation was encouraged by the exportation of law from the West, but all exports were not equally successful and law importation was therefore not a passive response or reception of exported law. This chapter has shown that the importers sought and chose particular models. Their reasons for their choice involved a complex combination of the prestige of a model, legal knowledge and the accessibility of the model, through linguistic knowledge and personal contacts with lawyers in the chosen system. In addition to these reasons, the choice of the model was also determined by the importers' own interests and agenda.

Law importation, however, is not imitation. Although the Hungarian Court imported many of the aspects of human dignity that exist in German case law, it very rarely followed the German Court's final conclusion in terms of the constitutionality of the challenged rules and, in this respect, Hungarian case law is autonomous from German case law. The next two chapters will consider this aspect more closely and will show that the differences existing between the German and Hungarian concepts of human dignity illustrate the Hungarian Court's instrumentalisation of the imported law.

5

Instrumentalising the Model

━━━━◦◦◦◦━━━━

TRADITIONALLY, THE STUDY of legal transplants seems to have been restricted to linking a model to the system into which it was transplanted. This was achieved by focusing on the similarities between the two systems, which were interpreted as a sure sign that one had 'received' the other. This might be partially explained by the historical approach of comparative law, from which the observation of the process of legal transplants is often derived. The emphasis on similarities supported the claim that the development of legal systems results from transplants from one system to another. Focusing on similarities further allowed scholars to map the spread of a particular body of law beyond the environment which generated it. As a result, some legal systems were deemed to belong to particular families and were grouped accordingly.[1] However, comparison of law has rarely taken place outside these categories and systems which differ too much have been deemed to be not comparable. More recently, the awareness that law develops in a particular cultural and social context has led commentators to acknowledge differences between legal systems, with a risk of cultural relativism being used as a blanket explanation for differences. Although some scholars have called for a constructive attitude in relation to differences,[2] these are still too often left out of the study of legal transplants. Frequently, divergencies have been assessed in terms of bad or good imitation. For some, differences are a good sign in that they show that the receiving environment has appropriated and digested the foreign rule, which can be interpreted as a sign of success. For others, differences are a bad sign because they reveal the inability of the receiving system to understand and accurately reproduce the foreign rule, leading to the conclusion that the transplanted rule is doomed to failure. Considering this process from theoretical heights, some have concluded that differences do not matter that much, as the transplant's main role is

---

[1] R David, *Les Grands Systèmes de Droit Contemporain* (9th edn, Paris, Dalloz, 1988).

[2] E Örücü, *Critical Comparative Law: Considering Paradoxes for Legal Systems in Transition* (Deventer, Kluwer Law International, 1999), 27: 'Comparative legal studies would itself benefit and therefore benefit scholars looking at the outcome of comparative legal research if it were to interest itself seriously in searching for and explaining divergencies, especially between the similars. This however, should not be done with the "negative" attitude of stressing "irreducible differences in *mentalité*" or "*summa differentia*" within the context of a contrarian challenge. It should be done with a constructive attitude in order to develop further a "critical comparative law." The findings of such would enhance our understanding of law and legal and social cultures.'

to trigger some reaction by 'irritating' the system into which it is introduced.[3] Revealingly, studies of legal transplants are often pitched at a level which is so general, or theoretical, that differences become invisible and are not even considered. The few case studies of transplanted law are often too short (a chapter in a book or an article in a law journal) to spend time on going beyond the visible similarities.

In contrast with the above mentioned approaches, I argue that the transformation of the original rule is an essential part of the process of law importation which cannot be restricted to a mechanical imitation. In fact, understanding and measuring the scope of the differences between the German and the Hungarian interpretations of the right to human dignity is necessary in order to deepen understanding of law importation. The starting point of this approach is therefore to consider that divergencies between the two bodies of case law on human dignity cannot be explained essentially by errors and misunderstandings (although a certain amount of these are almost inevitable given the complexity of the operation).

Identifying the differences requires a deeper comparison between German and Hungarian case law on human dignity and the general personality right. As explained in this chapter, the scope of the differences in fact reveals that the Hungarian Court, although it imported human dignity from German case law, has given it a meaning which is autonomous from that given to it by the German Constitutional Court.

1.   IMPORTING IS NOT IMITATING

Some differences are particularly visible and they are explained by the fact that Hungarian and German constitutional provisions on human dignity are not identical, which has led the Hungarian Court to adapt German case law in order to fit it into the Hungarian constitutional framework.

1.2.   Minimal Adjustments

The first and probably most visible difference between the German Basic Law and the Hungarian Constitution is a matter of number. The Hungarian Constitution only contains one provision on human dignity and no provision on the general personality right, whereas the German Basic Law contains two provisions: Article 1 on human dignity and Article 2 on the free fulfilment of one's personality. In addition there are significant differences in the phrasing of each provision. Article 54 of the Hungarian constitution reads:

---

[3] G Teubner, 'Legal Irritants: Good Faith in British Law and How Unifying the Law Ends Up in New Divergencies' [1998] *Modern Law Review* 11.

1—In the Republic of Hungary everyone has the innate right to life and to human dignity, of which no one can be arbitrarily deprived.

2—No one shall be subjected to torture or to cruel, inhuman or degrading treatment or punishment; it is particularly prohibited to conduct medical or scientific experiments on human beings without their consent.

Article 1 of the German Basic Law reads:

1—The dignity of human beings is inviolable. It is the duty of all state authorities to have regard to it and to protect it.

2—The German people therefore acknowledge inviolable and inalienable human rights as the basis of every community, of peace and justice in the world.

3—The following basic rights shall bind the legislature, the executive and the judiciary as directly enforceable law.

The general personality right was developed by the German Court under Article 2 of the Basic Law which is often associated in German case law with Article 1:

1—Everyone has the right to a free fulfilment of his personality, in so far as he does not injure the rights of others or violate the constitutional order or the moral law.

2—Everyone has the right to life and to the inviolability of his person. These rights may be restricted only on the basis of a statute.

(a) The Nature of Human Dignity: a Principle and a Right

In Hungarian case law, human dignity does not have the same nature as in German case law. In German case law, human dignity is considered as being a supreme value or a fundamental principle, as summarised by Donald Kommers:

The principle of human dignity, as the Constitutional Court has repeatedly emphasised, is the highest value of the Basic Law, the ultimate basis of the constitutional order, and the foundation of all guaranteed rights.[4]

In Germany, the combination of the position of the human dignity provision (ie the very first article of the Basic Law) and the Court's jurisprudence gives human dignity a constitutional status superior to that of a fundamental right: it is the highest principle in the constitutional order (*'der höchste Rechtswert innerhalb der verfassungsmäßigen Ordnung'*).[5] This is reinforced by the solemn

---

[4] D Kommers, *The Constitutional Jurisprudence of the Federal Republic of Germany* (Durham and London, Duke University Press, 1997), 32 and C Starck, 'Menschenwürde als Verfassungsgarantie im modernen Staat'[1981] *Juristenzeitung* 36.

[5] BVerfGE 45, 187, [227] *Life Imprisonment*. Some commentators have also considered human dignity to be a subjective right.

and general style of Article 1(1) of the Basic Law.[6] Human dignity is a value on which the whole German constitutional order rests. It binds 'all state authorities,' it is the guideline that constitutional judges (as well as other state organs) have to bear in mind when interpreting and implementing the Constitution. It can also be considered as an aspiration: when making decisions about the present and the future, the German Federal Republic should ensure that human dignity is never violated or restricted.[7]

In Hungarian case law, the question of the nature of human dignity arose in case 23/1990 on the death penalty and in particular in the concurring opinion by two constitutional judges, T Lábady and Ö Tersztyánszky:

> [3] Human dignity, as the integrity of personality, means along with human life the essence of man. Dignity is the elevating quality of our human existence and value: it is worthy of an unconditional respect, the honour of our human essence. It is an a priori value in the same way that life is, and it expresses the human dimension of life. Being a human and human dignity are inseparable from one another. Both are inalienable, immanent, essential properties of man. To be worthy of life means to be worthy of being a human person, and that is why human life and human dignity may in fact not be handled separately.
>
> [4] *The existence and dignity of man, as the unity of man, is not really a right, because human essence is in fact transcendent for the law—i.e., it is beyond the reach of the law.* Human life and dignity are, therefore, included in the catalogue of human rights and in modern constitutions as the sources of rights or as values beyond the reach of law which are inviolable, rather than as fundamental rights. Law should ensure that such inviolable values are respected and protected.[8] (emphasis added)

In this extract, the phrase 'catalogue of fundamental rights' refers to the list of fundamental rights contained in the constitution and it originally applied to the German Basic Law. The choice of terminology, as well as the general idea expressed in this opinion, further echo German case law. The Hungarian Court, however, did not adopt a clear-cut position on the nature of human dignity and it kept repeating its first definition of human dignity as a 'mother right.' In addition, unlike the German Court, the Hungarian Court did not refer to human dignity as a supreme constitutional value beyond the death penalty case. Consequently, the Hungarian Court seemed to consider human dignity as a fundamental right, albeit of a particular strength.

---

[6] ' "The dignity of man is founded upon eternal rights with which every person is endowed by nature.", read the first draft of Article 1 produced by the Herrenchiensee conference. Later, in the Main Committee of the Parliamentary Council, Christian Democratic delegates sought to characterise these "eternal rights" as "God-given". Social Democrats and Free Democrats resisted the use of such language because of its implications for constitutional interpretation. The result was a succinct and neutral formulation': Kommers, above n 4, at 301.

[7] To reinforce this protection, the Basic Law contains an explicit prohibition on amending fundamental rights provisions. Article 79(3) reads: 'Amendments of the Basic Law affecting the division of the Federation into *Länder*, the principle of participation of the *Länder* in legislation, or the basic principles laid down in articles 1 and 20, shall be inadmissible.'

[8] L Sólyom and G Brunner (eds), *Constitutional Judiciary in a New Democracy: the Hungarian Constitutional Court* (Ann Arbor, University of Michigan Press, 2000), 124.

(b) The Link Between Human Dignity and the General Personality Right

A second important distinction flowing from the different wording of the constitutions is the link (or absence thereof) existing between human dignity and
the general personality right. The German Basic Law contains two provisions
(Articles 1 and 2), which are clearly distinct, with autonomous meanings and
with different scopes and restrictions. In contrast, the Hungarian Constitution
only contains one provision on human dignity with which the Hungarian Court
associated, by way of importation, the general personality right.

Under German case law, Articles 1 and 2 have three possible combinations.[9]
First, the German Court has often interpreted human dignity under Article 1 on
its own. In those cases, the court has emphasised that dignity is the highest value
and supreme principle of the German constitutional order. In particular, this
emphasis was developed in the field of criminal law: famous cases include one
on life imprisonment in 1977[10] and one on the use of a lie detector to establish
the truth in criminal proceedings in 1982. Secondly, the German Court construed the general personality right under Article 2 in connection with Article
1.[11] The general personality right was often used on its own in a number of cases
where it appeared to have two aspects: the right to a private sphere and the right
to informational self-determination, including the famous case on the population census (as seen in chapter 3). Thirdly, Article 2 on its own, that is the right
to the free fulfilment of one's personality, encompasses the general freedom of
action, freedom of economic action and the right to fair proceedings in compliance with the rule of law.

It is true that under German case law Articles 1 and 2 are intertwined so that
it becomes difficult to associate one particular case with either Article 1 or
Article 2, considered separately.[12] Differences between the two interpretations
of human dignity, however, remain significant. Under the German Basic Law,
human dignity is not twinned with the right to life (although it was subsequently

---

[9] I Müller and GF Schuppert (eds), *Casebook Verfassungsrecht* (München, CH Beck Verlag,
1996), 63–126.

[10] BVerfGE 45, 187, *Life Imprisonment*: 'An assessment of the constitutionality of life imprisonment from the vantage of Article 1(1) and the principle of the rule of law shows that a humane
enforcement of life imprisonment is possible only when the prisoner is given a concrete and realistic-
ally attainable chance to regain his freedom at some later point in time; the state strikes at the very
heart of human dignity if [it] treats the prisoner without regard to the development of his personality and strips him of all hope ever of earning his freedom. The legal provisions relating to the grant-
ing of pardons do not sufficiently guarantee this hope, which makes the sentence bearable in terms
of human dignity' as translated by D Kommers, *Constitutional Jurisprudence of the Federal
Republic of Germany* (Durham and London, Duke University Press, 1997), 309.

[11] See ch 3, also D Jarass, 'Das allgemeine Persönlichkeitsrecht im Grundgesetz' [1989] *Neue
Juristische Wochenschrift* 857–62.

[12] See ch 3. D Kommers highlights the link between Arts 1 and 2: 'The human dignity clause is
almost always read in tandem with the general liberty interests secured by the personality, inviolability and right-to-life clauses of Article 2. The relationship between Article 1 and Article 2 is
symbiotic; all of their provisions nourish and reinforce one another. As capstones of the Basic Law,
they contain ringing declarations of human freedom': above n 10, at 298.

associated with that right by the German Court in its rulings on abortion). By contrast, the Hungarian Constitution clearly links the two rights under Article 54(1).[13] In a similar vein, in German case law, the general personality right is not necessarily associated with human dignity (although it has been combined with it in a number of cases). In fact, in Germany the general personality right was read into the fulfilment of one's personality under Article 2. Articles 1 and 2 have strengthened each other in German case law, but they also have clearly distinct scopes: human dignity is inviolable and it is the highest value of the constitutional order, whereas the general personality right and the other rights branching out from fulfilment of the personality can be submitted to a number of restrictions under Article 2 ('the rights of others,' 'the constitutional order' and 'the moral law').

In Hungarian case law, the general personality right, which was associated with human dignity, is not linked to any other constitutional provision. Indeed, its only raison d'être rests in its equivalence to the right to human dignity. The link established by the Hungarian Court between human dignity and the general personality right was not clarified. The Court presented as a matter of fact that human dignity is one aspect of the general personality right and repetition of the association seemed to substitute a better explanation. In other words, the general personality right became a constitutional right by a process of assertion and reification. In addition, the Hungarian Court, when establishing the equivalence between human dignity and the general personality right, never mentioned the right to life despite the fact that the two are linked under Article 54(1). Inevitably, the Constitutional Court had to clarify this position. In case 4/1993 on restitution of Church property, the Court made the distinction between human dignity and the general personality right explicit for the first time:

> The Constitutional Court laid down two aspects of the right to human dignity. On one hand, the right to human dignity—together with the right to life and legal capacity—is considered as a right which determines the person's legal status (*See Dec. 64/1991 (XII.17) AB: MK 1991/139, ABH 1991, 297.*) On the other hand, according to the practice of the Constitutional Court—from *Dec. 8/1990 (IV.23)* AB (MK 1990/35; ABH 1990, 42)—the right to human dignity is the 'general personality right,' which includes the free development of one's personality. The Constitutional Court also interpreted the freedom of conscience in *Dec. 64/1991 (XII.17)* AB as a right to personal integrity. (The state cannot compel anyone to accept a situation which sows discord within, or is irreconcilable with, those fundamental convictions which mould that person's identity.)
>
> The freedom of conscience and religion acknowledges that the person's conviction and, within this, in a given case, religion, is a part of human quality, so their freedom is a pre-condition for the free development of personality.[14]

---

[13] The wording of the Hungarian Constitution could have led to the interpretation that the right to human dignity was only a sort of psychological complement to the physical dimension of the right to life.

[14] L Sólyom and G Brunner (eds), *Constitutional Judiciary in a New Democracy: the Hungarian Constitutional Court* (Ann Arbor, University of Michigan Press, 2000), 251–52.

The Court acknowledged that human dignity could have two clearly distinct aspects, namely the right to life on one hand and the general personality right on the other. In this case, however, the Court used human dignity to emphasise the importance of freedom of religion under Article 60 of the Constitution.[15] It took the Hungarian Court another two years and another case (75/1995) to articulate the logical consequences of this split: different levels of protection apply to each aspect of human dignity. In this case, the Court was caught in the complexities of its convoluted case law on human dignity. Case 75/1995 was about procedural rules in a paternity suit. The petitioner questioned one aspect of these complex rules, namely the power of a court to impose certain medical tests on the man who might turn out to be the father of the child at the centre of the proceedings. This man is not considered as a witness and he does not enjoy the usual protection granted to witnesses or the parties in such proceedings. As a result, the judge can force him to undergo a blood test even—and this is important—against his will. This brought two aspects of the general personality right into conflict. On the one hand, the child had a constitutionally protected right to question and ascertain his biological origins: the right to self-identification set out by the Hungarian Court in an earlier case (57/1991). On the other hand, there was the potential father's right to self-determination in judicial proceedings, as established by the Court in cases 9/1992 and 1/1994. For the first time, two aspects of the general personality right conflicted with each other. Both rights, obviously, could not be enforced to the same extent since the realisation of one led automatically to the restriction of the other. In order to strike a balance between the two rights, the Court had to acknowledge that human dignity, when it is associated with the general personality right, is neither absolute nor inviolable:

> The right to human dignity only as far as it determines the human status and as far as it forms a unity with the right to life is absolute and without restrictions (case 64/1991, 17 December). *However, each partial right derived from the mother-right (for instance the right to free self-determination and the right to physical integrity) can be restricted just as any other fundamental right under art. 8(2) of the Constitution.*[16] (emphasis added)

This case completed the separation between the two branches of human dignity and clarified the status of the general personality right, in that it could from

---

[15] Art 60 reads: '1—In the Republic of Hungary everyone has the right to freedom of thought, conscience and religion. 2—This right shall include the free choice or acceptance of a religion or belief, either alone or in community with others, in public or in private, to manifest his/her religion or belief in religious acts and observances or in other ways, to refrain from its manifestation, to practise and to teach it. 3—In the Republic of Hungary, the Church shall operate in separation from the State. 4—A majority of two-thirds of the votes of the Members of Parliament present is required to pass the statute on the freedom of belief and religion.'

[16] Art 8(2) reads: 'In the Republic of Hungary rules pertaining to fundamental rights and duties shall be determined by statute, which however, may not limit the essential contents of any fundamental right.'

then on be subjected to constitutional restrictions. In subsequent case law, however, such a situation of clear conflict between two constitutional rights did not arise.

(c) Human Dignity for Legal Persons?

In case 24/1996, the Hungarian Court extended human dignity and the general personality right to legal persons, namely to an association. In this case, the petitioners challenged a governmental decree from 1982, which established the complex system of controls over cultural and artistic life that prevailed under communism. Under that decree, cultural associations were not absolutely free to handle works of art. The decree required such associations to obtain and comply with the opinion of a 'committee of experts,' emanating from the Ministry of Culture, as to the value of a work of art before they could obtain, use or commercialise it. The reasoning of the Court took into account the constitutional provisions on freedom of expression (Art 61) and freedom of scientific and artistic life (Art 70D).[17] In addition, an essential part of its reasoning focused on the general freedom of action, which is one of the numerous aspects of the general personality right.

The Hungarian Court ruled that the general freedom of action protected the 'freedom to engage in legal transactions, that is the right to make decisions in such transactions without any constraining influence and in an independent manner.' Interestingly, the Court related this new aspect of the general personality right to human dignity by referring to the founding case, which was about the right to self-determination of employees (8/1990). After briefly referring to three previous cases (21/1990, 7/1991 and 28/1994) which involved the protection of human persons, the Court recognised for the first time that 'human' dignity could extend to legal persons, ie non-human beings. According to the Court, the Constitution grants associations a certain autonomy of action. Having crossed this conceptual Rubicon, the Court cautiously added some precisions. In the Court's opinion, while human dignity applied to human beings is absolute, the autonomy of action of moral persons is not: it is determined and hence circumscribed by their founding text. In addition, as is the case for the

---

[17] Art 61 reads: '1—In the Republic of Hungary everyone has the right to freedom of expression, and furthermore to receive and impart information of public interest. 2—The Republic of Hungary recognises and protects the freedom of the press. 3—A majority of two-thirds of the votes of the Members of Parliament is required to pass the statute on the public access to information of public interest and the statute on the freedom of the press. 4—A majority of two-thirds of the votes of the Members of Parliament present is required to pass the statute on the supervision of public radio, television and the public news agency, as well as the appointment of the directors thereof, on the licensing of commercial radio and television and on the prevention of information monopolies.' Art 70G reads: '1—The Republic of Hungary shall respect and support the freedom of scientific and artistic life, the freedom of learning and of teaching. 2—Only scientists are entitled to decide on questions of scientific truth and to determine the scientific value of research.'

fundamental rights of human beings, the autonomy of action of legal persons can be restricted by statute in order to protect another constitutional value or right. Such a restriction has to be proportional for it to be considered constitutional.

Chapter 3 explained this surprising and in many ways contradictory development by noting that the German Court has made a similar use of the general freedom of action and, indeed, that in German case law this right is also developed in relation to legal persons. There is, however, a fundamental difference between the two courts' reasoning which can be explained by the difference in the phrasing of both constitutions. Under German case law, there is no contradiction in recognising that the Basic Law can also protect legal persons against the violation of their general freedom of action and autonomy in contractual relations. This flows from Article 2(1) and Article 19(3) of the Basic Law, which are not exclusively concerned with human persons.[18] In Hungary, by contrast, there is only one constitutional provision from which the Court creatively derived the general personality right and, among others, the general freedom of action (Article 54(1)). Moreover, Article 8(2) of the Hungarian Constitution explicitly focuses on the protection of the 'rights of man,' thus presumably excluding other legal persons. Finally, as it will be recalled from chapter 3, until case 24/1996, the Hungarian Court had consistently applied human dignity and the related personality right to human persons. The Court had clearly held so far that human dignity was an exclusively human attribute and even that enjoyment of the right to life and human dignity was the crucial conceptual (and constitutional) difference between human persons and other non-human persons enjoying a legal status (case 23/1990).

The examples above illustrate the Court's efforts to adjust German case law to the Hungarian Constitution. This involved twisting German case law as the Hungarian constitution differs from the German Basic Law on a number of points for the interpretation of human dignity. This further involved a constant adaptation of Hungarian case law in order to iron out the inconsistencies and to clarify the aspects of human dignity which were imported hastily in the very early cases. There exist, however, a number of differences between the two interpretations of human dignity which cannot be understood as a mere effort of judicial adjustment.

1.2. Significant Differences

One crucial element of the definition of human dignity is the determination of who is protected. This becomes more complicated in cases where humanity is

---

[18] Art 19(3) reads: 'The basic rights shall apply to domestic *legal persons* to the extent that the nature of such rights permits.'(emphasis added). See also D Kommers, above n 10; I Richter and GF Schuppert (eds), *Casebook Verfassungsrecht* (München, CH Beck Verlagbuchhandlung, 1996), 48–57 and 93–103 and Bundesverfassungsgericht (ed) *Nachschlagewerk der Rechtsprechung des Bundesverfassungsgerichts* (Heidelberg, Decker Verlag and Müller Verlag, 1997).

harder to define, ie before birth and after death and, in relation to such sensitive issues, the case law of the Hungarian Court is very different from that of the German Court.

(a) Dignity Before Birth

Both constitutions clearly protect the right to life and human dignity. The Hungarian constitution does so under one single provision, Article 54 and the German Basic Law achieves this through the combination of Article 1 (human dignity) and Article 2(2) (the right to life and physical integrity). In addition, both legal systems prohibit capital punishment: while the German Basic Law contains a provision explicitly prohibiting capital punishment,[19] the Hungarian Constitutional Court abolished the death penalty in a famous case (23/1990).[20]

In relation to the beginning of life however, each constitutional court reached a different conclusion. The German Court considered the constitutionality of abortion on two occasions. The first ruling was delivered in 1975, when abortion was liberalised following the Abortion Reform Act of 1974. In 1975, the German Court clearly established that the foetus had a right to life, ie a right to be born. The second ruling was provoked by the German reunification and the subsequent need to harmonise the two sets of legislation, due to the fact that rules in the former East Germany were more permissive than in West Germany. This second German case is particularly interesting because the German and the Hungarian Courts found themselves in an unusually similar situation, having to adjudicate on the more liberal regulations of abortion existing under the previous communist regimes. Although the provisions which were challenged before both courts were probably as similar as they can ever be and raised very similar constitutional issues, the Hungarian and the German Courts held very different views in relation to the foetus's right to life and human dignity.

The German Court held in its first case in 1975 that the right to life under Article 2(2) extends to the life developing within the mother's womb:

> The developmental process thus begun is a continuous one which manifests no sharp demarcation and does not permit any precise delimitation of the various developmental stages of the human life. Nor does it end with birth; for instance, the phenomena of consciousness specific to human personality do not appear until some time after birth. Therefore [we] may not limit the protection of Article 2(2)[1] of the Basic Law either to the 'completed' human being after birth or to the independently viable nasciturus [. . .] Additionally, [the obligation of the state to protect all human life]

---

[19] Art 102 of the German Basic Law provides that 'Capital punishment shall be abolished.'

[20] L Sólyom and G Brunner (eds), *Constitutional Judiciary in a New Democracy: the Hungarian Constitutional Court* (Ann Arbor, University of Michigan Press, 2000), 118–38. See ch 3, and see also T Horváth, 'Abolition of Capital Punishment in Hungary' [1991] *Acta Juridica Hungarica* 153–56. Two years after this case, Hungary accepted the European Convention on Human Rights together with Additional Protocol No 6, prohibiting the death penalty.

follows from the express provision of Article 1(1) of the Basic Law; for the developing life also enjoys the protection which Article 1(1) accords to the dignity of man. Wherever human life exists, it merits human dignity; whether the subject of this dignity is conscious of it and knows how to safeguard it is not of decisive moment. The potential capabilities inherent in human existence from its inception are adequate to establish human dignity.[21] (my editing in italics)

In 1975 the German Court did not have a single hesitation: the foetus is protected by the human dignity clause and has a right to life, a position that the court maintained in its 1993 ruling. In 1975 the Court did acknowledge, however, the conflict between this position and the rights to self-determination, to an intimate private sphere, to physical integrity and dignity of the pregnant woman. According to the German Court, the antagonism of such conflicting rights was 'resolved' through a careful balancing exercise in which the court found in favour of the foetus:

> No compromise is possible that would both guarantee the protection of the unborn life and concede to the pregnant woman the freedom of terminating the pregnancy, because termination of pregnancy always means destruction of the prenatal life. In the ensuing balancing process, 'both constitutional values must be perceived in their relation to human dignity as the centre of the Constitution's value system.' When using Article 1(1) as a guidepost, the decision must come down in favour of the preeminence of protecting the foetus's life over the right of self-determination of the pregnant woman. Pregnancy, birth and child-rearing may impair the woman's [right of self-determination] as to many personal developmental potentialities. The termination of pregnancy, however, destroys prenatal life. Pursuant to the principle of carefully balancing competing constitutionally protected positions, and considering the fundamental concept behind Article 19(2) of the Basic Law, [the state] must give the protection of the unborn child's life priority. In principle, this preeminence lasts for the entire duration of the pregnancy and may not be questioned for any particular phase.[22]

As a result, under German law, in 1975 abortion was unconstitutional in principle and punished by criminal law when performed outside the very strictly defined permitted cases. The criminalisation of abortion was questioned again after German reunification. Former East and West Germany maintained their specific regulations for a transitional period, but as soon as the all-German parliament had to agree on a compromise between the two positions, the statute (Pregnancy and Family Assistance Act) was challenged before the Constitutional Court. Under the Act, abortion was decriminalised during the first 12 weeks. The statute further contained numerous measures to support and inform women in matters such as contraception, education and family planning. The German constitutional judges essentially maintained the principle set

---

[21] BVerfGE 39, 1, *Abortion I*, 1975, as translated by D Kommers, *The Constitutional Jurisprudence of the Federal Republic of Germany* (Durham and London, Duke University Press, 1997), 337–38.

[22] Kommers, above n 21, at 339. Art 19(2) reads: 'In no case may the essential content of a basic right be encroached upon.'

out in their previous ruling and complemented it by a set of guidelines addressed to the legislator for the subsequent enactment of a statute on abortion.[23]

In stark contrast to the German position, the Hungarian Constitutional Court did not consider that the right to life and human dignity under Article 54 meant that the foetus had a right to be born. In case 64/1991, the Hungarian Court considered that this issue could not be settled by way of constitutional adjudication and called on parliament to enact a new statute:

> The question of whether the foetus is a legal subject cannot be resolved by interpretation of the Constitution. Accordingly, only after the legislature's decision concerning the foetus's legal personality and depending thereon would the Constitutional Court be able to make a substantive evaluation of the constitutionality of abortion regulations.[24]

As will be recalled from chapter 3, the Court nevertheless held that the (communist) governmental decree regulating abortion was unconstitutional, because it violated the requirement under Article 8(2) of the 1989 Constitution that restrictions to fundamental rights had to be regulated by statute.[25] In an attempt to provide guidelines for the legislator, the Hungarian Court adopted a very interesting line of hypothetical reasoning. Without deciding whether the foetus had a legal status, the Court considered the requirements for a constitutional statute on abortion in both possible instances: if the legislator were to decide that the foetus is a human person; or on the contrary, if it were to decide that the foetus has no legal capacity. The Court emphasised that, whatever the constitutional status of the foetus, the state had an objective duty to protect all life, including that of the unborn.[26] Further, this duty of protection had to be carefully balanced with the other (obvious) conflicting rights, namely the pregnant woman's right to self-determination and to a private sphere.

Parliament reacted fairly quickly to the Court's 1991 ruling and passed Act LXXIX on the protection of the embryo in 1992. It took the Court far longer to address the numerous petitions that this statute triggered. The second abortion case (48/1998) was decided by the same judges, not long before three of them, A Ádám, G Kilenyi and significantly, the president L Sólyom, reached the end of their mandate and left the Court.[27]

The new statute did not consider that the foetus had the same status as a human being. The legislator, while excluding legal capacity for the foetus, listed

---

[23] On this case, see Kommers, above n 21 at 349–55.

[24] L Sólyom and G Brunner (eds), *Constitutional Judiciary in a New Democracy: the Hungarian Constitutional Court* (Ann Arbor, University of Michigan Press, 2000), 184.

[25] Art 8(2) provides: 'In the Republic of Hungary rules pertaining to fundamental rights and duties shall be determined by statute, which, however, may not limit the essential contents of any fundamental right.'

[26] In Hungarian the word '*magzat*' (used in case 64/1991) can mean either 'embryo' or 'foetus.'

[27] The article of H Küpper provides a particularly useful insight into the reasoning of the Court, 'Das Zweite Abtreibungsurteil des ungarischen Verfassungsgerichts' [1999] *OsteuropaRecht* 155–69.

a number of cases in which abortion could legally be carried out. The most problematic of these, on which the Court focused its reasoning, was the situation of social crisis and extreme hardship affecting the woman which, under the new Act, could justify abortion during the first three months of pregnancy. The Hungarian Court ruled that this was unconstitutional, because it gave a disproportionate weight to the woman's right to self-determination and so the Court asked the legislator to reconsider its position on this particular matter.[28]

In its two abortion rulings, the Hungarian Court significantly departed from German case law. The gap between the two interpretations of human dignity appears to be even wider because it originates from constitutional provisions which are very similar, as well as from legal issues expressed in very similar terms. This arguably shows at least two things about law importation. First, it confirms that importation is not a sort of mechanical imitation of all aspects of a chosen foreign legal system. Secondly, these differences do not follow from a random or erroneous replication. On the contrary, the selection carried out by the Hungarian Court was deliberate and corresponded to specific reasons. I would suggest that one reason here, although it is not made explicit as such by the Hungarian Court, is the different social, cultural and political context in which these cases were decided. More precisely, the Court was very probably aware of public opinion and of the 'cultural and social' legacy of communism under which abortion was quite liberally permitted and not seriously objected to. Importing the German interpretation of the right to life and dignity which leads to abortion being constitutional in a very restricted number of cases would have probably caused public outrage and hence would not have been a politically tenable position for the Court.

(b) Dignity After Death

In a well-known case, called the *Mephisto* case after the title of the novel which gave rise to it, the German Court extended the scope of the general personality right to protect people after they have died.[29] As no similar case arose before the

---

[28] The Hungarian Court accompanied its ruling with a deadline: parliament had to enact a new statute by 30 June 2000. The latest development of the abortion 'saga' will not be considered here. A third ruling by the Court would however be most interesting for at least one reason, namely it would be delivered by the new Court, ie the Court with a substantially new composition after the change of staff in 1998. The new Court does seem to have a different approach to its function, see KL Scheppele, 'The New Hungarian Constitutional Court' (1999) 8 *East European Constitutional Law Review* 81–87.

[29] BVerfGE 30, 173, *Mephisto* case, 1971, translation of D Kommers *The Constitutional Jurisprudence of the Federal Republic of Germany*, (Durham and London, Duke University Press, 1997), 302–3. 'The courts [below] properly referred to Article 1(1) in order to determine the late actor Gründgens's protected sphere of personality. It would be incompatible with the constitutional commandment that human dignity is inviolate—a commandment which acts as the foundation for all basic rights—if a person, possessed of human dignity by virtue of his personhood, could be degraded or debased . . . even after his death. Accordingly, the obligation that Article 1(1) imposes on all state authority to afford the individual protection from attacks on his dignity does not end with death.'

Hungarian Court between 1990 and 1998, it is difficult to compare the position of the two Courts on this issue. However, on the basis of the Hungarian interpretation of the general right to personality, that is a right which has no existence independently of the right to human dignity and thus to life, it might be assumed that the extension of this right to protect the dead is not possible. Moreover, the general personality right was always applied to people who were alive and although a petition on the constitutionality of euthanasia was pending, the Court did not rule on it during its first term.[30]

The implications of the right to life and human dignity after death were considered in one instance between 1990 and 1998, in a case on compensation for deaths inflicted on political grounds. The emphasis in this instance was not so much on the scope of Article 54(1) and on the general personality right, as on the equality of humans and therefore of human deaths. Case 22/1996 was brought about by a Bill introduced in 1992 on 'compensation for persons illegally deprived of their lives on political grounds.' In one of the rare preventive reviews of legal norms, the Court had to decide whether it was constitutional to distinguish between causes of death for the purpose of assessing amounts of compensation. The Bill in question provided for three categories of persons and corresponding compensation: persons who were killed, persons deported and interned in a Soviet work camp and persons deprived of their liberties for other reasons. Whereas in earlier rulings on compensation the Court accepted that the state could discriminate, ie distinguish between various categories of persons in order to establish a compensation scheme,[31] in this case the Court's interpretation of Articles 54 and 70A made it impossible to reach such a conclusion. Instead, the Court held that the various categories established by the Bill were unconstitutional:

> Although deprivation of liberty can in general be conceived of as one type of injury, there have been so many different typical modes of captivity in respect of the severity of the injury and the extent of suffering that it renders it not only permissible but constitutionally required that the compensation be different. This was the result of the previous constitutional review of the third Compensation Act.
>
> When, however, captivity caused death, the finality and absolute weight of this 'result' minimises the significance of the difference in injuries and suffering preceding death. This loss absorbs all previous injuries.
>
> From a theoretical point of view, departing from the capital punishment and abortion decisions of the Constitutional Court, the absolute nature of the right to life makes the different appreciation of the loss of life impossible in a system of compen-

---

[30] A Sajó and J Sándor, 'Legal Status of the "Terminally Ill" under Hungarian Law' (1995/96) 37 *Acta Iuridica Hungarica* 1–21.

[31] See, eg the first compensation case (21/1990) on expropriated property, L Sólyom and G Brunner (eds), *Constitutional Judiciary in a New Democracy: the Hungarian Constitutional Court* (Ann Arbor, University of Michigan Press, 2000), 108–17. Also P Paczolay, 'Judicial Review of the Compensation Law in Hungary' [1992] *Michigan Journal of International Law* 806–31. More generally, see I Pogany, *Righting Wrongs in Eastern Europe* (Manchester, Manchester University Press, 1997).

sation based not on responsibility but on caused injuries. 'The right to equal dignity in unity with the right to life secures that there can be no differences made among the value of human lives' (*Dec. 64/1991 (XII.17)AB:* MK 1991/139 at 2815; ABH 1991, 297 at 309).

Considering the equally immeasurable value of the lives of the deceased, there can be no differentiation made as regards the actual circumstances of their deaths or the ideological commitment of the regimes by which they were killed.

Thus there is no need and—in a system of compensation based on the injuries caused—no legal possibility for a comparison, which is anyhow inexecutable and contradicts human dignity, that different kinds of compensation would be given for death in a Nazi death camp, a Soviet gulag or in the cellar of the AVH [State Defence Authority in Hungary].[32]

According to this ruling, human dignity in combination with the equality provision also applies to people after their deaths. More precisely, it can be used to assess the 'value' of their deaths: that is, to refuse to distinguish between causes of death in order to grant compensation. This solution was, in many ways, a brave effort to address the questions of history (are you entitled to more money when your (grand)father died in a Nazi concentration camp or when he died in a Soviet work camp?). Although it is not couched in such terms, this ruling might also be understood as a recognition that both ideologies were equal in their horror. This egalitarian stand is likely, however, to lead to more questions which will be difficult to answer if and when they arise before the Court. That is, if lives and deaths are all equal, it might mean that it is constitutionally impossible to distinguish, for compensation purposes, between a death 'for ideological reasons' and a death resulting from a medical error for instance. However, mercifully no such case was brought before the Court between 1990 and 1998. In case 22/1996, it has to be noted that, unlike the German Court, the Hungarian Court did not base its reasoning on dignity and the general personality right, but on the argument of equality. As a result, the general personality right does not protect the dead in Hungarian case law.

Interestingly, in the cases where the Hungarian Court differed most visibly from German case law, that is essentially in the abortion cases, the Hungarian Court did not refer to 'modern constitutions and their practice' as it did in most other decisions (as seen in chapter 4). It seems that in such cases, the Hungarian Court deliberately sought to depart from the German model, which was otherwise a source of inspiration. This arguably indicates that the Hungarian Court deliberately selected what it wanted to import from German case law, in order to develop its own conception of human dignity.

---

[32] L Sólyom and G Brunner (eds), *Constitutional Judiciary in a New Democracy: the Hungarian Constitutional Court* (Ann Arbor, University of Michigan Press, 2000), 352–53.

2. INSTRUMENTALISING THE MODEL: AN ISOLATED INDIVIDUAL

A crucial aspect of the definition of individuals lies in their relationship with the state, as well as their status within society. With regard to this second aspect, the Hungarian Court selected those elements from German case law which emphasised the individuality and the autonomy of individuals.

2.1. Importing Rights Without the Corresponding Restrictions

In German law, the right to the free fulfilment of the personality is perhaps, together with the human dignity provision, the right which the German court has construed in the most creative manner. However and significantly, this right is also subject to three restrictions clearly spelled out in the Basic Law under Article 2:

> Everyone shall have the right to the free fulfilment of his personality *in so far as he does not violate the rights of others, or offend against the constitutional order or the moral code.* (emphasis added)

The broad and open phrasing of these restrictions has led to numerous developments in case law and has been widely commented on by the academic community. Yet, the exact meaning and scope of the restrictions is still surrounded by much debate. This brief presentation loosely follows that of Adalbert Podlech in his *Kommentar zum Grundgesetz der BRD*.[33] First, 'the rights of others' is probably the easiest restriction to understand. Its meaning is almost self-evident: 'rights of others' represent a requirement of symmetry for the realisation of the free fulfilment of the personality and the rights derived therefrom. The exercise of these rights stops where it breaches the rights of others. 'The rights of others' acknowledges the fact that the individual claiming the benefit of Article 2(1) is not alone in society. The Court has to ensure that no one individual dominates the community; in other words, that no right can be exercised while disregarding or even breaching other rights enjoying the same constitutional status. Beyond this, the legal order (or more precisely statutes) cannot create situations where the right to fulfilment of one's personality dominates other rights or the rights of other people. Secondly, 'the constitutional order' is a more general restriction and arguably more difficult to understand. The phrase 'constitutional order' could also be translated as the constitutionality of the order established by the German Basic Law, or maybe by the constitutional order on which the German Federal Republic is based ('*die verfassungsmäßige*

---

[33] A Podlech, 'Art. 2 GG', in R Wassermann (ed), *Kommentar zum Grundgesetz der Bundesrepublik Deutschland* (Darmstadt, Luchterhand, 1984), 348–56. In his book on the jurisprudence of the German Constitutional Court, Kommers does not mention the restrictions contained in Art 2(1) of the Basic Law.

Ordnung'). As a result, this phrase embraces formal and substantial requirements of constitutionality. The 'constitutional order' can be determined by the written provisions of positive law, but it is not restricted to those written norms.[34] Thirdly, the 'moral code' ('*das Sittengesetz*') cannot be determined solely in relation to written law, and here the word 'code' has to be understood in its wider sense ('*Gesetz*' also means law in a general sense). The 'moral code' refers rather to what is morally acceptable and hence constitutional at a given time. As a result the definition of the 'moral code' has varied over time and the German Court is keen not to impose or even to propose a precise and substantial definition of the 'code.'

The German Court has probably been as creative with this set of restrictions ('*Schrankentrias*') as it has been with the interpretation of the right itself.[35] Indeed, constitutional restrictions provide a sort of negative definition of a right which reflects the society or the perception of what matters at a given time. This constant adjustment can be illustrated by the varying perceptions of the last restriction, the respect for the 'moral code' ('*das Sittengesetz*'). With its broad phrasing, the 'moral code' was open to many different interpretations. Back in 1957 the Karlsruhe Court ruled that sexuality fell within the scope of the fulfilment of the personality and thus could benefit from the constitutional protection of Article 2. However, the court ruled that the petitioner could not invoke this provision to protect his own sexual life, because homosexual behaviour was against the 'moral code'.[36] Nowadays, the German Court would probably take a difference stance on this matter to reflect the social and legal changes regarding the perception of homosexuality. Kommers offers perhaps the clearest and briefest summary of the role of the general personality right in German jurisprudence:

> . . . the general right to personality is not a shorthand expression of other guaranteed rights. The personality right is so broad in its phrasing that almost any content could be poured into it, and it could easily function as the first and last resort of constitutional arguments. Recognising this, the Constitutional Court has sought to confine its reach. As a general rule, the personality clause is subordinate to those positive rights of liberty expressly mentioned in the Basic Law. A complainant may invoke the personality clause only when he or she challenges a governmental act that invades a liberty interest vital to the exercise of personality outside the protection of any particular right. In addition, the personality clause can be invoked only to vindicate a fundamental liberty interest against intrusive state activity.[37]

---

[34] See BVerfGE 6, 32, [37] *Elfes* case.

[35] On the restrictions, see also I Richter and GF Schuppert (eds), *Casebook Verfassungsrecht* (München, Beck Verlagbuchhandlung, 1996), 111–27.

[36] BVerfGE 6, 289, (403), 10 May 1957.

[37] Kommers, above n 29, at 313–14. In 1977 in the *Life Imprisonment* case (BVerfGE 45, 187), the German Court held that: 'The free human person and his dignity are the highest values of the constitutional order. The state in all of its forms is obliged to respect and defend it. This is based on the conception of man as a spiritual-moral being endowed with the freedom to determine and develop himself. This freedom within the meaning of the Basic Law is not that of an isolated and self-regarding individual but rather [that] of a person related to and bound by the community. In the light of this community-boundedness it cannot be "in principle unlimited." The individual must

By contrast, in Hungarian case law the general personality right appeared in the first cases as a right without restrictions. In fact, the Hungarian Court never referred to any of the restrictions existing under the German Basic Law. Furthermore, in most cases, the Hungarian Court never considered the rights of others, or that their rights presumably and almost inevitably conflicted with the general personality right of one particular person. A particularly clear illustration of this pattern is the abortion case of 1991: when the conflict between the pregnant woman's rights and the foetus's rights could not be ignored, the Court set the issue aside and waited for the legislator to decide the matter.[38] This reinforced the impression that Article 54(1) was a sort of all-powerful provision: an open-ended number of rights could be discovered under it, very few restrictions were allowed and invoking it almost always led to a ruling of unconstitutionality and subsequent nullification of the norm examined by the Court.[39]

2.2. Individualistic Humanity

The importation of rights without their corresponding restrictions led to the development of a very different picture of the human person in Hungarian case law. In Germany, the elaborate system of restrictions and values has allowed the German Court to consider that the individual is involved in a complex network of social relations and is not isolated. In Hungary, the representation of the individual is very different: it is that of a person considered in isolation and fighting against the state to protect her rights.

(a) Focusing on Autonomy and Self-Determination

Although German case law on human dignity has (too) often been reduced to the Kantian maxim according to which man is a subject and not merely an object, German cases and indeed the Basic Law itself are not solely based on this principle and endeavour to protect and reflect a multitude of (competing) values. As Kommers summarised, German case law is not a glorification of individual autonomy:

> In seeking to advance human dignity as a constitutional value, both court and commentators have relied on three politically significant sources of ethical theory in post

allow those limits on his freedom of action that the legislature deems necessary in the interest of the community's social life; yet the autonomy of the individual has to be protected.' As translated by Kommers, above n 29, at 307–8.

[38] Strangely enough, the whole case focused on the status of the foetus which remained unsettled and uncertain. The Court did not elaborate on the various rights of the pregnant woman which do exist: their scope might vary in relation to the foetus's status, but a (pregnant) woman arguably has a legal status that is clearly defined under the 1989 Constitution.

[39] I will come back to the quasi-systematic nullifications on the basis of Art 54 in ch 6 in more detail.

war Germany—Christian natural law, Kantian thought and social democratic thought—present in the constitutional text as a whole. . . . These orientations have converged in German constitutional case law to produce an integrated conception of the human person as an individual possessing spiritual autonomy, which—in a properly governed society—is to be guided by social discipline and practical reasonableness.[40]

Furthermore, although fundamental rights are given priority in the German Basic Law, they are by no means absolute. Their number and variety clearly imply the need for reaching an equilibrium between rights as most of the time they cannot be enforced while breaching conflicting rights. Indeed, the core of German constitutional jurisprudence is about establishing a balance between the rights of the person seeking redress and those of other people or institutions concerned by the issue at stake. This search for an equilibrium is probably best known (although not necessarily best summarised) by the proportionality test, that is the requirement that the restriction of a particular right be proportional to the aim that the state seeks to achieve through that restriction.

In contrast, the Hungarian interpretation of human dignity is focused on individuality and autonomy. The Hungarian Court only considered an individual's interaction with other people when an immediate conflict emerged between two incompatible rights. In such instances, in order to determine whether the questioned rule was constitutional, the Court had to solve the conflict by deciding in favour of one of the rights involved. In most cases, however, when the conflict of rights was less urgent and visible, the Court was oblivious to potentially conflicting rights and, indeed, to other people. The Constitutional Court consistently emphasised the autonomy of the individual. In fact, the very function of human dignity and the general personality right is to protect individual autonomy in the absence of a specific right in the 1989 Constitution, as the Court decided in its very first case on this issue (8/1990):

> The Constitutional Court considers the right to human dignity as one of the formulations of the general personality right. Modern constitutions and constitutional case law name the general personality right in terms of several of its aspects, such as the right to free fulfilment of personality, the right to self-determination, the general freedom of action or the right to a private sphere. The general personality right is a 'mother-right,' that is a fundamental subsidiary right on which *the Constitutional Court as well as other Courts can rely in order to protect individual autonomy in instances where no specific named fundamental rights can apply to the facts of the case.* (emphasis added)

This function of protecting individual autonomy was subsequently reiterated in all cases referring to human dignity and in which the Court imported another right from German case law in the wake of the general personality right.[41] In

---

[40] Kommers, *The Constitutional Jurisprudence of the Federal Republic of Germany*, (Durham and London, Duke University Press, 1997), at 304.
[41] Ch 6 will come back to the function of 'subsidiarity' of human dignity.

fact, each of the imported rights can be seen as a particular illustration of individual autonomy. In other words, the rights derived from Article 54(1) illustrate several manifestations of individual autonomy, and this is particularly clear with the right to self-determination. This right, which is the most frequently invoked by the Court, was conjugated into many variations: the right to self-identification and to ascertain one's biological origins, the right to marry freely and the right to take an active role in judicial proceedings.[42]

When reading Hungarian cases, there is no indication that individuals are part of a community or society and that they interact with each other. Similarly, there is no sense that the (proportional) restrictions of some rights might be beneficial for the wider community. One illustration of this point is found in case 23/1990 on the abolition of capital punishment. The death penalty reflects a clear conflict of interests or rights between an individual, whose best interest is arguably to remain alive, and the community, which may be said by some to need retribution or protection against the criminal deeds of the person sentenced to death. However, in that case the Hungarian Court only considered the individual life at stake: the life of the criminal sentenced to death. Nowhere in the course of its reasoning did the Court consider the implications of its ruling for the wider community.[43] The Court could have (at least) raised the issue of the gravity of the crimes committed or indeed examined more closely criminal regulations providing for the death penalty. All that seemed to matter was ruling out the death penalty as a constitutional punishment. It is true that Hungary was due to abolish capital punishment anyway as it was in the process of ratifying the European Convention on Human Rights, together with its additional protocols.[44] This probably prompted the Constitutional Court to nullify the provisions on capital punishment. Hypothetically, even if the Court had considered the rights of others and the interests of the community, it could nevertheless have decided that the death penalty was unconstitutional.

---

[42] Ch 3 proposed an overview of these rights, see Table 1.

[43] Under the Law Decree 1979, the death penalty could be enforced as a punishment for crimes, such as genocide, aggravated cases of violence against civilian populations, aggravated cases of criminal warfare, aggravated cases of homicide, aggravated cases of terrorist activity and some military crimes, such as aggravated cases of desertion, mutiny and disobedience.

[44] L Sólyom commenting on this case, pointed out that: 'The decision of the Hungarian Court was not received without debate. A favourite argument against the Court contends that it exceeded its competences because elimination of the death penalty was necessarily a matter for Parliament to address. This position lacks a legal basis. During the long process, which was well known to the public, there was no relevant initiative in the Parliament for such an Act. Following a series of infamous murder cases, reinstatement of the death penalty was regularly called for. Some political parties turned this into a campaign issue in the 1994 election and even on the eve of the 1998 one. According to the receptivity of the people to such slogans and the repeated attempts to organise a referendum on the reintroduction of the death penalty, it would appear that a large majority of the population remains in favour of it. On the other hand, elimination of the death penalty is in accordance with the European Convention on Human Rights and its Sixth Protocol, which Hungary ratified after the Constitutional Court's decision in 1993': L Sólyom and G Brunner (eds), *Constitutional Judiciary in a New Democracy: the Hungarian Constitutional Court* (Ann Arbor, University of Michigan Press, 2000), 53, n 20.

The emphasis on self-determination and autonomy is such that these two notions might summarise the essential meaning of human dignity. The Court did not provide a substantial definition of human dignity, but such a definition can nevertheless be reconstructed from the body of case law decided between 1990 and 1998, according to which human dignity is limited to the individual considered in his singularity. It empowers the individual to take control over his life without any interference, or indeed any help, from others or from the state. Human dignity in Hungarian jurisprudence, unlike in German case law, does not essentially facilitate interaction and relationships between people.[45] Instead, human dignity surrounds the individual in a sort of protective sphere, and thus isolates individuals from each other. This leads to a selfish picture of human beings as solely preoccupied by the realisation and protection of their own interests and achievements.

(b) Individuals Fighting Against the State

The social dimension is largely missing from Hungarian case law on human dignity, which does not refer to the society in which people live and develop. In German case law however, individuals are part of society and society shapes their lives both positively and negatively, that is by allowing them some personal space, or a private sphere,[46] as well as encouraging interaction. As Kommers eloquently summarised:

> Society, the court affirmed [in the *Mephisto* case], is more than an aggregation of isolated individuals motivated by self-interest and a desire to manipulate one another for purely personal ends. Neither did the court offer a blanket endorsement of the value of autonomy as against competing social goods. Indeed, the notion of a simple opposition between person and polity is alien to the court's jurisprudence and the political theory of the Basic Law itself. The court's vigilant defence of personal freedom is embodied in the larger context of common life. Human dignity resides not only in individuality but in sociality as well. Such dignity requires the protection of the personality and freedom of the individual, but must also promote the goods of relationship, family, participation, communication, and civility.[47]

In contrast, when interpreting human dignity and the general personality right, the Hungarian Court never referred to, or considered, society in its dimension of developing towards the common good, or simply as Kommers says

---

[45] While following, or rather claiming the Kantian legacy, the Hungarian Court produced an image of man in society opposite to that developed by the philosopher of the Enlightenment for whom human dignity was both the requirement and the means for human interaction and communication necessary for the establishment of democracy.

[46] In German constitutional jurisprudence, the private sphere surrounding individuals has several dimensions: while in the less private sphere there is room for interaction and state interference, the intimate private sphere guarantees the individual a complete protection from external interventions. See R Scholz, 'Das Grundrecht auf freie Entfaltung der Persönlichkeit in der Rechtssprechung des Bundesverfassungsgerichts', (1975) 100 *Archiv für Öffentliches Recht* 80–130.

[47] Kommers, *The Constitutional Jurisprudence of the Federal Republic of Germany*, (Durham and London, Duke University Press, 1997), at 305.

(above) for the promotion of 'the goods of relationship, family participation, communication, and civility'. Society is not entirely absent from Hungarian case law, even though it is represented in a very truncated manner. In its reduced manifestation, society appeared as troublesome people, ie those people whose rights conflict with the petitioner's or as an over powerful state which claims dictatorial control over individual lives. This produced the impression that the isolated individual is constantly fighting for her freedom against the state, or rather against various emanations of the state: the trade unions, the judiciary, the public prosecutors, institutions of higher education, the army, the civil service and so on. The picture of the state, or more precisely of the relations between individuals and the state, is both negative and Manichean. While the individual is good and enjoys absolute human dignity, the state is bad and its powers have to be tightly controlled.

Naturally, the image of the state partly reflects the type of petitions submitted to the Court and these, during the first years of its operation, were essentially concerned with getting rid of the overwhelming powers that the state, ie the former one party state, could exercise over individuals and their rights. In addition, under communism, society was largely absorbed into the state structures and this partly explains the way in which society was pictured in Hungarian case law in the immediate aftermath of communism. However, the image of individuals fighting against the state also reflects the selective importation from German case law. As seen above, this selection applied to certain aspects of the interpretation of human dignity together with the general personality right. The selection arguably extended to other elements of German case law, such as the quadruple identity (functions or roles) of the state as '*Parteienstaat*' (political party state), '*Sozialstaat*' (welfare state), '*Rechtsstaat*' (state based on the rule of law) and '*streitbare Demokratie*' (militant democracy),[48] which is largely missing from Hungarian case law (with the exception of the state based on the rule of law).

3. CONCLUSION

The imported interpretation of human dignity in Hungarian case law is considerably simplified and it represents only a much reduced idea of the meaning of human dignity in German case law. The Hungarian Court selected only certain aspects of human dignity and the general personality right, such as the numerous rights derived therefrom, the extension of the general freedom of action to moral persons, the importance of autonomy and the perception of human dignity as a supreme value of the constitutional order. At the same time, the Hungarian Court did not import the constitutional restrictions associated with the general personality right and it was oblivious to the social and relational

---

[48] Kommers, above n 47, at 34.

dimensions of human dignity. As opposed to German case law, in which the complexity of the interpretation of human dignity produced an elaborate picture of the individual considered in his relations with the state as well as with other people, the Hungarian interpretation of human dignity insists on individualism and antagonism between the state and individuals.

This comparison, some would argue, is unfair to the Hungarian Court because in only nine years of functioning (however intensively), its case law could in no way match the complexity and sophistication of the German interpretation of human dignity which rests on over 50 years of constitutional adjudication. In 50 years' time, the concept of human dignity might be just as complex and rich in Hungarian case law as it is in its German counterpart. Arguably, however, rather than this lack of equivalent complexity illustrating a lack of jurisprudential sophistication due to shortness of time, the Hungarian Court's approach to human dignity reveals a deliberate choice to import only the aspects of German case law that suited it.

To some extent the selection operated by the Hungarian Court reflected its priorities in the context of the early (and uncertain) years of transition from communism: emphasising the requirement of fundamental rights protection, the creation of new rights to protect new situations and, last but not least, the need to curb and control the mighty influence of the state (the former Communist Party) over individual lives. To a certain extent as well, I would suggest that this simplified picture of human beings in their society, namely the ideological message that individualism is good and state is bad, reflected the general spirit of transitions from communism.

6

Overcoming the Communist Legacy

⟫⟨

A S SEEN IN the previous chapter, the main reason for importing foreign law
is not to imitate a foreign model. This chapter argues that the main reason is
instead to use the foreign model to solve problems facing the importer. It explores
the rationale at the root of this use of law importation: the crucial factor in the
context of transition in Central and Eastern Europe was the urgent need to face
up to the legacy of communism.[1] Law and in particular public law or 'state law,'
as it was called under communism, left its mark on the legal system as a whole.
This is particularly visible at the constitutional level in Hungary because, as it will
be recalled from chapter 1, Hungary did not adopt a brand new constitution in
1989 or after, but amended the existing communist one after the Round Table
Talks held over the summer of that year. Although the constitutional amendments introduced very substantial changes, the compromise reached between the
communist government at the time and the opposition is visible throughout, but
is particularly well illustrated by the section on fundamental rights and duties.

This chapter proposes that the reason why the Court imported human dignity
and construed it in a very individualistic way, emphasising the autonomy of the
individual, is because it sought to address the communist legacy in the
Constitution and, in particular, to reorient the conception of fundamental rights
in a liberal sense. In this process of reorientation, the human dignity provision,
as construed through law importation, proved to be a very powerful tool for
switching from a communist concept of rights to a liberal one.[2]

1. RIGHTS INHERITED FROM COMMUNISM

Communist states recognised rights which were enshrined in their constitutions.
Indeed rights were one of the bones of contention between capitalist and communist regimes, each claiming to have the best type.[3] Despite its generally poor

---

[1] Z Barany and I Volgyes (eds), *The Legacies of Communism in Eastern Europe* (Baltimore,
Johns Hopkins University Press, 1995).

[2] It is beyond the scope of this chapter to consider the legacy of the pre-communist era. On some
aspects of this legacy, see I Pogany, *Righting Wrongs in Eastern Europe* (Manchester, Manchester
University Press, 1997).

[3] J Halász, *A Socialist Concept of Human Rights* (Budapest, Akadémiai Kiadó, 1966), also
A Erh-Soon Tay, 'Marxism, Socialism and Human Rights', in E Kamenka (ed), *Ideas and
Ideologies, Human Rights* (London, Edward Arnold Press, 1978), 104–13.

record regarding the protection of political rights, a certain culture of rights developed under communism that was characterised by expectations to be protected and supported by the state in a range of situations, such as work, retirement, illness, maternity and education. Furthermore and interestingly, communist constitutions did contain a number of important political rights and personal freedoms in a formal sense. While the protection of these rights had improved since the 1970s, their conceptual basis and their understanding were still determined by communist ideology.[4] Therefore, the liberal rights introduced in the post-communist constitution did not develop in a context of *tabula rasa* and their addition to a pre-existing body of rights that had been supported and framed by a different ideology and logic was problematic for the Constitutional Court, which had to interpret them. In Hungary, this communist legacy is particularly important due to the fact that the 1989 Constitution inherited a number of rights from the 1975 Constitution, as Table 3 illustrates.

Table 3: The communist legacy

1975 Constitution	*1989 Constitution*
Art 4(3): 'The trade unions shall protect and strengthen the power of the people and shall protect and represent the interests of the workers'.	Art 4: 'Trade unions and other representative organisations shall protect and represent the interests of employees,members of cooperatives and entrepreneurs'.
Art 15: 'The Hungarian People's Republic shall protect the institutions of marriage and the family'.	Art 15: 'The Republic of Hungary shall protect the institutions of marriage and the family'.
Art 16: 'The Hungarian People's Republic shall take special care of the development and socialist education of the youth; it shall protect the interests of youth'.	Art 16: 'The Republic of Hungary shall make special efforts to ensure a secure subsistence, education and the raising of the young, and shall protect the interests of the young'.
Art 66: 'The Hungarian People's Republic shall guarantee the personal freedom and inviolability of citizens, the respect of the secrecy of correspondence, and the privacy of the home'.	Art 59(1): 'In the Republic of Hungary everyone has the right to the good standing of his/her reputation, the inviolability of his/her private home and the protection of his/her personal secrets and data'.
Art 63(1): 'The Hungarian People's Republic shall guarantee the freedom of conscience of citizens and the right to the free practice of religion'.	Art (1): 'In the Republic of Hungary, everyone has the right to freedom of thought, conscience and religion'.
Art 65: '1—The Hungarian People's Republic shall guarantee the right of association. A special law shall regulate the right of association.	Art 63: '1—On the basis of the right of association, everyone in the Republic of Hungary has the right to establish organisations for any purpose not

[4] G Brunner (ed), *Before Reforms: Human Rights in the Warsaw Pact States, 1971–1988* (London, Hurst and Co, 1990).

1975 Constitution	1989 Constitution

2—Workers may form mass organisations and mass movements to protect the order and achievements of socialism, to promote increased participation in the socialist work of construction and public life, to expand culture and educational work, to ensure the rights and duties of the people, and to promote international solidarity'.

prohibited by law and to join such organisations.
2—The establishment of armed organisations with political objectives shall not be permitted on the basis of the right to association'.

Art 57: '1—The citizens of the Hungarian People's Republic shall have the right to protection of life, physical safety and health.
2—The Hungarian People's Republic shall implement this right through organising labour safety, health institutions, and medical care, as well as protecting the human environment'.

Art 70D: '1—Everyone living in the territory of the Republic of Hungary has the right to the highest possible level of physical and mental health.
2—The Republic of Hungary shall implement this right through the organisation of safety at work, health care institutions, medical care, through securing the opportunities for regular physical activity, as well as for the protection of the built and natural environment'.

Art 59: '1—The Hungarian People's Republic shall assure the right to education of the citizens.
2—The Hungarian People's Republic shall implement this right through extending public education to all in free and compulsory general schools, as well as through secondary and higher education, extension training of adults, and through giving financial assistance to persons who receive an education'.

Art 70F: '1—The Republic of Hungary shall ensure the right of education for all its citizens.
2—The Republic of Hungary shall implement this right through the extension and general access to public education, free compulsory primary schooling, secondary and higher education being available to all persons on the basis of their ability, and furthermore through financial support for training'.

Art 60: 'The Hungarian People's Republic shall assure the freedom of scientific work and artistic production'.

Art 70G: '1—The Republic of Hungary shall respect and support the freedom of scientific and artistic life, the freedom of learning and of teaching.
2—Only scientists are entitled to decide on questions of scientific truth and to determine the scientific value of research'.

Sources: 1975 Constitution: W B Simons (ed), *The Constitutions of the Communist World* (Alphen aan den Rijn, Sijthoff and Nordhoff, 1980), 196, translated by William Sólyom-Fekete; 1989 Constitution: as available on the Constitutional Court's website www.mkab.hu.

Table 3 offers a comparison between the 1975 and the 1989 constitutional provisions on fundamental rights. The Hungarian Constitution of 1975 was amended again in 1983 when the Council for Constitutional Law was established, but the provisions relating to rights were not modified then and, for reasons of convenience, I have decided to refer readers to the 1975 Constitution which was translated into English, whereas the 1983 constitution was not.[5] The provisions included in Table 3 were chosen for the striking similarity of the phrasing in both versions of the Constitution and for their relevance to human dignity case law. As two translators were involved, this similarity is not quite accurately reflected in Table 3. Nevertheless, the communist legacy in the wording of the 1989 Constitution is clearly visible. For instance, the right to inheritance, the right to marry and the protection and education of youth were incorporated in the 1989 version without change. Furthermore, Table 3 reflects particularly well the style of the 1989 amendment and its spirit of compromise with the Communist Party that was still in power at the time. As shown above, the most typical socialist phrases, such as 'People's Republic' or 'consistent with the interests of socialism and the people' were removed from the post-communist amendment. For instance, the only difference in the 1989 version of Article 15 on the protection of the family is the change in the republic's name. In addition other provisions not mentioned in Table 3 include social rights which, although they are enshrined in the constitutions of some liberal democracies, are more typical of socialist countries, such as the right to social security (Art 70E) and the right to rest, free time and regular paid holidays (Art 70B(4)). Some provisions had already been deprived of the socialist 'hallmark' in their phrasing when the constitution was amended in 1983, but this alone did not transform them into liberal rights. They include the right to secrecy and privacy (Art 59(1)), freedom of thought, conscience and religion (Art 60(1)), freedom of expression (Art 61(1)) and, maybe to a lesser extent, freedom of association (Art 63(2)).

Despite a phrasing similar to that of rights recognised in Western liberal democracies, these rights were understood and implemented in conformity with the socialist concept of rights, with priority being given to socio-economic rights. As a result, the rights introduced in the communist constitutions were subject to two general restrictions: first, these rights could only be exercised in relation to corresponding duties and secondly, communist ideology postulated a general harmony between the interests of individuals and of society, with the latter superseding the former in case of conflict.[6] In a study of human rights in

---

[5] It will be recalled from ch 1 that the Hungarian Constitution was adopted in 1949. It was subsequently amended a number of times. Two substantial amendments were introduced in 1975 and 1983 and I refer to these as being the '1975 Constitution' and the '1983 Constitution.' The same applies to the '1989 Constitution' which technically and formally is the amended Constitution of 1949.

[6] See G Brunner (ed), *Before Reforms: Human Rights in the Warsaw Pact States, 1971–1988* (London, Hurst and Co, 1990). In particular, see the contributions on freedom of expression and information by D Blumenwitz, on voting rights by W Weidenfeld, and freedom of religion by O Luchterhandt.

the Warsaw Pact countries between 1971 and 1988, Hans von Mangoldt summarised the communist concept of civil rights:

> According to the Communist conception of basic rights, the latter, and also the basic duties of the citizens which are seen as being inseparably linked to them, are granted by the State, and their legal source is exclusively to be found in State law, usually the constitution. Basic rights and basic duties are conceived so as to establish the citizen's fundamental legal status on principle, the fundamental relationship between the community and the individual under the conditions of the Socialist State system and social order.
>
> The granting of rights and the imposition of duties by the State, so it is claimed, takes place in consonance with the needs of the Socialist society and the interests of the individual's personality; the criteria for establishing legal standards are the objective historical mechanism of the development of society as recognised by Marxism-Leninism.[7]

At such a level of generalisation, this presentation of communist rights does not take into account the national variations between countries, such as Poland, Hungary and the USSR. Nor does it allow for a more nuanced picture of the evolution of the conception of communist rights. For instance, in Hungary in the 1980s, the approach to human rights was more 'liberal' than in many other communist countries, although political and civil rights were not granted the same quality of protection as in Western liberal democracies.[8] Von Mangoldt's presentation nevertheless has the merit of proposing an archetypical picture of communist rights which highlights the conceptual gap existing between them and liberal rights, together with the weighty influence of ideology on human rights.

Article 54 of the 1989 Hungarian Constitution itself has a weighty past which the Court could not ignore. The first provision of the chapter on rights and duties in the Hungarian Constitution has always heralded the particular concept of rights that the Constitution recognised and protected. In 1949 the chapter on rights and duties began with Article 45 which, in a typical communist way, enshrined the right to work and to rest in proportion to the quality and quantity of the work done,[9] thus setting the tone for the other rights. In 1975, the amended and renumbered chapter on rights and duties pushed the right to work

---

[7] H v Mangoldt, 'The Communist Concept of Civil Rights and Human Rights under International Law', in G Brunner (ed), *Before Reforms: Human Rights in the Warsaw Pact States, 1971–1988* (London, Hurst and Co,1990), 32. See also J Halász, *A Socialist Concept of Human Rights* (Budapest, Akadémiai Kiadó, 1966).

[8] M Katona Soltész (ed), *Human Rights in Today's Hungary* (Budapest, Mezon, 1990). Originally published in Hungarian in 1988 to commemorate the 40th anniversary of the United Nations Universal Declaration of Human Rights, this volume was subsequently translated into English and updated in order to reflect the 1989 changes.

[9] Art 45 of the 1949 Constitution: '1—The Hungarian People's Republic guarantees for its citizens the right to work and the right to remuneration in accordance with the quantity and quality of the work done. 2—This right is implemented by the Hungarian People's Republic by means of the planned development of the forces of production and by a manpower policy based on economic planning.'

into second place and started with Article 54, which reflected the orthodox conception of socialist rights:

> 1—The Hungarian People's Republic shall respect human rights.
>
> 2—*The rights of citizens in the Hungarian People's Republic shall be exercised in accordance with the interests of socialist society; the exercise of rights shall be inseparable from the fulfilment of the duties of citizens.*
>
> 3—Rules pertaining to the basic rights and duties of citizens in the Hungarian People's Republic shall be established by law. (emphasis added)

In the early years of the transition, the Constitutional Court's task in interpreting the rights enshrined in the 1989 Constitution was, I suggest, twofold. It had to elaborate a new concept of rights based on a liberal understanding, while at the same time it had to break away from the legacy that communism had left in the Constitution, as well as arguably in the legal and judicial community.

2. HUMAN DIGNITY AS A RUPTURE WITH COMMUNIST LAW

The Hungarian Court addressed this challenge by using its imported concept of human dignity in order to eliminate possible confusion with the concept of rights inherited from the previous communist constitution and to spell out a liberal concept of rights. In so doing, the Court replaced or reinterpreted the rights inherited from communism on the basis of human dignity, ie (as seen in the previous chapter) individual autonomy. The new concept of rights developed by the Court led judges to nullify, almost systematically, the rules enacted under communism which were challenged before the Court.

2.1. Setting Aside the Rights Inherited From Communism

Since the very first case (8/1990) the Hungarian Court consistently emphasised that it intended to use human dignity in situations which were not protected by a specific constitutional right. This was referred to by the Court as the subsidiary nature of human dignity.[10] While this corresponds to the use of human dignity and the general personality right in German constitutional case law, a closer analysis of Hungarian cases shows that, in fact, the Hungarian Court used the argument of human dignity in order to set aside the provisions inherited from the communist constitution or to reinterpret them in a liberal way. This is an additional aspect of the use made of human dignity (as seen in chapter 5) which highlights the instrumentalisation of imported law.

---

[10] 'The general personality right is a "mother-right," that is a fundamental subsidiary right on which the Constitutional Court as well as other courts can rely in order to protect individual autonomy in instances where no specific named fundamental rights can apply to the facts of the case': case 8/1990.

This is well illustrated in the case on trade unions in which the Court used human dignity for the first time. While setting out the subsidiary nature of human dignity, the Court set aside the two constitutional provisions which were arguably specific to the issue at stake and more directly relevant than human dignity:

> The Constitutional Court did not find the disputed provision unconstitutional either under Art. 4, or Art. 70/C(1) of the Constitution: Art 4 extends the trade unions' right to engage in the protection of interests and representation, *which appears also in the former Constitution*, to other organisations formed for the protection of interests. Neither this rule nor the provision of Art. 70/C(1) pertaining to the freedom of forming trade unions and other organisations for the representation of interests prescribe what interest protection and representation activities include. . . .
>
> *The Decision of the Constitutional Court is based on the interpretation of the right to human dignity.*[11] (emphasis added)

The reasons why the Court set aside Articles 4 and 70C(1) of the Constitution, which are about trade unions and their powers, are at first difficult to understand. These provisions, it seems, are both relevant and specific to the issue examined by the Court. In any event, they seemed more relevant than the right to human dignity which was interpreted by the Court in a very convoluted manner so as to make it fit the case. In addition, having read the first part of this reasoning and, in particular, the reference to the existing constitutional provisions, the justification which followed is hardly convincing.

The Court's reference to the fact that these provisions existed under the previous communist constitution sheds a different light on this reasoning. In fact under communism trade unions were an essential pillar of the legal system and of society. They were so central to the understanding of communist law that they were mentioned at the very beginning of the Constitution together with provisions stating that Hungary is a People's Republic (Art 1), that it is a socialist state (Art 2), that the leading force is the Marxist-Leninist Party (Art 3) and that Hungary 'shall fight against any form of exploitation of the people by the people and shall organise the forces of society to complete the building of socialism' (art. 5). Article 70C(1), which is also mentioned by the Court, was not directly inherited from the communist constitution. However, the right to found organisations to protect one's economic interests is a typical social(ist) right. In this sense, it still bears the stigma of socialism and hence is a potential source of confusion and ambiguity.[12] This first case established a pattern for the use of

---

[11] L Sólyom and G Brunner (eds), *Constitutional Judiciary in a New Democracy: the Hungarian Constitutional Court* (Ann Arbor, University of Michigan Press, 2000), 106–7.

[12] Art 65 of the 1975 Constitution read: '1—The Hungarian People's Republic shall guarantee the right of association. A special law shall regulate the right of association. 2—Workers may form mass organisations and mass movements to protect the order and achievements of socialism, to promote increased participation in the socialist work of construction and public life, to expand culture and educational work, to ensure the rights and duties of the people, and to promote international solidarity.'

human dignity: it was used not so much in the absence of more specific constitutional provisions, as the Court claimed, but to set aside all rights inherited from communism. This pattern is illustrated in Table 4.

Table 4: Setting aside rights inherited from the communist constitution

Cases	Issues Decided Under Art 54(1)	Alternative provisions referred to by the Court and inherited rights*
8/1990	self-determination, power of representation vested in trade unions	Arts 4*, 70C(1)
23/1990	right to life, unconstitutionality of capital punishment	Art 54 (1)
27/1990	general freedom of action, right to take part in sports competitions	Arts 70D(2)*, 63(1)*
15/1991	right to a private sphere, personal identity number, processing of personal data	Art 59(1)*
46/1991	right to a good reputation, enforced payment of a debt	Art 59(1)*
57/1991	self-determination, self-identification, questioning and ascertaining identity of one's biological father	Art 67(1)
64/1991	self-determination of the mother, right to life, protection of the foetus, abortion	Art 54(1)
9/1992	self-determination in civil proceedings, powers of the public prosecutor, protest of illegality	Art 57(1)
22/1992	self-determination, right to marry freely for firemen and soldiers	Art 15*
4/1993	general freedom of action, freedom of conscience, freedom of religion	Art 60*
23/1993	right to marry freely, self-determination for policemen	Art 15*
1/1994	parties' self-determination, public prosecutors' powers to intervene in judicial proceedings to protect 'important state and social interests'	Arts 57(5), 2(1)
28/1994	right to a healthy environment in connection with the right to life	Arts 18, 70D(2)*
36/1994	freedom of expression, ie right to criticise official persons	Art 61
56/1994	right to a private sphere for civil servants outside work	Art 59*
35/1995	free fulfilment of the personality in relation to the right to access higher education institutions	Art 70F*

Cases	Issues Decided Under Art 54(1)	Alternative provisions referred to by the Court and inherited rights*
43/1995	protection of the right to life in relation to benefits for mothers and children	Arts 15*, 16*, 66(2)*, 67(1) and 70E
75/1995	right to self-determination of the alleged father vs. child's right to self-identification	Arts 67(1), 57(5) and 50(1)
12/1996	right to self-fulfilment of one's personality in relation to access to higher education institutions	Art 57(5)
24/1996	general freedom of action for some moral persons, ie associations dealing with works of art	Art 70G(1)*
20/1997	public prosecutors' power to ban or restrict the publication of certain matters	Arts 61(2), 51

The last column lists the alternative rights referred to by the Court, which are often provisions that are more specific to the issue at stake than human dignity, as seen with the example of case 8/1990. Most of these rights, as the similarity of their phrasing indicates (see Table 3), were directly inherited from the 1983 Constitution (indicated in Table 4 by an asterisk). The communist legacy is also detectable arguably in the fact that some of these are social rights which prominently featured in communist constitutions. These rights include, for instance, Article 67 on children's right to receive assistance and care from their family, state and society: this right echoes two provisions of the 1975 Constitution, Article 16 on the protection of youth and Article 62(2) on child-care institutions. Similarly, Article 60 on freedom of thought, conscience and religion echoes Article 63(1) of the 1975 Constitution on the 'freedom of conscience of citizens and the free practice of religion.'

Table 4 illustrates two crucial aspects of the use of human dignity. First, the Court almost always set aside the rights more specific to the case. Secondly, Table 4 shows that the more specific right was in most cases directly inherited from the previous communist constitution, or is reminiscent of rights enshrined in it. Case 57/1991 on the right to ascertain and to question one's biological origins provides a clear example of this pattern of interpretation. In that case, the Hungarian Court set aside Article 67(1) which provides for children's 'right to receive the protection and care of their family, of the State and of society which is necessary for their physical, mental and moral development'.[13] In a typical manner, the Constitutional Court held:

[13] Article 67: '1—In the Republic of Hungary all children have the right to receive the protection and care of their family, of the State and of society which is necessary for their proper physical, mental and moral development. 2—Parents have the right to choose the education to be given to their children. 3—Separate regulations shall establish the responsibility of the State with regard to the situation and protection of the family and youth.'

In the Constitutional Court's opinion *the provisions of Art. 67(1) of the Constitution may not be interpreted to contain a child's right to ascertain his or her parentage.* From the aforementioned constitutional provision only a right to receive actual family care can be derived. And this encompasses not only the consanguineal but also the so-called sociological family unit and protection and care from that family.

However, the Constitutional Court points out that *the right to ascertain one's parentage, and to challenge and question the legal presumption relating to it, are everyone's most personal rights which fall within the scope of 'general right of personality' found in Art. 54(1) of the Constitution.* According to Art. 54(1) of the Constitution, in the Republic of Hungary everyone has the inherent right to life and human dignity, of which no one can be arbitrarily deprived . . .[14] (emphasis added)

Chapter 3 explained that the choice of Article 54 in this context was dictated by the existence of a very similar case decided by the German Constitutional Court. Yet this is only part of the explanation and the reason for the importation of the right to self-identification may further be understood as an illustration of the Hungarian Court's effort to avoid confusion with the communist understanding of the protection of children. In case 57/1991 Article 67(1), under which 'all children have the right to receive the protection and care of their family, of the State and of society, which is necessary for their proper physical, mental and moral development,' was briefly considered by the Court before being set aside. This provision is not directly inherited from the communist constitution. However, its phrasing echoes that of Article 16 of the 1975 Constitution which was directly inherited in the 1989 constitution (see Table 3). As a result, the Court's choice in favour of human dignity may be interpreted as an attempt to move away from a possible connection with a communist reading of this right.

This logic also applies to the right to marry freely and arguably explains why the Court did not construe this right in relation to firemen and the military (case 22/1992) and to policemen (case 23/1993) on the basis of Article 15 on the freedom to marry. It seems that the Court was seeking to avoid confusion with a socialist understanding of this right, which was contained in very similar terms in both versions of the constitution (see Table 3). A similar pattern further applies to the right to education, ie the right to access institutions of higher education in cases 35/1995 and 12/1996. In the first case, while upholding the idea of a right to higher education, the Court based its reasoning on the imported right to human dignity rather than on the specific provision on education inherited from the communist constitution, Article 70F which explicitly guarantees the right to higher education (see Table 3):

The fundamental right to education, and within it the subjective right guaranteed to Hungarian citizens capable of pursuing higher educational studies in national institu-

---

[14] L Sólyom and G Brunner (eds), *Constitutional Judiciary in a New Democracy: the Hungarian Constitutional Court* (Ann Arbor, University of Michigan Press, 2000), 176.

tions of higher education, according to the act on higher education, is in direct rela-tion with the general component of the general personality right to human dignity guaranteeing the fulfilment of the personality, which includes a right to free determin-ation of the person and a private sphere, as well as the possibility to achieve one's con-stitutional aspirations and to assert oneself. The essential and absolute content of the right to human dignity is embodied in the equal dignity of each person. The second component of the general personality right to human dignity allowing the free fulfil-ment of the personality implies that Hungarian citizens capable of pursuing higher educational studies can have the right to do so. (emphasis added)

In this definition, in accordance with its own logic, the Court did not refer to Article 70F on the right to education and based its construction of this right on the imported right to human dignity, by linking it with free self-determination and the general personality right. In so doing, it emphasised the individual dimension of this right, as opposed to its social scope, which was put forward under communism.[15]

Two cases mentioned in Table 4 seem to represent exceptions to this logic, in that Article 54 was the main constitutional provision relevant to the issue exam-ined by the Court and was not used by the Court to set aside a more specific right: case 23/1990 on the death penalty and case 64/1991 on abortion.[16] These cases, however, are only apparent exceptions for two reasons. First, Article 54 is the only constitutional provision relevant to the issues at stake, ie different aspects of the right to life. Secondly, in those cases the construction of Article 54 made it possible for the Court to emphasise novel aspects of its understanding of human rights, as will be explained in more detail in the third section below. A final group of cases involved the public prosecutors' powers (9/1992, 1/1994, 75/1995 and 20/1997). According to Table 4, the related constitutional provi-sions are not directly inherited from the communist constitution. However, as will be explained below, the same logic applies to this issue, that is the Constitutional Court used Article 54(1) to clarify the scope of the prosecutors' powers and to nullify those powers which were inherited from communism.

Finally, the use of human dignity in place of a more specific provision evolved in that the Court began to use Article 54 as a way to complement and emphasise the importance of the more specific provision. In case 46/1991 on the enforced payment of a debt, the Court also mentioned the right to honour and a good rep-utation under Article 59. However, it did not elaborate on this right, and the

---

[15] 'The safeguarding of the right to education is basically effected through the introduction of free, compulsory, unified elementary schooling. . . . Schools at all stages are run by the state in people's democratic countries. . . . The tenet that the material safeguards of citizens' rights are tied up with the level attained in socialist construction applies also to the regulation of free schooling. . . . Another over-all guarantee of the right to education in the socialist constitutions is the provision on the incessant expansion of the network of secondary and higher education establishments': J Halász, *A Socialist Concept of Human Rights* (Budapest, Akadémiai Kiadó, 1966), 223.

[16] In case 23/1990, the Court also relied on international law. See Chapter 7 and I Pogany, 'Human Rights in Hungary' [1992] *International and Comparative Law Quarterly* 676.

core of the reasoning was based on the right to privacy derived from Article 54. In case 4/1993 on the restitution of Church property, Article 54 is clearly used by the Court to support the freedom of religion under Article 60. Although in this case Article 54 did not replace the more specific provision, the general pattern is the same in that it is used to insist on the importance of the individual dimension of the specific right (as will be recalled from chapter 5) and in so doing to move away from the understanding of this right under communism. The same is true of case 43/1995 which was about maternity and child benefits and allowances. In this case, although the Court referred to the specific provisions on the protection of the family (Art 15), of youth (Art 16), of mothers after birth (Art 66(2)) and on the protection and care for children (Art 67(1)), it nevertheless referred to Article 54 to reinforce the need for the protection of life and self-determination of mothers. Finally, in the last case mentioned in the table (20/1997, on the public prosecutors' powers), the Court used Article 54, ie the right to self-determination, to highlight the importance of Article 61 on freedom of expression, that is, it is unconstitutional for public prosecutors to ban the publication of certain printed matter.

In all these cases, whether human dignity was used instead of a more specific right or in order to strengthen the meaning of the specific right involved, it was always used to ensure that the inherited provisions from the communist constitution were clearly not understood in a communist manner. This interpretation and use of human dignity led the Court to nullify most of the provisions which were challenged by the petitioners.

2.2. Nullifying Communist Rules

During the first years of the transition from communism the vast majority of rules challenged before the Court had been enacted under the previous communist government and they obviously no longer complied with the new values and principles. In relation to pre-1989 norms, the Constitutional Court in an early case clarified its position and held that each contested rule had to be considered on its own merits and had to comply with the new constitutional benchmarks.[17] The Court nullified most of these provisions after establishing that they did not comply with human dignity and the rights derived therefrom. Table 5 illustrates the systematic character of this enterprise.

---

[17] Case 11/1992: 'The change of system has been carried out on the basis of legality. The principle of legality imposes on the state under the rule of law the requirement that legal regulations regarding the legal system itself should be abided by unconditionally. The politically revolutionary changes adopted by the Constitution and all the new fundamental laws were enacted, in full compliance with the old legal system's procedural laws on legislation, thereby gaining their binding force. The old law retained its validity. With respect to its validity, there is no distinction between 'pre-Constitution' and 'post-Constitution' law. The legitimacy of the different (political) systems

Table 5: Breaking with the communist past

Cases	Issues	Date of the challenged rule	Nullification
8/1990	power of representation vested in trade unions	1967	Yes
23/1990	capital punishment	1978	Yes
27/1990	right to take part in sports competitions	1988	Yes
15/1991	creation of a personal identity number and processing of personal data	1986	Yes
46/1991	enforced payment of debt and right to honour	1979	Partial
57/1991	filiation, ie right to question and ascertain one's biological origin	1952	Yes
64/1991	abortion, protection of the foetus and of the pregnant woman's rights	1972	Yes
9/1992	public prosecutors' powers to initiate a 'protest of illegality'	1973	Yes
22/1992	requirement for the military and firemen to receive the authorisation of their superior officer before marrying	1982	Yes
4/1993	clarification of the meaning of freedom of religion in relation to the issue of restitution of some real estate to churches who owned them before the communist nationalisation	1991	Yes
23/1993	requirement for policemen to receive the authorisation of their superior officer before marrying	1990	Yes
1/1994	public prosecutors' powers to intervene in judicial proceedings in the name of 'important state and social interests'	1952, 1972	Yes

during the past half century is irrelevant from this perspective; that is, from the view point of the constitutionality of laws, it does not comprise a meaningful category. Irrespective of its date of enactment, each valid legal rule must conform with the new Constitution. Likewise, constitutional review does not admit two different standards for the review of laws. The date of enactment can be important in so far as previous laws may have become unconstitutional when the new Constitution entered into force.', L Sólyom and G Brunner (eds), *Constitutional Judiciary in a New Democracy: the Hungarian Constitutional Court* (Ann Arbor, University of Michigan Press, 2000), 220.

Table 5: Breaking with the communist past *cont.*

Cases	Issues	Date of the challenged rule	Nullification
28/1994	rules on redistribution (as part of the process of compensation and privatisation) of landed property and on regulations on the protection of nature	1992, 1993	Yes
36/1994	freedom of expression, ie right to criticise official persons	1978, 1993	Yes
56/1994	power to impose disciplinary sanctions on civil servants because of their behaviour outside work	1992	Yes
35/1995	exclusion from higher education of persons subject to a prohibition on participation in public affairs	1993, 1978 (Penal Code)	Yes
43/1995	reform of social security system as part of a programme of economic austerity resulting in the abolition of a number of benefits/allowances for mothers and children	1995	Yes
75/1995	rules concerning the 'witness' in proceedings aiming at determining the paternity of a child, when the 'witness' might turn out to be the father, power of the court to order certain medical tests	1952	Yes
12/1996	requirement to produce a certificate of good morals issued by the Ministry of the Interior to be admitted to some higher education institutions	1988, 1996	Yes
24/1996	restriction of freedom of action for associations dealing with works of art, in particular, requirement to receive the authorisation of a panel composed of 'experts' appointed by the Ministry of Culture	1982	Yes
20/1997	powers of public prosecutors to ban the publication of any printed matter when 'it infringes the rights of others' or it incites crime	1986	Partial

Table 5 shows the outcome of cases decided on the basis of Article 54 between 1990 and 1997. The vast majority of the contested provisions dated from the communist era, ie before 1989. Some provisions despite being enacted after this date were nevertheless linked to communist rules, in that they were amendments of rules enacted under communism. As a result, in challenging the more recent rules, petitioners often asked the Court to examine the constitutionality of an earlier communist rule, as in case 23/1993. The remaining cases involved statutes enacted under the post-communist government and they concerned issues which are very sensitive, such as restitution and redistribution of property (4/1993 and 28/1994) and economic reforms affecting the social security system and abolishing certain benefits that existed under communism (43/1995). Table 5 shows that human dignity was used by the Court to nullify some of the typical features of communist law. Broadly, three groups of issues can be identified.[18]

(a) Freedom of Association

The first group contains a small number of cases which involve freedom of association: trade unions (8/1990), sport associations (27/1990) and cultural associations (24/1996). In all cases, the Court nullified the challenged communist provisions. Although freedom of association improved slightly in Hungary in the 1980s,[19] its exercise remained very limited. In fact, associations were a privileged channel used by the Communist Party in order to control the population. Freedom of association as such was not recognised, as Brunner pointed out in his survey of rights in the Warsaw Pact countries:

> In the area of freedom of association and trade union membership . . . the Warsaw Pact States have set up a self-contained system of party-controlled social organisations, with varying degrees of scope for independent action which is, however, in all cases restricted and tied to a specific function. The establishment of private associations requires State approval or registration, the granting or effecting of which is either placed by law at the discretion of the administrative authorities, or made contingent upon the absence of grounds for refusal, these being formulated so vaguely that the decision amounts in practical terms to the exercise of discretion.[20]

---

[18] Privacy is another issue that the Court considered under Art 54(1), but the reasoning of the Court in this respect fluctuated and the Court referred as well to Art 59 which enshrines the protection of the home and personal data. See Chapter 3 on this.

[19] G Brunner noted in his study on 'Legal Remedies against Public Authorities' that: 'It must be said, however, that in Hungary it has been possible since 1981 to contest in court both refusal of the registration needed to found an association and also dissolution of an association, and since 1986, it has been possible there as well to take court action against the refusal and withdrawal of press permits.', in G Brunner (ed), *Before Reforms: Human Rights in the Warsaw Pact States, 1971–1988* (London, Hurst and Co, 1990), 441.

[20] G Brunner, 'Individual Human Rights', in Brunner, above n 19, at 473.

In particular, party control was exercised on cultural life through the infamous 'three Ts system' of control set up by Kádár's ideological-cultural deputy, György Aczél.[21] Under this system, associations dealing with works of art had to get the authorisation of a committee of experts appointed by the Ministry of Culture before obtaining, using or selling any piece. Not surprisingly, this rule set out in a governmental decree of 1982 was challenged before the Court (case 24/1996). The Court explicitly referred to the infamous control as being a typical aspect of communism and the judges nullified this rule on the basis of the imported general personality right, ie the general freedom of action derived from human dignity (as seen in chapters 3 and 5).

(b) Public Prosecutors

The public prosecutors' powers constitute the second group of issues examined by the Court under the human dignity provision. Like the others, some of their most significantly communist features were nullified by the Court, as clearly illustrated by cases 9/1992 and 1/1994. The prosecution service was a key institution of communist legal systems and it allowed for a very tight control of judicial decisions (there was no independence of the judiciary under communism). This was generally called the 'supervision of legality' and it is described by Brunner in the following terms:

> Finally, traditional Communist public law doctrine points to the general supervision of legality by the public prosecution service, guaranteed by the constitution and regarded as lessening the practical need for special judicial protection. According to the Leninist concept, the public prosecution service should exercise a comprehensive checking function in respect of the legal system, and in this context also voice criticism of violations of the law by the authorities . . . The whole cast of the constitutional order to be found in the Warsaw Pact States . . . produces a tendency to view with reserve the average citizen's entitlement to legal redress, and to attach primary importance instead to a centralised monitoring system, marked above all by party control, a hierarchical process of internal supervision between the different parts of the system, the general legality 'brief' held by the prosecuting service, and external spot checks carried out by special supervisory authorities.[22]

---

[21] R Tőkés outlines the strategy developed by the Communist Party to control intellectual and cultural life under Kádár as follows: 'Kádár kept an eye on the "men on the street," and his ideological-cultural deputy György Aczél orchestrated, quite brilliantly, the score, the players and the instruments of the cultural scene. The policies of the "three t's" (*tiltás* [ban], *tűrés* [toleration], *támogatás* [support]) paid the expected dividends. Though dissonant tunes and defiant voices could never be eliminated, the policies worked well enough, that is, until the late 1970s': *Hungary's Negotiated Revolution: Economic Reform, Social Change and Political Succession* (Cambridge, Cambridge University Press, 1996), 16.

[22] G Brunner, 'Legal Remedies against Public Authority', in Brunner, above n 19, at 435. The author explained the particular function of public prosecutors further: 'According to a tradition normally attributed to Lenin, but which is in fact a Tsarist one established in Russia by Peter the Great in 1722, the department of public prosecution is intended to be not only a prosecuting authority, but also an institution with a wide general supervisory responsibility in matters of law. . . . In

In Hungary, this function was given constitutional prominence and inserted in the chapter on the powers of the public prosecutors. Article 51 of the 1975 Hungarian Constitution read:

1—The Chief Prosecutor of the Hungarian People's Republic and the organisation of public prosecution shall ensure the consistent prosecution of every act violating or jeopardising the legal order of society or the security and independence of the state, as well as the protection of the rights of the citizens.

2—Public prosecutors shall exercise supervision over the legality of the investigation and represent the state in criminal court proceedings.

3—Public prosecutors shall cooperate to assure that state, social, and cooperative agencies, as well as citizens, comply with the laws and shall make others comply as well. In case of any violation of the law, they shall take steps to defend legality.[23]

These constitutional provisions were completed by two statutes, Act V/1972 and Act I/1973 on the Code of Criminal Procedure. The latter statute granted public prosecutors the power to appeal final judgments when they thought that they breached the law. This particular form of appeal, called the 'protest of illegality,' was discretionary: it could not be appealed and could be filed at any time during proceedings, even after the final ruling was made. This rule was challenged before the Constitutional Court, which nullified the provisions on the protest of illegality in case 9/1992, on the basis of human dignity under Article 54(1):

The violation of this fundamental principle of civil procedure constitutes a violation of the constitutional right to self-determination (see case 8/1990, 23 April). Following the established line of constitutional case law, the right to self-determination is a component of the right to human dignity, and thus the protest of illegality conflicts with art. 54(1) of the constitution. The deprivation of the parties' right to self-determination also violates art. 57(1) of the constitution. The constitutional right of the parties involved in the judicial proceedings to bring their case before a court—like other fundamental freedoms—also includes the freedom not to use this right. Such a rule [the protest of illegality], which independently of both parties' wishes and in all cases makes it possible to continue proceedings and to change a decision affecting the parties, cannot be a necessary or proportional restriction of this right.

order to cope with this immense task, the public prosecuting service has a large number of powers to investigate and criticise, the most effective of which is the so called "protest" which can be made against illegal administrative measures and in its legal effects, corresponds to an administrative complaint': 450–51.

[23] In the 1989 version this provision reads: '1—The Chief Public Prosecutor and the Office of the Public Prosecutor of the Republic of Hungary shall ensure the protection of the rights of the citizens, and shall steadfastly prosecute any act which violates or endangers the constitutional order, and the security and independence of the country. 2—The Office of the Public Prosecutor shall exercise powers in relation to investigations as provided for by law, represent the prosecution in court proceedings and supervise the legality of the implementation of punishments. 3—The Office of the Public Prosecutor shall contribute to ensuring that all organisations of society, government bodies and citizens comply with the law. When the law is violated, the Office of the Public Prosecutor shall act to uphold the law in the cases and manner specified by statute.' The constitutional amendment has not solved all the problems caused by the communist legacy on prosecutors' powers: see on this I Szikinger, 'The Procuracy and its Problems: Hungary' [1999] *East European Constitutional Review* 85.

As in many other cases, the human dignity argument came before the more specific provision guaranteeing a fair trial under Article 57(1).[24] The two constitutional provisions seemed to overlap. The parties' right to self-determination, however, is clearly derived from human dignity as another aspect of the right to self-determination recognised by the Court in earlier cases (case 8/1990 on trade unions and case 57/1991 on the right to ascertain one's origin). Alongside other principles such as the rule of law and legal certainty, the right to self-determination is one of the key arguments used by the Court in order to nullify the typical socialist features of the general supervision of legality vested in the public prosecutors.

The Constitutional Court used human dignity in another case (1/1994) in relation to the powers of public prosecutors under socialism to intervene in civil proceedings in the name of 'important state and social interests.' This ground of intervention, as one can guess, enabled the ruling party to control the process of judicial decision-making. Public prosecutors under communism also had powers similar to those of prosecutors in the West, that is they could represent people's interests and require criminal punishment. Those powers were also challenged before the Court which, however, did not nullify them because they did not infringe the principle of the rule of law. This case is a clear illustration of the use of human dignity to filter out communist law and to retain only those provisions which comply with the new liberal benchmarks and concept of law.

(c) Social Rights

The last group of issues targeted with human dignity by the Court involved a range of rights whose wording refers to the support provided by the state or society, such as children's right to care and protection from the state and society (case 57/1991 and 75/1995), the right to a healthy environment (28/1994), the right of access to institutions of higher education (35/1995 and 12/1996) and the right to some maternity and child-care benefits (43/1995). In all these cases the petitioners questioned the scope of social rights. As these rights are enshrined in the 1989 Constitution, the Court could not deny their existence altogether, but it did not consider them as being enforceable or justiciable as such. Instead, it reinterpreted them by using human dignity to highlight their individualistic, rather than social, dimension.[25] In so doing, the Court moved

---

[24] Art 57(1) reads: 'In the Republic of Hungary everyone is equal before the law and, in the determination of any criminal charge against him/her or in the litigation of his/her rights and duties, everyone is entitled to a fair and public hearing by an independent and impartial court established by statute.'

[25] The cases related to the so-called 'Bokros package,' decided in June and September 1995, were decisive for the determination of social rights and in particular for the right to social security. This issue provoked much debate and disagreement within the Court. The Court rejected an interpretation of social rights primarily relying on state support through appropriate institutions and/or benefits and allowances, as had been the case under communism and which was challenged by the

away from the socialist approach to these rights and construed them, not as social rights as they were intended to be under communism (and perhaps after the change of regime), but as individual rights, ie as rights whose purpose is to protect the free fulfilment of the personality and self-determination. In short, the imported human dignity concept was used by the Court as a tool to perform the switch from social rights, as they were understood under communism, to individual rights.

3. INTRODUCING A NEW CONCEPT OF RIGHTS

The imported interpretation of human dignity enabled the Hungarian Constitutional Court to develop new rights, which were not contained in the 1989 Constitution, in order to replace the socialist understanding of rights by a concept of individual rights, as illustrated by the various aspects of human dignity. In so doing, the Court reversed the communist understanding of rights. Although in practice, as a new legal culture emerges, constitutional case law may not be consistently successful in influencing the implementation of fundamental rights in Hungary, the new *theoretical* architecture of fundamental rights was clearly set out by the Constitutional Court. The following section highlights the main elements of this new conception of rights.

3.1. Reversing the Communist Understanding of Rights

As shown in chapter 5, the Hungarian understanding of human dignity and its related rights is more individualistic than that developed by the German Constitutional Court, according to which the individual is considered in his or her relationships with fellow individuals and with society as a whole. The insistence on the individual and on the inherent character of constitutional rights hammers home the fact that the Hungarian Court was deliberately turning away from the communist concept of rights which was not centred on the individual, but on society and on the achievement of social goals. This radical shift is probably best illustrated by case 23/1990, in which it was held, as will be recalled, that the rules providing for the death penalty were unconstitutional:

austerity measures. Instead of this the Court, acknowledging the need for protection in some situations, developed an interpretation of the social rights involved based on the notion of protection of acquired rights and the requirement of legal certainty (which is part of the rule of law principle). As the president of the Court made clear: 'the Constitutional Court did not handle the austerity package of the government and the plans to reform the social security system on an ideological basis and *less with any intent to conserve the old socialist paternalistic allocation of benefits*' (emphasis added): L Sólyom and G Brunner (eds), *Constitutional Judiciary in a New Democracy: the Hungarian Constitutional Court* (Ann Arbor, University of Michigan Press, 2000), 37.

Human life and human dignity form an inseparable unity and have a greater value than anything else. Accordingly the rights to life and human dignity form an indivisible and unrestrainable fundamental right which is the source of and the precondition for several other fundamental rights. A state under the rule of law shall regulate fundamental rights stemming from the unity of human life and dignity with respect to the relevant international treaties and fundamental legal principles and in the service of public and private interests defined by the Constitution.[26] (emphasis added)

This extract is at the heart of the Court's reasoning on the abolition of the death penalty. While the emphasis on the absolute nature of the right to life and dignity led to the ruling that capital punishment was unconstitutional, it also enabled the Court to clarify essential aspects of the new concept of human rights and in so doing to break clearly with the 1975 phrasing of that provision, which read:

1—The Hungarian People's Republic shall respect human rights.

2—The rights of citizens in the Hungarian People's Republic *shall be exercised in accordance with the interests of socialist society; the exercise of the rights shall be inseparable from the fulfilment of the duties of citizens.* (emphasis added)

The contrast between these two definitions of fundamental rights highlights the Court's efforts to substitute the socialist understanding of rights with a liberal and individualistic one.

3.2. Inherent Individual Rights

According to the Constitutional Court, human dignity is absolute, inherent, illimitable and the supreme value of the constitutional order. These new characteristics broke with a firm and well-established understanding of rights. Under communism, rights were conditional: they had to be 'exercised in accordance with the interests of socialist society' and they were tied to 'the fulfilment of duties.' They were not inherent and socialist constitutions rejected the idea of a natural law justification of rights; instead, rights were granted by the state to fulfil certain purposes (eg 'to complete the building of society') and controlled by the ruling party. Finally, individual life and human dignity were not supreme, whereas society was, ie the achievement of communism and the abolition of the exploitation of the working people by certain classes.

As seen in the previous chapter, the Constitutional Court has insisted on the individual dimension of rights. People are not granted rights because they are part of society aiming at achieving certain goals. Individuals are born with rights and they can use them in order to fulfil their potential and to achieve certain personal aims, for instance getting married, studying in higher education institutions and knowing who their biological father is. Significantly, the right to self-

---

[26] L Sólyom and G Brunner (eds), *Constitutional Judiciary in a New Democracy: the Hungarian Constitutional Court* (Ann Arbor, University of Michigan Press, 2000), 122–23.

determination, closely followed by the right to the free fulfilment of one's personality, is by far the most frequently cited by the Court, as seen in chapter 3.

The Hungarian Court has hardly developed the social dimension of the imported rights. In fact, those rights were often used in place of a type of rights which would be understood as a 'social right'. This is particularly visible with the right to education which is guaranteed under Article 70F(2) through:

> the extension and general access to public education, free compulsory primary schooling, secondary and higher education being available to all persons on the basis of their ability, and furthermore through financial support for training.

In two cases involving access to institutions of higher education (35/1995 and 12/1996) the Constitutional Court changed the focus of this provision by reading this right in connection with human dignity. According to the Court, each individual has the right to the free fulfilment of their personality through higher education. As a result, higher education institutions should not exclude those individuals who are banned from participation in public affairs (case 35/1995). A year later, in case 12/1996, the Court referred to its earlier ruling and repeated that the right of access to institutions of higher education is a component of the general personality right and human dignity. Consequently, the Court ruled that everyone should have access to higher education, because it enables them to fulfil their personality and the Court also held that the requirement to produce a certificate of good morals, issued by the Ministry of the Interior and needed in order to register with such institutions, is unconstitutional.

Similarly, in case 57/1991 the Court reoriented the focus of children's 'right to receive the protection and care of their family, of the State and of society which is necessary for their proper physical, mental and moral development' under Article 67. In that case, as it will be recalled, the Court had to decide whether a child should be able to challenge the outcome of judicial proceedings determining the identity of his real father when he reaches the age of majority. The Court's emphasis was not on the 'protection and care of [their] family, of the State and of society.' Instead, the core of the ruling rested on the child's individual right to self-determination which, for the purpose of the case, was construed as meaning a right to self-identification and hence a right to question and ascertain his biological origins. In that case, the Court clearly moved away from the social(ist) logic of children's right to receive protection from the state and society and adopted the perspective of individual children.

In these cases, as in most cases involving human dignity, the rights imported from German case law and read into Article 54(1) did not really add brand new rights and Table 4 showed that in most cases the 1989 Constitution already contained a relevant provision. The imported and transformed understanding of human dignity was used by the Hungarian Court to turn those rights, whose phrasing sounded more like that of social(ist) rights, into individual rights similar to those recognised in Western liberal democracies. The imported interpretation of human dignity made this radical transformation possible in that it introduced into the case law, and hence as constitutional benchmarks, the characteristic features of individual rights which had not always been spelt out clearly in the constitutional amendment of 1989. This went together with the elaboration of mechanisms of protection, such as the requirement that fundamental rights have to be regulated by statute and that they can be protected and enforced by the judiciary.

3.3. Statutory Requirement

Matters concerning fundamental rights can only be regulated by statute. This follows from the Constitution itself and in particular from Article 8(2). The Hungarian Court gave this requirement a prominent role in case 64/1991 on abortion when it ruled that this matter could only be regulated in a statute, as opposed to the various ministerial decrees challenged by the petitioners. In this case the nullification of the challenged provisions was essentially based on this formal requirement.

This requirement, which derived from the combined interpretation of Articles 54(1) and 8, was at the heart of the Court's reasoning.[27] Again for Western lawyers, the statutory requirement seems self-evident.[28] For postcommunist lawyers, however, such a requirement represented a major innovation and a break with the communist era which was characterised by a different hierarchy of norms. Under communism, rules were very often adopted by the administration without—needless to say—democratic debates, or even in most cases publicity.[29]

In case 64/1991 on abortion, the Court argued that the contested ministerial and governmental decrees were unconstitutional and called for parliamentary action to remedy this situation. However, the Court narrowed down the statutory requirement and held that:

---

[27] Art 8 reads: '1—The Republic of Hungary recognises the inviolable and inalienable fundamental rights of man; to respect and to protect these rights is a primary obligation of the state. 2—In the Republic of Hungary rules pertaining to fundamental rights and duties shall be determined by statute, which, however, may not limit the essential contents of any fundamental right. 3—(*repealed.*) 4—During a state of national crisis, state of emergency or state of danger, the exercise of fundamental rights may be suspended or restricted, with the exception of the fundamental rights enshrined in Articles 54–56, Article 57(2)–(4), Article 60, Articles 66–69 and Article 70E.' Although confusion was hardly possible, it is interesting to note that the 1975 version of Art 8 read: '1—State property forms the assets of the entire nation. 2—The following shall be, above all, in state ownership: the deposits within the bowels of the earth, the land holdings of the state, natural resources, significant plants and mines, railroads, public roads, waterways and airways, banks, the post, telegraph, telephone, radio and television. 3—A special law shall determine the scope of state ownership, as well as the scope of the exclusive economic activities of the state.'

[28] It is probably even more self-evident for a French lawyer because the French Constitution explicitly states that liberties and rights have to be regulated by an act of parliament (Art 34 of the 1958 Constitution).

[29] See Act XI 1987 on the hierarchy of sources of law.

Statutory regulation is required *for any direct and significant restriction of fundamental rights* and, *in certain instances, the determination of the content of such rights and the manner of their protection.* However, where the relationship with fundamental rights is indirect and remote, administrative/executive (i.e., non-statutory) regulation is sufficient, as otherwise everything would have to be regulated by statute.[30] (emphasis added)

The Court then ruled that there was a direct and significant link between abortion and a pregnant woman's rights and the rights of the foetus (namely its legal capacity) although the Court did not decide on their precise scope.

The Court applied this reasoning in a later case, involving a very different type of issue. In case 12/1996 as discussed above, the petitioners questioned the constitutionality of a ministerial decree which required a certificate of good morals, issued by the Ministry of the Interior, for registering with some higher education institutions. The Court held that this restriction on the right of access to higher education and on the free fulfilment of one's personality could not be prescribed in a decree and that a statute was required to decide the scope of these rights. Therefore, the Court considered that the decree was no longer a constitutional source of law for regulating the right of access to higher education.

3.4. Judicial Protection Against the State and Public Bodies

The second element of the new system of protection lies in the role of the judiciary, on which the Constitutional Court kept insisting. The very existence of the Constitutional Court, with its wide-ranging jurisdiction that enable it to intervene on virtually any issue and practically any situation, makes the realisation of this principle possible.[31] Although there is a specific remedy to protect fundamental rights, the constitutional complaint, it was not used very often. This is probably because there was little need for a specific remedy since the violation or restriction of fundamental rights was a regular aspect of constitutional review. In fact, most cases before the Constitutional Court were initiated by the very open remedy of subsequent review of legal norms. Between 1990 and 1996 this amounted to 3,170 cases before the Court, while the specific procedure of constitutional complaint only led to 102 cases.[32]

In addition as it will be recalled from the first chapter, the Hungarian Constitutional Court was granted powers to nullify unconstitutional norms, which transformed constitutional review into a very powerful tool for acting against unconstitutional legislation. This completely altered the nature of

---

[30] L Sólyom and G Brunner (eds), *Constitutional Judiciary in a New Democracy: the Hungarian Constitutional Court* (Ann Arbor, University of Michigan Press, 2000), 179.

[31] See the introduction and ch 1 on the powers of the Constitutional Court.

[32] Data quoted from L Sólyom and G Brunner (eds), *Constitutional Judiciary in a New Democracy: the Hungarian Constitutional Court* (Ann Arbor, University of Michigan Press, 2000), 72.

constitutional review in Hungary which had operated to a very limited extent under communism. The Council of Constitutional Law introduced in 1983 and that some consider to have been an embryonic version of a constitutional court, was a major innovation at the time. However, as seen in chapter 1, its scope was considerably limited by the principle of unity of powers. In particular, it never had the power to protect rights, nor to nullify 'unconstitutional' provisions. At best, it could raise the issue but had no power to constrain the ruling party's actions.[33] The powers of nullification were explicitly granted to the Constitutional Court by the 1989 Constitution, in Article 32A:

> 1—The Constitutional Court shall review the constitutionality of laws and perform the tasks assigned to [it] by statute.
> 2—The Constitutional Court shall annul the statutes and other legal norms that it finds to be unconstitutional.

The Court, which never hesitated to use its powers fully, also called upon the ordinary courts to protect fundamental rights. The Constitutional Court, when it explained in case 8/1990 and subsequent cases how it used human dignity, made it clear that ordinary courts could (and should) also rely on it to protect individual autonomy. In so doing, the Constitutional Court encouraged the judiciary to incorporate in their own reasoning the imported rights derived from human dignity. Although the 1989 Constitution sets out that the judiciary's most important function was to protect rights, it was a major innovation which was only made possible by the change of systems. This can best be seen by comparing Article 50 on the judiciary in its 1989 and 1975 versions. The 1989 version reads:

> 1—The courts of the Republic of Hungary shall protect and guarantee the constitutional order, as well as the rights and lawful interests of citizens, and shall punish those who commit criminal offences.
> 2—The courts shall supervise the legality of the decisions of public administration.
> 3—Judges are independent and answer only to the law. Judges may not be members of political parties and may not engage in political activities.
> 4—The administration of the courts shall be the task of the National Council of the Judiciary; self-government organs of the judges shall also participate in the administration.
> 5—A majority of two-thirds of the votes of the Members of Parliament present is required to pass a statute on the organisation and administration of courts, as well as on the legal status and remuneration of judges.

Article 50 in the 1975 version of the Hungarian Constitution read:

> 1—The courts of the Hungarian People's Republic shall protect and assure the state, economic, and social order [and] the rights and lawful interests of citizens, and punish perpetrators of criminal acts.
> 2—Judges shall be independent and subject only to the law.
> 3—Rules pertaining to the courts shall be established by law.

---

[33] See ch 1 and Gy Antalffy, 'Modification de la Constitution en Hongrie' [1984] *Revue de Droit Hongrois* 5–19.

The new phrasing of the first section of Article 50 summarises the radical change that took place in 1989. Judges are no longer the guardians of 'the state, economic and social order,' instead their primary function is to protect the 'rights and lawful interests of the citizens'. The independence of the judiciary is reinforced by the statement of incompatibility between judicial and political functions and the creation of a council to remove judicial appointments from governmental influence. In addition, Brunner reminds us that although words might sound similar, the reality that they describe is entirely different. Indeed, communist systems were characterised by their 'cautious attitude to judicial redress' to say the least:

> The traditional view is that basic rights should be ensured first and foremost by means of political, ideological and economic safeguards, i.e. essentially via the absolute power of the Communist Party, the binding nature of the Marxist-Leninist ideology underlying the prevailing system, and the 'socialist' economic system (in particular the planned economy and nationalisation of the more important means of production).[34]

The 1989 constitutional amendment alone was not enough to change judicial practice and culture. The work of the Constitutional Court and, in particular, its emphasis on the importance and protection of fundamental rights have been one of the mainsprings in initiating the ongoing process of change in this area.

4. CONCLUSION

Law importation was not an easy option for post-communist judges. The process started with the importation of a synthetic definition of human dignity: a definition which contained all the components of this right long before they were elaborated by the Court. In many ways, this first definition is an academic reconstruction and a synthesis of several cases decided over a period of time by the German Constitutional Court. While the Hungarian Court kept referring to this key definition, in subsequent case law it enriched it by 'discovering' more rights derived from human dignity. At the same time, the Hungarian Court was faced with the difficult task of adjusting the imported definition to its new environment and, in particular, to the differences between the German and Hungarian constitutional settings and the phrasing of fundamental rights.

Once it had imported a reconstructed definition of the right to human dignity, the Hungarian Court had to achieve two tasks simultaneously: one was to find a solution for each constitutional question brought before it, while the other was to try to establish a relatively coherent core of principles integrating imported law and the existing domestic constitutional norms. This is well illustrated by the Hungarian Court's efforts to refine its position in relation to the restrictions on human dignity. The Court started to state very strongly the

---

[34] G Brunner, 'Legal Remedies' in G Brunner (ed), *Before Reforms: Human Rights in the Warsaw Pact States , 1971–1988* (London, Hurst and Co, 1990), 434–35.

'illimitable' character of this particular right, but it soon realised that this logic could not be followed for the rights derived from human dignity. It took the Court a number of cases before it managed to differentiate between the two aspects of human dignity, namely the right to life and the general personality right. In addition, the importation of human dignity is vulnerable in that it rests on the equivalence established by the Hungarian Court between human dignity and the general personality right, which is not comprised in the Constitution. Repetition and reliance on common sense seem to replace a clear explanation of this equivalence.

While importing German law, the Hungarian Court selected the aspects of German case law which best supported its agenda: breaking with communist rules and introducing a new concept of rights. This led to a very different image of the human person in both sets of case law. Surrounded by other persons and interacting with them within society in Germany, the Hungarian individual is isolated and fighting against the state for the fulfilment of his personal aims. This arguably shows that in importing the law from Germany, the Hungarian Court was not so much seeking to import individual pieces of a legal system, as it was seeking to import values or principles on the basis of which the Court could lay the foundations of a new constitutional order. The Hungarian Court used imported law as a source of new criteria for constitutional justice.

PART III

THE GENESIS OF A NEW LEGAL SYSTEM

The collapse of communism led to the creation of new legal systems and gave lawyers the rare opportunity to observe the birth of law. In the very early stages of this process, choices were not always made according to a legal logic. Previous chapters have shown the crucial role played by non-legal elements, such as the general political context in which the reconstruction of post-communist law took place and which determined its pace and its general aim, as well as the people and their experience.

Law importation was perceived as the safest strategy to carry out such a daunting transformation in the little time available to post-communist countries. Beyond reconstructing the law of a particular country, or a particular aspect of this law, such as Hungarian constitutional case law, law importation also aimed at going back to the West from which post-communist countries had been cut off. This endeavour to join the family of Western democracies can also be seen in Hungarian constitutional case law, where the use of imported law is presented as a modern substitute for natural law and is supported by a rhetoric of global law.

The conclusion considers the non-legal elements involved in the strategy of law importation, such as the importance of the language of law, and the need to renew the importing élite. Crucially, the success of the importation of Western law relies on the sustained enthusiasm for the West and the belief that 'West is best' for post-communist countries.

7

Imported Law: Between Natural Law and Globalisation

———∗◦∗———

T HE HUNGARIAN CONSTITUTIONAL Court relied on law importation to
develop its case law in a foundational period when almost everything still
had to be invented. Importing law from abroad and in particular from Germany
enabled the Hungarian Court to discover new rights in the wake of human dignity and the general personality right. More fundamentally, as seen in the previous chapter, beyond the legal development of specific rights derived from
human dignity, the importation of law enabled the Court to bring in a new value
system. Each new right, as has been shown, was in fact a vehicle for illustrating
specific aspects of these values, the most important of which was individual
autonomy. These new values were absolutely essential in the early years of transition where the legal system had to move away from communism.

The Hungarian Court, however, like other constitutional courts, cannot
overtly make decisions or base its reasoning on a value system that is not given
to it by the legislature or by the constitution, without facing criticism of its
apparent adoption of law-making powers. This chapter argues that, in order to
avoid such criticism, the Hungarian Court used imported law in its early case
law as a modern substitute for natural law, in that it enabled the Court to base
its reasoning on new supra-constitutional values, while presenting them in a
legal guise. At the same time, the use of imported law is couched in a discourse
of globalisation or *ius commune*, in which the Court presents itself as an active
participant.

1. IMPORTED LAW AS A MODERN SUBSTITUTE FOR NATURAL LAW

In the early years of the transition, the Hungarian Constitutional Court found
itself in a difficult situation: while the essence of the transition was ideological,
the Court could not rely on ideological arguments to support its reasoning. I
suggest that the Court eased itself out of this situation by using imported law
as a legal justification for its reasoning and for the creation of new constitutional rights. Consequently, imported law performed the function of a modern
form of natural law.

1.1 By-Passing the Taboo of Ideology

Constitutional courts are always trapped between law and politics and are often, as a result, under a taboo against apparently ideologically-based decisions. In fact, although they have been criticised for this, one of the great advantages of constitutional courts is their ability to turn political controversies into legal arguments to which they provide a legal solution. In so doing they have often had a certain calming effect on heated political debate and this is particularly true when referrals to the courts are made by political actors, be they members of parliament or members of government. Constitutional Courts in Western democracies have a number of tools that they can use to present a legal answer to a political debate. General principles of law, historical declarations such as the 1789 Declaration of the Rights of Man and the Citizen in France, the case law of ordinary courts and even academic writings are among the many legal sources of inspiration to which they can turn in cases where a strict legal interpretation does not provide an immediate solution.

The situation of post-communist constitutional courts in relation to politics is no different from that of Western courts, in that inevitably they have had to propose legal solutions to political controversies. In fact, many of the cases decided by the Hungarian Constitutional Court were prompted by particularly sensitive political crises, such as the President of the Republic's powers of appointment, the huge issue of compensation and restitution of property, or the reform of social security and the benefits system. However, the ideological taboo facing a post-communist court is exacerbated by a number of factors. First, post-communist transitions are by their very nature ideological and constitutional courts almost inevitably have to propose a new ideological interpretation of law. Therefore, the choice they are faced with is not between various political shades of meaning, but rather between a liberal interpretation or a communist interpretation of law. In fact, as seen with the Hungarian Court, they have to reinterpret communist law in a liberal sense. As Herman Schwartz noted, post-communist courts played a key role in proposing a new set of values:

> Like the U.S. Supreme Court, they lack the power of either the purse or the sword. Unlike their American counterpart, however, they have no established prestige, tradition or long-standing public acceptance to support them. If they are to survive and if their actions are to command respect and obedience, they must somehow persuade their respective society, both its people and its leaders, that their decisions are based not on partisan political considerations but on neutral, objective law, even when the issue in dispute obviously has very contentious political origins and consequences. They must do what U.S. Chief Justice Marshall is credited with having done: transform public policy disputes into questions of constitutional interpretation that can be decided by texts, procedures, principles, and rules that are generally accepted as legal and not political, by a means that former president of the Hungarian Constitutional Court László Sólyom has called 'legal argumentation.' And even though values— some ethical and some which reflect political inclinations—inevitably enter into the

decision-making process, *the introduction of such values must be justified by being drawn from governing texts* (e.g., statutes, the nation's constitution), established legal principles that are generally accepted by lawyers and judges (e.g., international custom or instruments), *and, ultimately, from fundamental values widely accepted by the society and identifiable as such.*[1] (emphasis added)

Secondly, although post-communist constitutional courts obviously need to construct an ideological, ie liberal, interpretation of the law, they cannot do this by explicitly referring to the ideology of liberalism, as ideology had been the ultimate justification for law under the previous regime. Most of the cases decided by the Court, in particular in the early years of the transition, were not simple cases of interpreting the Constitution (supposing that this is a simple task): those cases were political, or more precisely ideological rulings. They were cases in which the Hungarian Court—the first of its kind in history—had to spell out its own adjudication policy; they were cases where the Court had to clarify the ideological basis of the 1989 Constitution. In the early years of transition, the Court had to give similar words, ie rights phrased in a similar way, a radically different meaning.

Finally, unlike Western constitutional courts, post-communist courts had very few alternative legal arguments to justify an ideological choice, such as the choice in favour of an individual interpretation of a given right, as opposed to a social reading of this right. As seen above, this is due to the fact that alternative arguments used by Western courts usually stem from domestic legal traditions, case law or academic writings which in the early years of post-communist transitions were not available to constitutional courts. There was, however, one argument on which post-communist courts could rely, namely natural law.

In constitutional adjudication, the natural law argument has been used in acute circumstances, such as the sudden collapse of a regime and the resulting necessity to reconstruct the law on a new legal basis, as was the case in immediate post-war Germany.[2] This involved reaching for supposedly universal values and principles of justice deemed to be common to humanity, rather than contained in any positive law or constitutional text. The reliance on law importation in post-communist case law (as seen in previous chapters) has been a

---

[1] H Schwartz, *The Struggle for Constitutional Justice in Post Communist Europe* (Chicago, University of Chicago Press, 2000), 5.

[2] 'With the *Götterdämmerung* in May, 1945, there fell what many jurists had regarded as "a regime of systematic injustice," a regime which had taught *ad hominem* the necessity of universal higher standards of objectively valid suprapositive principles for the lawmaker. Accordingly, from the middle of 1946 on, a revival of natural law thinking took hold of the intellectual world, especially the jurists and the members of the constituent assemblies of the *Länder*. . . . At the same time, all attempts at passive and active resistance to the regime were necessarily grounded on natural law ideas or on divine law, for legal positivism as such could offer no legal foundation': H Rommen 'Natural Law in the Decisions of the Federal Supreme Court and of the Constitutional Courts in Germany' [1959] *Natural Law Forum* 5. See also W Friedman, 'Übergesetliche Rechtsgrundsätze und die Lösung von Rechtsprobleme' [1955] *Archiv für Rechts-und-Sozialphilosophie* 348–71, and P Schneider, 'Naturrechtliche Strömungen in Deutscher Rechtsprechung' [1956] *Archiv für Rechts-und-Sozialphilosophie* 98–109.

response to similarly extreme circumstances: breaking with communist law and laying the foundations of a new conception of rights and their protection.

A natural law type of reasoning has also been used by many constitutional courts in a normal set of circumstances, to enable them to discover new rights, also called the 'unwritten rights' because they are not enshrined in written constitutions.[3] Constitutional courts do not, of course, actually call upon natural law, but the logic of their reasoning is similar in that they add new positive rights by 'discovering' them into a particular provision of the constitution. Typically, a constitutional court would use a right phrased in particularly broad terms to derive from it a number of subrights. Almost any right can play this role, but provisions on personality rights are particularly suited to the discovery of such an open-ended list of rights.[4] This can be illustrated for instance by Article 2 of the German Basic Law on the free fulfilment of one's personality, into which the German Court read a number of additional personality rights (as seen in chapter 3). This kind of reasoning rests on the assumption that the law, as it is recognised in a set of positive rights enshrined in the written constitution, is bound to have loopholes or to become out of date and it is the constitutional court's role to improve the law by increasing the number of positive rights to protect people in situations that were not foreseen by the constitution when it was drafted.[5]

From the point of view of post-communist courts, the natural law approach had at least two advantages. The first was that it enabled the courts to craft the much needed ideological (re)interpretations while avoiding criticism for doing so, by relying on apparently universal principles rather than by overtly substituting a new political ideology for the old one. The second advantage of this approach was that the supposedly universal principles on which the Court drew did not have to be rooted in domestic law, as they were deemed to exist beyond and before positive law. In fact, the natural law argument made it possible for the Hungarian Constitutional Court to seek inspiration outside its own legal system. Of course, as in Western constitutional case law, the phrase 'natural law' was not used by the Hungarian Court. It was arguably substituted by the phrase 'modern constitutions' which reflects a similar logic and fulfils a similar function as natural law arguments in constitutional adjudication. It asserts unquestionable truths and values which are presented as having always existed, ie even before their selection by judges, who as a result cannot be criticised for creating new rights or introducing new values and thus for making law.

---

[3] A Grisel, 'Droit public non écrit' in *Mélanges Max Imboden* (Bâle, Verlag Helbing und Lichtenhahn, 1972), 139; H Huber, 'Über die Konkretisierung der Grundrechte' in *Mélanges Max Imboden* (Bâle, Verlag Helbing and Lichtenhahn, 1972), 191; M Rossinelli, *Les libertés non écrites, contribution à l'étude du pouvoir créateur du juge constitutionnel* (Lausanne, Payot, 1987).

[4] H Mota, 'Le principe de la liste ouverte en matière de droits fondamentaux' in P Bon *et al* (eds), *La justice constitutionnelle au Portugal* (Marseille, Economica PUAM, 1988), 177.

[5] M-C Ponthoreau, *La reconnaissance des droits non écrits par les cours constitutionnelles italienne et française, Essai sur le pouvoir créateur du juge constitutionnel* (Marseille, Economica, 1994).

1.2. An Alternative Set of Values . . .

Imported law in Hungarian case law has similar characteristics to those commonly attributed to natural law. As by definition it comes from outside, imported law is exterior to the existing positive rules in Hungary. At the same time, imported law is anterior to Hungarian law or, more precisely, to the construction of new rights by the Constitutional Court, ie it is not construed by judges who remain interpreters and do not become law-makers. In addition, as it was presented by the Court in the guise of 'modern constitutions,'[6] imported law is not linked to any particular temporal or national context.

Furthermore and crucially, imported law like natural law embodied an ideal of justice and a reliable set of constitutional values that were much needed in the uncertain times of transitions. They were presented by the Court as so many unquestionable truths that are valid in all 'modern constitutions' and, therefore, in Hungary too. It will be recalled that the Hungarian Court rarely discussed the relevance or the substance of these 'modern constitutions' and that this argument was used to support very strong claims, such as the workers' right to decide not to be represented by trade unions (case 8/1990), or the children's right to find out who their biological father is (57/1991). Imported law represented the alternative ideal of justice, ie an alternative ideological justification to that prevailing under communism. In most post-communist countries, arguably, the change of regime had left people no time to elaborate an alternative set of values on which to rebuild their societies. If people clearly knew what they no longer wanted, ie an almighty and authoritarian ruling party, their positive desires were perhaps less clearly articulated. At the time when constitutional courts started operating, those values were not sufficiently well developed to be used by courts in support of their reasoning.

One thing, however, was clear, namely the wish to embrace and benefit from a liberal type of democracy. Imported law served the purpose of introducing a set of liberal values, such as individual autonomy and individualism, without a single reference being made to the ideology of liberalism. Significantly, those values, because they were presented by way of references to 'modern constitutions' or 'international standards' did not appear to be ideological claims. In fact, although 'modern constitutions' only comprise liberal constitutions, the Hungarian Court never referred to them as such, preferring instead the ideologically neutral term of 'modernity.' In addition, the values imported through 'modern constitutions' already had a legal form, in constitutions and international instruments. This arguably anticipated any criticism of apparently ideologically-driven adjudication and prevented it.

---

[6] See ch 4.

1.3. ... Exterior to the Work of the Court

Imported law is by definition not Hungarian: it is a body of law which is exterior and thus not marked by the stigma of communist law, unlike most domestic law in the early years of transition. The exteriority of law is expressed by the reference to *foreign* legal systems or *international* law. Like natural law, imported law was not created by judges: it was there before the Court even started operating. In fact, 'modern constitutions' are not associated to a particular temporal context and the idea of modernity refers to the quality of a constitution rather than to the time of its adoption. The dates of foreign legislation or constitutions were rarely mentioned. When they were indicated by the Court (in particular in the case on personal data, 15/1991), the Court did not associate them with a particular political or legal context. It follows from this way of portraying 'modern constitutions' that imported law is meant to be atemporal, ie a body of law which has always existed and is valid without consideration of a particular time span. As such it is deemed to comprise values and norms which are eternally valid and which are not presented as a reaction to a particular social context at a particular moment.

Consequently, constitutional judges cannot be suspected of creating new rights: they merely saw the new law in the pre-existing 'modern constitutions.' The vocabulary chosen by the Court illustrates this visual effort: the Court 'regards' human dignity as being associated to the general personality right. In fact the Court, following a phrase coined by its president Sólyom in the death penalty case, has the remarkable gift of seeing the 'invisible constitution':

> The Constitutional Court has to develop its own interpretation of the right to life. In this context the starting point is the constitution as a whole. The Constitutional Court must continue its efforts to explain the theoretical basis of the constitution and of rights included in it and to form a coherent system with its decisions, *which as an 'invisible constitution' provides for a reliable standard of constitutionality beyond the Constitution* which nowadays is often amended out of current political interests; therefore this coherent system will probably not conflict with the new Constitution to be established or with future constitutions.[7] (emphasis added)

The 'invisible constitution' provoked much controversy in Hungary because commentators, not without reason, feared that the Court was giving itself *carte blanche* to interpret the Constitution according to a supposedly higher body of law, which was invisible to everyone other than constitutional judges.[8] The attraction of this 'invisible constitution', as highlighted above in italics, is its permanence and reliability in a constitutional context marked by uncertainties: as it will be recalled, the Constitution was an interim document in 1990 and there were many inconsistencies due to the temporary overlap between two

---

[7] Case 23/1990, L Sólyom and G Brunner (eds), *Constitutional Judiciary in a New Democracy: the Hungarian Constitutional Court* (Ann Arbor, University of Michigan Press, 2000), 126.

[8] A Sajó, 'Reading the Invisible Constitution' [1995] *Oxford Journal of Legal Studies* 253–69.

fundamentally antagonistic systems in the early stage of the transition. Due to the outcry provoked by the 'invisible constitution,' the phrase was not developed by the Court beyond this well-publicised separate opinion. The Hungarian Court nevertheless kept elaborating the invisible constitution by importing foreign law, thus making some of its aspects more visible, such as new fundamental rights or constitutional principles. Imported law has a third feature in common with natural law: this is its universality.

2. IMPORTED LAW: AN EXAMPLE OF GLOBALISATION AT WORK?

In addition to its exteriority and anteriority, one of the crucial qualities of imported law is that it is presented as being universally shared and accepted. Although this is also a feature of natural law, the emphasis in Hungarian case law is not on abstract universality but on the development of legal systems towards a common set of rights and standards. The importation of law from 'modern constitutions' may be understood as an attempt by the Hungarian Court to reach their level of legal development, as well as to be part of the process of elaboration of a sort of modern *ius commune* or global law. Without engaging with current debates on the existence of such *ius commune* as they are not particularly helpful for present purposes, this section argues that in Hungarian case law this corresponds to a constructed discourse which was aimed at legitimising the work of the Court.

2.1. The Rhetoric of Global Law

The universality of imported law is clearly reflected in the Court's cases and the Court's rhetoric in this respect was explained by its president on several occasions outside the Court. Sólyom elaborated the argument of universality by emphasising the common development of law in Europe.

(a) Universality

In Hungarian case law, the universality of imported law is expressed in several ways. First, as seen in chapter 4, the Court referred to a set of 'modern constitutions,' that is not one single constitution but a plurality of constitutions. The phrase seems to encompass all modern constitutions and the plural is meant to indicate that a particular interpretation of a right is in fact shared by all 'modern constitutions' and that it is universal. This claim of universality was reinforced by references to international human rights conventions, such as the European Convention on Human Rights, the International Covenant on Civil and Political Rights, or the Universal Declaration of Human Rights, which were the most frequently cited. It seems that in referring to these international instruments, the Court was not so much concerned with their precise binding force as with highlighting that imported law exists in all the signatory states, ie virtually the whole world (at least the world which the Court aims to resemble). For instance in the death penalty case, the Court listed a number of international instruments protecting the right to life or prohibiting capital punishment without considering their binding force, nor their legal ranking within the Hungarian system:

> Article 6(1) of the International Covenant on Civil and Political Rights—which was signed by Hungary and promulgated by Law Decree 8/1976—declares that 'every human being has the inherent right to life. This right shall be protected by law. No one shall be arbitrarily deprived of his/her life.' Paragraph (6) of the same article states that '[n]othing in this article shall be invoked to delay or to prevent the abolition of capital punishment by any State Party to the present Covenant.'
>
> The Covenant, therefore, recognises a development towards the abolition of capital punishment. While art 2(1) of the European Convention on the Protection on Human Rights and Fundamental Freedoms, signed in Rome on 4 November 1950, had recognised the legitimacy of capital punishment, art 1 of the Sixth Additional Protocol thereto adopted on 28 April 1983 provides that '[t]he death penalty shall be abolished. No one shall be condemned to such penalty or executed.' Also the Declaration on 'Fundamental Rights and Fundamental Freedoms' adopted by the European Parliament on 12 April 1989 declares the abolition of capital punishment.[9]

At the time when the case was decided only the International Covenant was legally binding in Hungary by virtue of the 1976 Law Decree. Interestingly—but the Court did not raise the issue—it had been binding on the previous communist regime which nevertheless maintained capital punishment for a number of offences. The other European instruments referred to by the Court were not binding on Hungary: the ECHR was not yet ratified[10] and the Declaration of the European Parliament is just that, a declaration. What arguably mattered here for the Court was not so much the strict binding force of these documents in the Hungarian legal system[11] as their mere existence, ie their existence in a great number of other legal systems. What further mattered was arguably both the accumulation and the generality of the instruments referred to: one of international scope and two of European scope. The picture so created was of an international consensus—and practice—on the abolition of capital punishment and the Court's ruling enabled Hungary to join in this universal practice.

---

[9] Case 23/1990, L Sólyom and G Brunner (eds), *Constitutional Judiciary in a New Democracy: the Hungarian Constitutional Court* (Ann Arbor, University of Michigan Press, 2000), 123.

[10] M Weller, 'Application of the ECHR in the Hungarian Legal System' [1999] *Acta Juridica Hungarica* 105–18.

[11] Art 7 of the 1989 Constitution states that: '1—The legal system of the Republic of Hungary accepts the generally recognised rules of international law, and shall further ensure the harmony between domestic law and the obligations assumed under international law. 2—The procedures for passing legislation shall be regulated by statute, for the passage of which a majority of two thirds of the votes of the Members of Parliament present is required.'

explain why the Court did not rely on it in its early cases. In response to this, two points can be made. The first is that Hungarian constitutional judges were clearly aware of the ECHR even before it was ratified. Its forthcoming ratification influenced their reasoning at least in one instance: the death penalty case in which the Court anticipated the effect that the ratification of Additional Protocol 6 would have on Hungarian law as pointed out by Hanna Bokor-Szegö and Mónika Weller:

> The first such decision to rouse a wide echo was the one declaring the unconstitutionality of the death penalty. The judgement was delivered a few days before the Convention was actually *signed* by Hungary. In item V/4 of the comments to this decision, reference is made to, among other documents of international law relating to death penalty, Protocol No. 6 of the European Convention on Human Rights as a demonstration of European legal development towards the abolition of the death penalty, but the decision was, of course, based on arguments stemming from the text of the Constitution itself.[22]

The second point that may be made is that German constitutional case law was not binding but, unlike the ECHR, was never going to have any binding force on Hungary. The fact that despite the 'advantages' of the ECHR, the Hungarian Court preferred German case law seems to confirm the existence of a process of learning the law, which involves at least two elements. The first consists of acquiring knowledge of a source of law. It might be assumed that the prior knowledge that some Hungarian judges had of German case law was at first better than the knowledge they had of the ECHR, thus making it easier for them to turn to German case law. The second element consists of developing a type of rationality which follows the rule only because of its binding force. This is where a legal type of reasoning begins to develop and the law becomes the law: rules are implemented not because of their prestige or knowledge but because they are legally binding. This point seems to be confirmed by the emergence of a trend in constitutional adjudication towards the end of the first term of the Court: the reliance on imported law decreased slightly and the references to the ECHR began to increase both in quality and in quantity.[23] The use of imported law did not stop altogether, but it was gradually complemented by increasing references to the law binding the Court, starting with the Constitution in the first place and then the ECHR. As seen in chapter 6, the Hungarian Constitutional Court used imported human dignity at first *instead of* the more specific constitutional provisions. Later, the use of imported law evolved from substituting ambiguous constitutional provisions by imported rights to clarifying and strengthening these provisions with imported rights. In

---

[22] H Bokor-Szegö and M Weller, 'Hungary' in R Blackburn and J Polakiewicz (eds), *Fundamental Rights in Europe: the European Convention on Human Rights and its Member States, 1950–2000* (Oxford, Oxford University Press, 2001), 389. See also ch 5.

[23] M Weller, 'Application of the European Convention on Human Rights in the Hungarian Legal System' [1999] *Acta Juridica Hungarica* 105 and H Bokor-Szegö and M Weller, 'Hungary' in Blackburn and Polakiewicz, above n 22, at 383.

The universality of imported law rests on a legal reality: most current constitutions enshrine similar rights and international conventions protect a (complementary and sometimes overlapping) wide range of rights leading to the development of 'international standards' in the protection of rights. The Court's description, however, remained very general and made the law of various countries appear to be fairly homogenous and in so doing the Court was oblivious to variations and dissenting views. In presenting those 'international standards' the Court ironed out the differences existing between national systems, as well as the controversies arising about the protection and the scope of certain rights. In fact, the Court often had in mind a very particular legal system and interpretation of a right and presented it as if this particular interpretation and use were recognised by all legal systems in the same manner. For instance, the interpretation of human dignity and the general personality right is clearly imported from German law and has not been developed in the same way anywhere else. The Court nevertheless presented it as an interpretation shared by all 'modern constitutions,' ie universally shared.

(b) The Argument of Global Law

This particular presentation of imported law, ie the generalisation of a national body of law, is supported by the view that law is increasingly becoming autonomous of individual legal systems. In the words of the former president of the Hungarian Court, this creates a sort of 'supra-national character for constitutional jurisdictions' which as a result are gradually becoming more independent from the 'constraints of national law':

> Moreover, as a study by the Hungarian Constitutional Court has shown, even the diversity of constitutions does not necessarily lead to different results in constitutional case law (despite the differences between the German constitution, which does not recognise the notion of social rights, but only that of welfare state based on the rule of law (*Sozialrechtsstaat*), and the Italian constitution which includes extremely detailed social rights, and the Hungarian constitution stipulating the state's obligation to grant social benefits, the constitutional courts of these three countries have almost reached the same conclusions regarding the constitutional means to allow the reduction of social benefits).
>
> This *independence* of constitutional justice from the constraints of national laws represents at the same time an extraordinary potential for integration. The relationship between the independence from national constraints and supra-national character of constitutional jurisdiction can be explained by professional-technical and historical reasons. We have already talked about the history of the globalisation of constitutional jurisdiction. The fact that the methods applied in constitutional review are few in number and that international case law in the matter of human rights is tending to become uniform, leads to a common language. This uniformity

represents a greater constraint on constitutional courts than national doctrinal traditions.[12]

This passage clearly expresses the assumption which guided the work of the
Hungarian Constitutional Court. It can be articulated in two claims. The first
claim is that law, and in particular human rights, are not national but global.
The second claim is that this global law binds national courts, in fact that its
binding force is superior to that of 'the constraints of national law,' ie individual constitutions. This speech was delivered at the Conference of European
Constitutional Courts held in Budapest in May 1996, which encouraged cooperation among constitutional courts. Importantly, this passage does not solely
represent the personal views of the former president of the Court; it reflects a
discourse shared by wider circles on the globalisation of law.

The discourse of global law has become more widespread since the end of
the Cold War, which meant the end of alternative and antagonistic types of
ideology, law and economy. The end of this dichotomy has very often been
translated as the triumph of liberalism and capitalism over communism.
Globalisation is a multi-functional term: descriptive and prescriptive, it is often
associated with a never-ending expansion of one ideology over the whole globe.
Heralded by the advocates of (ultra) liberalism, globalisation means the end of
now outdated state borders, which merely represent so many obstacles for a
prosperous free market economy that these advocates trust to provide a just and
democratic society.

Following these assumptions, law is no longer developing within the closed
boundaries of national legislations. Moreover, the collapse of the Iron Curtain
and the immediate reconstruction of new democracies led to an unprecedented
movement of export/import of law in which states were no longer essential
actors.[13] In addition, the creation of post-communist democracies has sped up
the process of Europeanisation, in the sense of increased European integration.
Both institutional poles of Europe, the European Union and the Council of
Europe, played a key role in the transformation process, by vigorously encouraging the new democracies to adopt constitutions and statutes which are both
'EU and ECHR compatible.' In the West, after five decades of existence, these
European institutions have begun to have a significant impact on domestic leg-
islation, as well as on domestic case law.

Certain areas of law are more affected than others by this so-called process
of globalisation, especially the areas that regulate activities which themselves
are rapidly expanding beyond the traditional state framework, such as inter-

---

[12] L Sólyom, 'Sur la coopération des cours constitutionnelles', *Introduction à la X Conférence des
Cours Constitutionnelles Européennes, Rapports Généraux sur la Séparation des Pouvoirs et la
Liberté d'Opinion dans la Jurisprudence des Cours Constitutionnelles* (Budapest, 6–9 May 1996, on
file with the author), 24–25. Author's translation from French.

[13] J Grugel (ed), *Democracy without Borders: Transnationalisation and Conditionality in New
Democracies* (London and New York, Routledge, 1999).

national trade and finance law.[14] Another branch of law, criminal law, has also left the boundaries of national states in an attempt to address the increasingly international nature of crimes of all sorts (from war crimes to smuggling and terrorism, for example) and this has led authoritative voices to call for a 'world law.'[15] Human rights too, by definition, are particularly prone to international-isation and to becoming global. The concept of natural rights, which was one of the first attempts to define rights, was based on the idea that rights were prim-arily derived from human nature and not from state legislation. The concept of naturally universal rights has been reinforced through the enactment of inter-national conventions for the protection of rights, particularly after the Second World War.

The Hungarian Court's claim that human dignity and the general personality right were understood in the same way in all modern constitutions was sup-ported by this propensity of rights to be perceived by definition as global, as well as by the existing international protection of rights. In fact, the Hungarian Court's approach to 'modern constitutions' went beyond simply trying to achieve the level of rights protection guaranteed in such constitutions; the Court also intended to play an active role in the converging development of rights.

(c) Taking Part in the Global Development of Law

Sólyom clearly perceived the need to bridge the gap existing between the 'old' constitutional courts and the 'new' post-communist ones and to foster commun-ication between them. In his introductory address to the Conference on the Cooperation of European Constitutional Courts, the president of the Hungarian Court insisted on the importance for European constitutional courts of elaborating a common language:

> The geographical position of the old courts and the new courts corresponds to the usual division, that is the distinction between EU members and non-EU members. The limit of integration will no longer correspond to the limit of constitutional cultures or to that of the different levels of achievement of the rule of law as it does at present. *All European constitutional courts speak the same language or at least they participate in elaborating its grammar.* The community sharing this culture is larger than the circle of countries which aim to join the European Union and which have good chances of doing so. *I do not believe that the constitutional courts that speak this language or that enrich its vocabulary, consider themselves as being very different because of their countries' position in the integration process.* This common language is not confined to Europe and is at most just a barely comprehensible dialect of an international lan-guage.

---

[14] This is the example chosen by Michel Guénaire to initiate a debate on the globalisation of law, 'Droit romain, common law: quel droit mondial?' [2001] *Le Débat* (August) 49.

[15] M Delmas-Marty, *Trois défis pour un droit mondial* (Paris, Seuil, 1998).

The development of a common constitutional language is therefore an important task, even for constitutional courts which consider this common development to be the preparation for the future 'European constitution.' *The influence and the strength of a constitutional court also depends on its ability to participate in the development of this legal culture.*[16] (emphasis added)

This extract highlights the fact that learning the language of Western courts is a deliberate strategy developed by the 'new courts.' One of the main points of this speech was to emphasise the sense that European constitutional courts are part of a community, which is not defined by current or future EU membership. Interestingly, although the divide between 'new' and 'old' courts clearly follows that of the Iron Curtain, Sólyom did not refer to 'post-communist courts' as these courts are perhaps more commonly labelled. In fact, he seemed committed to bridging the gap left by the half-century of ideological war and to ending the quarantine to which some of the 'new courts' might feel they are subjected until they have successfully passed all the tests for EU membership. All courts are set on an equal footing and they are presented as equally active participants in the construction of a common language. As a result, the 'new courts' are not learning *from* the West, they are learning and creating a common language *with* the West. More precisely, the president of the Hungarian Constitutional Court referred to the elaboration of a 'common grammar.' In relation to constitutional adjudication, this can be understood as a common set of rights, tests and approaches to constitutional justice. In the view of Sólyom, crafting a grammar common to all European courts will bring those courts together and erase the stigma left by communism and the Cold War. The last sentence of this passage aptly summarises the implications of this for all courts and for the new courts in particular: they can no longer operate in complete oblivion to each other, and judicial reasoning, while obviously addressing domestic issues, adds a brick to the construction of this common language. It is clear from this sentence that the two processes are interdependent and that being part of the common language, far from making the operation of constitutional adjudication more difficult, will facilitate it.

2.2. Global Law or Selected Law?

There is no doubt that over the past 10 years in particular the development of European *ius commune* has become less of an abstract or historical phenomenon.[17] Constitutional courts in Europe (with the exception of the French

---

[16] L Sólyom, 'Sur la coopération des cours constitutionnelles,' *Introduction à la X Conférence des Cours Constitutionnelles Européennes, Rapports Généraux sur la Séparation des Pouvoirs et la Liberté d'Opinion dans la Jurisprudence des Cours Constitutionnelles* (Budapest, 6–9 May 1996, on file with the author), 23. Author's translation from French.

[17] AS Hartcamp, MW Hesselin and EH Hondius, *Towards a European Civil Code* (Nijmegen, Ars Aequi Libri, 1994) and M Capelletti (ed), *New Perspectives for a Common Law of Europe* (Leyden and Brussels, Sijthof and Bruylant, 1978). More recently, A-J Arnaud, *Entre modernité et mondialisation, Cinq leçons de la philosophie du droit et de l'État* (Paris, LGDJ, 1998).

Constitutional Council which can only carry out an abstract review of Bills) have a similar range of competences and some of their techniques of interpretation are broadly similar. In addition, the constitutional rights which they foster and protect are often phrased in a similar way and this trend was reinforced with the creation of the post-communist courts. Finally, constitutional judges, as never before, have started discussing their cases in formal as well as informal ways. The 'common grammar' which is developing is, however, used by an extremely small number of people and courts, and, when considered more closely, is not as global as some perceive it to be.

(a) Some Rights are More Global than Others

Some rights are more global than others; social rights in particular do not seem to globalise easily. The example given by Sólyom in the above quoted address is, tellingly, about constitutional techniques to reduce social benefits. The rights which are more uniformly protected (and one might say global) are individual and political rights. They are the rights, such as rights to fair and free elections, freedom of expression, freedom of thought, the prohibition of discrimination, and of torture, right to privacy and to a fair trial, which were conditional to joining the Council of Europe (let us not mention Russia) and the European Union. However, in comparison to the efforts made to foster individual and political rights and the financial support provided in these areas, little importance was granted to social and economic rights. While the policies of transition advocated by European and international institutions sped up the collapse of the safety net provided by the existence of various social benefits and institutions, almost no alternative was proposed to secure some of these basic social rights.

Furthermore, it is striking that the globalisation of rights in the communist transitions was a one-way process: whereas post-communist states had to adopt liberal rights, the West did not feel the urge to learn from the system of protection of social rights, which existed in the communist states.[18] However, social rights, one could (maybe somewhat naively) argue, were one of the few achievements of communist systems, and they are (there is no *naiveté* here) currently

---

[18] In her preface to H Schwartz's book, PM Wald, who has served for 20 years on an appellate federal court in the USA, observed that: 'In [her] view, the chronicles of Eastern European constitutional courts go a long way in settling a fervently held but up to now undocumented dispute among Western consultants and commentators about the wisdom of including positive economic or social rights in constitutional norms. *The majority view among Americans has been that it is dangerous to load a constitution with such affirmative rights*; the U.S. Constitution limits citizens' rights basically to negative protection against arbitrary government interference in their lives. To enshrine "aspirational" goals such as the right to subsistence, maternal care, decent housing, or a healthy environment, it is argued, invites widespread cynicism when economic conditions do not allow government to fulfil those broadly worded promises' (emphasis added), in H Schwartz, *The Struggle for Constitutional Justice in Post-communist Europe* (Chicago, University of Chicago Press, 2000), preface, xii.

much in demand by people in the West. While the Hungarian Constitutional Court imported the right to human dignity from German constitutional jurisprudence and in its wake a number of individual rights, there is no sign yet that the German Constitutional Court (not to mention the US Supreme Court or the House of Lords) has acknowledged in its case law the importance of rights, such as the right to rest, to retirement, or to education, which are all enshrined in the Hungarian Constitution.

This shows that globalisation of rights does not appear to be the organic process, as it is sometimes described, through which rights are returned to their original nature, namely global, once the obstacle of state borders has been lifted. Globalisation is far more about the selection of rights driven by the ideology of liberalism. The impact of ideology and politics on the definition of rights, ie their differentiation, is particularly visible for one right, which one would have thought, is the most widely shared and hence global: the right to life. Although all human beings on the planet are alive and have a life, there are great discrepancies in the level of protection of their right to life. In fact Europe—and it is a fairly small part of the world—is the only place where the death penalty is banned, thanks to the Council of Europe. However, universality of the right to life, even within this relatively small space, stops when considering another of its aspect, namely its application to the foetus. Constitutional courts (and indeed legislatures) have reacted very differently to the issue of abortion. The French Constitutional Council decided it was not an issue at all, more precisely that deciding on the compatibility of the Abortion Bill with Article 2 of the ECHR did not fall within its jurisdiction. It thus left (with a sigh of relief?) the ordinary courts to decide on this matter, neither of which found that the contested abortion regulations infringed the right to life.[19] In contrast, as it will be recalled from chapter 5, while the German Constitutional Court firmly asserted that the foetus had a right to life, ie to be born, the Hungarian Court did not grant the foetus a right to be born. Unlike the Hungarian Court, the Polish Constitutional Court ruled that abortion was unconstitutional.[20] More examples of constitutional rulings on this issue would only strengthen the point that there is no global right to life and that, in practice, its protection depends on a set of political, cultural, social and religious considerations, which are differently influential in different states.

[19] Conseil Constitutionnel, 15 January 1975, Cour de Cassation, 15 June 1975 and Conseil d'Etat (Assembly), 21 December 1990. See C Dupré 'France' in R Blackburn and J Polakiewicz (eds), *Fundamental Rights in Europe: the ECHR and its Member States, 1950–2000* (Oxford, Oxford University Press, 2001), 316–17. See also Cons. Const. 27 June 2001, constitutionality of abortion within the first 12 weeks of pregnancy.

[20] Constitutional Tribunal, 28 May 1997 (K 26/96), Constitutional Tribunal (ed), *A Selection of the Polish Constitutional Tribunal Jurisprudence from 1986 to 1999* (Warsavia, Constitutional Tribunal, 1999), 184.

(b) Not Global but German

Although the Hungarian Court relied on 'modern constitutions' for its interpretation of human dignity, its source of inspiration was quite clearly not global but German. As it will be recalled, this was never made explicit by the Court which, having faith in global law, stuck to 'modern constitutions.' The choice of terminology though, as well as the pattern of interpretation, unambiguously pointed to German constitutional jurisprudence and this source of inspiration, despite never being spelled out, actually served to legitimise the imported interpretation, because of the German system's prestige. The reliance on one specific legal system while claiming to rely on many systems illustrates two complementary points. The first is a very practical one: the impossibility of identifying (yet?) a global right to human dignity which really exists in all modern constitutions and the fact that the German Court is the only constitutional court to have elaborated human dignity as an essential constitutional argument. The second point is that, at the same time, in the absence of a truly global jurisprudence on human dignity, it was essential for the Hungarian Constitutional Court to be able to support its reasoning with at least one (as it happens the only) specific body of case law. Without such support, the Hungarian Court would have put itself in a perilous situation because judges— unlike legislators—cannot invoke rights that are nowhere (yet) to be seen and therefore they need some textual and tangible basis for their interpretation. Construing the Hungarian constitutional provisions on the basis of global law would have proved right the critics of the 'invisible constitution.'

This shows that global rights that may be invoked by judges to support and to legitimate their reasoning, particularly in cases where they added new rights to those already existing, or interpreted them in a way that departs from established case law, cannot exist *in abstracto*. When judges used the argument of global law (as with the natural law type of reasoning), they had in mind a very precise constitutional system which provided them with some tangible and textual basis for their interpretation. While it was necessary for judges to base their interpretation on a particular test, or a pre-existing body of law, the reliance on 'modern constitutions' for the purpose of interpreting the Constitution of Hungary raises some questions relating to the binding mechanism of law in the early years of the transition.

3. FROM PRESTIGE TO BINDING FORCE: LEARNING THE LAW

As was explained in chapter 2, the reliance on imported law for the purpose of constitutional adjudication cannot be explained by its binding force on the importing Court and the choice of a foreign body of law is based on different criteria, such as its prestige, its suitability and the knowledge that the importers had of it. The two previous sections have shown the efforts made by the Court to present and integrate this body of foreign law into its case law and both the natural law type of reasoning and the global law argument are intended to justify and legitimate the reliance on 'modern constitutions.' This paragraph attempts to address the question 'why rely on a body of law which is not binding when there are alternative sources of law, such as the Constitution or the European Convention on Human Rights, which are binding in Hungary?' This section considers three possible hypotheses which may provide an answer to this question, highlighting the most realistic one, ie that the use of and the reliance on a particular body of law do not necessarily nor exclusively depend at the outset on whether or not it is binding in principle. It takes time and a learning process for law to become the law.

3.1. The Neo-Colonialism Hypothesis

This hypothesis rests on the observation that massive law importation had generally only taken place previously in the context of colonisation, or more broadly domination by one country—such as the winner of a war or a country in a position of economic and political power—of another (theoretically sovereign) country. This hypothesis further rests on the massive exportation of Western law and the way in which it was promoted, especially considering that post-communist countries were left with no option but to conform with Western law and to import it if they wanted to be taken seriously and ultimately to join the European Union. Western law was of course not—strictly speaking—legally binding on the post-communist countries. However, if the post-communist countries were to get some political and financial support from the West, it was made clear to them that they had to comply with its law. In relation to the Hungarian Constitutional Court, this does not mean that Germany or the German Court imposed German case law for the interpretation of human dignity. Hungarian judges, I would argue, chose German case law for the reasons set out in the previous chapters. However, the general relationship of Hungary (like other post-communist countries) with the West was characterised by inequality. Hungary (like other post-communist countries) was expecting a range of things from the West (for instance, recognition, economic support, foreign investment and of course EU membership) that the West was in a position to refuse or to grant under certain conditions. This relationship of unequal power between the West and post-communist countries greatly determined the general orientation and features of their legal systems, which, as it will be recalled from chapter 2, were put under very strong pressure to achieve certain results within a given period of time.

For the time being, the hypothesis has to be left open. Hungary is of course not a German colony but an independent and sovereign state. The hypothesis of neo-colonialism itself needs to be refined and better phrases need to be put forward to characterise this phenomenon. Similarly, far more research needs to be done on the exportation of law to post-communist countries. In particular it would be interesting to know more about the precise channels and mechanisms of exportation. Arguably exportation was not essentially carried out through a network of personal and friendly contacts. Furthermore, law exportation was arguably part of a wider web of agreements and the way in which it was promoted (for instance, lobbying, promises of financial or economic support, or even a privileged relationship with the exporter) needs to be more systematically studied. Until this hypothesis is convincingly disproved, one has to bear in mind that the strict mechanisms of the binding force of a body of law (be it the Hungarian Constitution or that of 'modern constitutions') did not operate in the early stages of the post-communist transitions as they are meant to in more normal circumstances.

3.2. The Failure of the Hungarian Constitution?

The second possible hypothesis to explain the preference for 'modern constitutions' over the Hungarian Constitution is not a very optimistic one, in that it considers that the 1989 Constitution failed to gain a proper binding force and to foster a legal culture different from that of communism, where the constitution was not considered to be the supreme law of the land. It would confirm the neo-colonialism hypothesis set out above, according to which it is less important to comply with the constitution than with the law of the 'dominating power.' In the early years of the transition, the Court's enthusiasm for foreign law and in particular German law, together with its tendency to be creative with the Constitution for the interpretation of fundamental rights provisions, might be understood as an indication that the Hungarian Constitution was less valued than German case law. The difficulty in transforming the Constitution into the supreme law of Hungary may be further illustrated by the painstaking process of constant amendments to the 1989 revised Constitution culminating, as it will be recalled from chapter 2, in the eventual failure to draft a brand new constitution. Hungary remains the only post-communist state which did not adopt a brand new constitution.

However, despite the fact that the Constitution did suffer from a number of handicaps in the early years of the transition, it has come to be respected as the fundamental law of Hungary for at least three reasons. First, one could argue that the process of gradual amendments did allow for some experimentation with new provisions and made it possible to refine the Constitution and remedy some of its weaknesses. Secondly, one could further argue that the 1989 revised Constitution did become stable when the government decided in 1997 to abandon the project of drafting a new constitution. Finally and crucially, although in its enthusiasm for German law the Court did not always include the Hungarian constitutional provisions in its interpretation of Article 54, it never disregarded the Constitution altogether. In fact, as was argued in chapter 6, the Court was acutely aware of the constitutional text. The early 'weakness' of the Constitution seems to indicate the existence of a learning process through which the law gradually becomes the law.

3.3. Learning the Law

The third hypothesis to explain the preference for 'modern constitutions' over domestic constitutional resources proposes that the law does not instantly become the law. In other words, there is an intermediary period when the choice of legal arguments does not flow from legal logic but can be explained by other (non-legal) motivations, such as prestige and prior knowledge and, better still, knowledge of a body of foreign law. Law importation was a response to the extreme set of circumstances surrounding the early years of transition. Importation arguably took place during the short interval when compliance with law was guided by prestige and knowledge rather than by the strict mechanisms of its binding force. Indeed, the frequent reliance on 'modern constitutions' shows that the binding force of the Hungarian Constitution itself was weak, by contrast with the prestige of Western law. This would also explain why law importation is rare in Western legal systems: these are systems where the binding force mechanisms of the law are well established and which have a much stronger sense of their legal identity.

The process of learning the law becomes even clearer if we consider the existence of another body of 'foreign' law which the Hungarian Court might have used instead of importing German case law, namely the European Convention on Human Rights (ECHR) and its case law. It is true that, unlike the German Basic Law, the ECHR does not enshrine human dignity and hence the ECHR was perhaps not the immediately obvious source of importation for Article 54 of the Hungarian Constitution. However, a number of rights that were imported in the wake of human dignity might also have been constructed by reference to the ECHR. They include the right to privacy, which the European Court has interpreted quite broadly under Article 8 ECHR, the right to life, which is clearly spelt out in Article 2 and Additional Protocol 6 and the right to a fair trial under Article 6 ECHR, which might have been used instead of the right to self-determination in judicial proceedings. In addition, if there is any '*ius commune*' or European standard in the protection of fundamental rights, it is likely to be found in the ECHR and its case law which has developed by integrating some aspects of the law of the member states.[21]

One could argue, of course, that the ECHR in 1990 was not binding on the Hungarian Court as Hungary ratified it three years later in 1993 and this would

---

[21] R Blackburn and J Polakiewicz (eds), *Fundamental Rights in Europe: the ECHR and its Member States, 1950–2000* (Oxford, Oxford University Press, 2001).

addition, from 1994–95 onwards the Court began to rely on the ECHR (ratified in 1993) in an increasingly effective manner. Whereas early references to the ECHR were limited to the occasional case, subsequent references became more systematic and more comprehensive and the Court started quoting relevant extracts from particular cases.

4. CONCLUSION

Imported law was essential for initiating the process of transformation of the communist legal system: while introducing a new set of individual rights, it replaced the communist foundations of the legal system with liberal ones. The Court justified its use of imported law in two ways: it presented it in the form of a modern type of natural law and it included it in a discourse of globalisation of law. As a result, the Court's creative approach to judicial reasoning was presented as a positive attempt to modernise Hungarian law according to legal standards and values deemed to be inherently good and universally shared.

Law importation, however, was only the initial step in the creation of a new legal system. While it proved to be a convenient and astute device for the purpose of constitutional adjudication in the early years of the Hungarian Constitutional Court's first term, its ability to influence the law beyond constitutional case law is less certain. The full success of law importation as a strategy to develop a new legal system depends on many factors, most of which are not of a legal nature.

8

Conclusion

————

I T IS RARE for lawyers to be able to witness the birth of a new legal system. As the current Western legal systems came into existence so long ago, our sources of information are often restricted to historical accounts and for Ancient Greece and Rome, often considered as the ancestors of our democracies, historical sources sometimes blend in with mythical or reconstructed accounts. The legal systems which emerged in Eastern and Central Europe after the collapse of communism have provided us with the opportunity of improving our understanding of the process by which the law becomes the law and to shed some light on the birth of a new legal system. Before considering this aspect however, one has to address the inevitable question: does the strategy of law importation work?

1. DOES LAW IMPORTATION WORK?

As shown in the previous chapter, the argument of global law was crucial for the legitimacy of the Hungarian Constitutional Court's work because, by relying on it the Court rose to a status equal to that of Western courts. In fact, in less time (less than 10 years) the Hungarian Court achieved a standard of protection similar to that existing in the older democracies after over five decades of existence. This shows that the reliance on imported law has certainly sped up the lengthy process of developing constitutional justice.

1.1. The Short Answer: Yes

The extensive reliance on law importation has undoubtedly contributed successfully to the transition from the communist legal system to the new one. As illustrated by the example of human dignity, the role of imported law was essential in several ways. It enabled the Court to lay the foundations of the constitutional order on liberal principles. It further enabled the Court to add a number of important constitutional rights to those existing in the Constitution in order to protect individual autonomy. Finally, and very importantly, it enabled the Court to filter out from the legal order some of the most significant characteristics of communist law. In less than 10 years after the collapse of the Kádár regime, Hungarian constitutional rights—on paper—are comparable to those existing in 'old' democracies.

Furthermore, the importation of 'ready-made rights' has certainly accelerated the process of creating a new legal order, allowing for a sort of short-cut in history, whereby far less time was needed in Hungary than in most Western democracies to achieve a similar degree of fundamental rights protection through constitutional adjudication. In fact, on some issues, such as the protection of the environment, the recognition of same-sex partnerships, and children's right to find out the identity of their biological father, the Hungarian Court is ahead of legal developments elsewhere in Western Europe. Law importation further provided a number of constitutional values that were needed to establish a constitutional framework to accompany and guide the various steps of the transition.

Finally, law importation is part of a two-way process. As will be recalled from chapter 2, it was partly triggered by Western involvement in the early stages of the transition and the similarity of Western law and imported law in post-communist countries has stimulated an ongoing exchange between constitutional judges, as observed by Schwartz:

> The fact that the West is watching and that its economic and other support is vital to the governing regimes, almost certainly helps as well. The Western influence is reinforced by the increasing interaction with constitutional court judges from Western countries. Since 1989, there has been a plethora of international conferences on law, constitutionalism, separation of powers, human rights, judicial independence and other matters. At these meetings, East European judges are warmly received by the judges from other parts of the world and other attendees (usually prominent academic and other experts) and regarded as distinguished and respected peers engaged in the especially difficult task of trying to establish a rule of law in the very difficult circumstances created by the wreckage and vestiges of Communist rule and, in some cases, continuing pressures from the government.[1]

This observation confirms that the Hungarian constitutional judges' efforts to establish communication with colleagues in the West were rewarded. It also highlights a particular consequence of importation of Western law: post-communist constitutional courts were successful in establishing communication with their Western counterparts because they managed to speak the language of Western law with their Western interlocutors. However, in so doing, the need to establish communication with the domestic ordinary judiciary may have been overlooked as priority was given to developing a type of reasoning that would make sense for Western lawyers and gain their approval.

1.2. The Long Answer: Caution and Vulnerability

The long answer to the question 'does law importation work?' is far more complex and highlights the vulnerability of this strategy of legal development.

---

[1] H Schwartz, *The Struggle for Constitutional Justice in Post-Communist Europe* (Chicago and London, University of Chicago Press, 2000), 240.

While in the short term as seen above, law importation proved an efficient tool for laying the foundations of the post-communist legal systems, the longer term success is less easy to assess. Law importation was triggered and supported by a very particular set of circumstances characteristic of the early years of the changes, and alterations to these circumstances, as well as the general fate of the countries involved, are influential.

(a) Waning Enthusiasm for the West

As seen in chapter 2, the process of law importation was sparked off by enthusiasm for the West, together with a strong institutional optimism characteristic of the early years of the transition. However, the euphoria of the first taste of freedom did not last as long as the time required to complete the transformation process. Although the picture is not altogether bleak and desperate, a growing criticism of the 'West is best' attitude has emerged as the living conditions deteriorated for many people who did not benefit from the changes.

For most post-communist people, the success of the transition, ie the adoption of liberalism, was not primarily measured by the new design of their institutions, nor the sophistication of their new constitutions. It was assessed against the improvement of their daily lives. The collapse of communist regimes was prompted by aspirations for more freedom and by the increasingly visible failure of a generation of ageing and ailing rulers desperately clinging to power. One of the catalysts of the transitions was indeed the general failure of state economies, which could no longer provide basic consumer goods.

In response to these challenges, Western economists prescribed shock therapies, which were presented as the best method for a speedy recovery. Under the close supervision of the International Monetary Fund, the World Bank and the European Union, austerity packages were implemented throughout the region, privatisations were energetically carried out and Western investors were made to feel welcome by extremely attractive deals and the promise of substantial profits. As a result, as political scientist Bennett Kovrig pointed out, Eastern European countries became 'guinea pigs' for a range of economic experiments:

> After serving as guinea pigs for state socialism, East Europeans must endure another historic experiment, the conversion of a bankrupt centrally planned economy into a prosperous market. The process began with much doctrinaire advocacy of free markets, partly in reflection of the Western fashion for denationalisation and deregulation. Yet state involvement in the economy, along French dirigiste or German neocorporatist lines, remains the European norm and most of the new regimes in the East, whatever their official label, are essentially social democratic. With no precedents to draw upon, politicians and economists are testing in practice the merits of the 'Big Bang' change versus incrementalism in relation to prices, subsidies, tariffs, and convertibility, and a wide variety of privatisation strategies. By generally adopting the restrictive fiscal and monetary policies recommended by the International Monetary Fund, governments did rein in runaway inflation, but disappearing markets, collapsing

industries, falling consumption, rising unemployment, and cutbacks in welfare state services are hardly conducive to the legitimation of market democracy.[2]

These strategies were not without success, but they have also had a very high cost: the substantial deterioration of daily life for many people in Central and Eastern Europe. Unemployment shot up while all the safety nets (in particular the welfare systems) that existed under communism collapsed. Consumer goods that were no longer provided by the intricate combination of exchange and import/export within the COMECON bloc started being imported from the West at Western prices. With the privatisation of gas, water and electricity, bills increased. As a result, most people suffered from needing to have several jobs at the same time to make ends meet. Although people genuinely enjoyed more freedom after the change of regime, the living conditions after the collapse of communism did not match the hopes and the promises; in some cases, they in fact became worse than they had been under communism. 'Poverty' was one entry in Jean-Yves Potel's welcome book *Les Cent Portes de l'Europe Centrale et Orientale* and I quote at length from his presentation of economic conditions, because he manages very well to link economic figures to the quality of people's lives:

First of all it has to be noted that, despite positive levels of GNP, the quality of life has declined for the majority of the population. This decline can be measured in terms of disposable income and actual consumption. . . . 1990 and 1991 were the most difficult years: in 1990 [private] consumption declined by 15.3% in Poland, 24.6% in the Czech Republic and by 33% in Slovakia; Hungary reached its record in 1991 (−9%), as did Romania (−22.6%) and Bulgaria (−15.7%), with a continuing decline for these three countries in 1992 and even in 1993. . . . Real salaries (which only formed part of people's income) declined in all countries from 1990 to 1995. . . . The growth in illegal or additional activities was spectacular in 1991 and in 1992, and was also measurable by the increase in temporary and insecure jobs. At the same time, the significance of non-monetary incomes also increased. [A UNICEF report] estimated that the proportion of non-monetary agricultural incomes rose from 21.3% to 37.3%. These two increases were not accompanied by a growth in social benefits, as is usually the case in Western Europe. The same trends were also revealed in Hungary, where a trade union report underlined the difficulty faced by workers in finding a second job (45% of families tried to increase their income through extra work) and the growth since 1990 in family production of vegetables, fruit, but also of clothes. This trend particularly affected children, all the more so since, throughout the country, the real value of family benefits (allowances, maternity benefits, etc. . . . .) did not stop decreasing. Between 1989 and 1995, public expenditure on families decreased in some cases from 50% to 20%. . . . Further signs of poverty were recorded by UNICEF and confirm these tendencies, notably the increase in private debts and the dispersal and decline of family wealth. In Hungary for example, the pawning of jewels increased threefold from 1990 to 1992. . . . *To sum up, the primary consequence of transition was the rapid and*

---

[2] 'Marginality Reinforced' in Z Barany and I Volgyes (eds), *The Legacies of Communism in Eastern Europe* (Baltimore and London, Johns Hopkins University Press, 1995), 37–38.

general deterioration in quality of life. The shock, according to UNICEF, was one of the most violent that has been observed since the Second World War.[3] (emphasis added)

From this perspective, it can be seen that the post-communist transitions were not exactly successful and in fact the introduction of market economy soon led to wide-spread disillusionment with the transition.[4] This disillusionment, together with the impression that the first liberal governments were failing to tackle the huge economic crisis successfully, led to the election of neo-communist governments in many countries, replacing the post-communist governments elected in 1990–91. Together with the hardship of people's lives, which certainly fuelled the increasing popularity of extreme political parties, the disillusionment with the 'West is best' motto arguably fragilised the legitimacy on which the strategy of law importation from the West rested. As seen above and by definition, the development of law through importation is not rooted in domestic soil, but it relies to a great extent on the prestige of Western law and its perception as being the best way forward for post-communist legal systems. In addition, law importation was only possible because the judges involved spoke the language of Western law, which however was not widely known beyond the very small circles of constitutional judges and specialised lawyers who took part in the importation process. Therefore, for law importation to continue to be accepted in the whole legal system in the face of social discontent with westernisation, it is important for the language of imported law to be disseminated more widely.

(b) Speaking the New Language of Law

Learning the language of the West and the ability of ordinary courts to make sense of it and use it in their own reasoning is crucial for the imported law to complete its integration into post-communist law. The success of this process can only be cautiously measured. It is of course hard to generalise, but as Schwartz noted:

> With respect to one matter—general court sensitivity to constitutional issues as reflected in referrals to the constitutional courts—the evidence is quite discouraging,

---

[3] J-Y Potel, *Les Cent Portes de l'Europe Centrale et Orientale* (Paris, Les Editions de l'Atelier, 1998), 214–18.

[4] 'Nowadays our own people are not getting the feeling that they are any better off. The fruits of the victory have gone sour. Already we can hear some people wondering why we have ever done it. Democracy is losing its supporters. Some people even say: "Let's go back to authoritarian rule." Reality has mocked all those who thought the overthrow of communism would move the Eastern world closer to its Western counterpart. . . . [The West] was supposed to help us in arranging the economy on new principles, but in fact . . . largely confined its efforts to draining our domestic markets . . . the richer part of Europe has shut itself from the poorer part': Lech Walesa, President of Poland, at the Council of Europe, 4 February 1992, quoted from B Kovrig, 'Marginality Reinforced' in Z Barany and I Volgyes (eds), *The Legacies of Communism in Eastern Europe* (Baltimore and London, Johns Hopkins University Press, 1995), 35.

for there has been very little. This may not be quite as ominous as it seems, for in Germany, where the rule of law is well established, referrals are also infrequent. But in Germany, the general courts are quite sensitive to constitutional issues, whereas in East Europe, such sensitivity is rare. Both anecdotal evidence from conversations with Bulgarian human rights lawyers in the summer of 1997, and recent incidents in the Czech Republic indicate that the general courts are either unaware of, or deliberately indifferent to, both the constitution and constitutional court rulings. In Bulgaria, the author was told that criminal court judges, for example, refuse to consider anything but the text of the Penal Code and turned a deaf ear to any constitutional talk. In the Czech Republic, Supreme Court Justices simply ignored a constitutional court ruling; it took pressure from both the Czech prime minister and the Supreme Court chairman to force two other Supreme Court judges to obey a Constitutional Court decision.[5]

Although it is not mentioned in the above quotation, a similar tension between the Constitutional Court and the ordinary courts existed in Hungary. In particular, the Supreme Court, which was the only higher court up to 1989, was not an enthusiastic follower of the Constitutional Court's rulings. The relationship between the Constitutional Court and the ordinary courts was characterised by a certain rivalry rather than by constructive cooperation, as both the Constitutional Court and the Supreme Court were keen to assert their scope of competencies.

Ordinary courts at first made little use of the concrete review of norms provided in Article 38(1) of the Act on the Constitutional Court, under which a judge who finds that a legal norm or an administrative provision is unconstitutional must stay the proceedings and obtain a decision on the matter from the Constitutional Court.[6] The Constitutional Court developed the approach of 'living law' (of Italian origin) to extend its control beyond the mere letter of the norm, that is to include the way in which a particular norm was constructed by the ordinary judiciary.[7] While following this doctrine in a number of cases the Constitutional Court sought to extend the scope of its power to exercise some control over the case law of ordinary courts as supervised by the Supreme Court, the Supreme Court rarely took the rulings of the Constitutional Court into

---

[5] Schwartz, above n 1, at 236–37.

[6] 'In the period 1990–96, only 140 judicial requests were forwarded to the Constitutional Court. In the beginning, most of them were not at the initiative of the judge but rather based on the authority of the parties to the proceedings to propose to the judge that the Constitutional Court be consulted which is specifically identified in art.38(2). Nonetheless, it appears that the reserved attitude of the judiciary is gradually changing, since the number of proceedings to review concrete norms continues to increase': G Brunner, 'Structure and Proceedings of the Hungarian Constitutional Judiciary' in L Sólyom and G Brunner (eds), *Constitutional Judiciary in a New Democracy: the Hungarian Constitutional Court* (Ann Arbor, University of Michigan Press, 2000), 82.

[7] 'Again, by way of interpretation, the Court introduced the concept of "living law". Since the decision on ancestry (57/1991), the Constitutional Court had not reviewed the language of the law itself as determining the contents of the norm but rather the meaning and the content that can be attributed to it from the consistent and unitary practice of applying the law. This is the "living law," the review of which leads to a decision on the application of the law by courts and agencies': L Sólyom and G Brunner (eds), *Constitutional Judiciary in a New Democracy: the Hungarian Constitutional Court* (Ann Arbor, University of Michigan Press, 2000), 4.

account. In his analysis of 'Statutory Interpretation and Precedent in Hungary,' Béla Pokol observed:

> When considering the core of the question, the most important statement in this respect to be put right from the outset into focus is that *interpretation that refers to constitutional basic rights and especially constitutional court judgements has an absolutely minimum role in the interpretation of law.* . . . A more complete view can be achieved by paying special attention to the cases of law interpretation performed on the grounds of constitutional rights. In these, the Supreme Court's and the high courts' attitude to these are defined more precisely. It occurred several times that the opposing parties referred to constitutional court decisions, but the court did not react to that, and that the judgement did not contain any position, neither negative, nor positive, that referred to them. Another distinction can be based on the fact that sometimes the court refers to constitutional basic rights in its law interpretation but does not refer to the relevant constitutional court decision(s). A further distinction should be made between criminal and civil cases. In criminal proceedings, the court also refers to constitutional basic rights, while in civil actions, the judges do not, only the parties refer to them in some cases.[8]

This observation shows that the importation of a particular right into constitutional case law can only be a first step in the process of integrating this right into the legal system. It furthers shows that importing a right from a foreign legal system is perhaps the easiest part of the process of reconstructing this legal system. It is true, however, that in legal systems where courts are not bound by the rule of precedent, it has taken some time before higher courts have begun to follow constitutional case law and to comply with it in a fairly systematic manner. Therefore, the reaction of the ordinary judiciary in Hungary is not surprising, nor is it particularly worrying. However, the necessity for the ordinary judiciary to change their legal reasoning and to bring it into line with that of constitutional courts is perhaps more pressing in the context of reconstructing a legal system after the collapse of communism.

In addition, as illustrated by the Hungarian situation, this task is perhaps more difficult to accomplish in post-communist systems for a number of reasons. One reason is the novelty of the Constitutional Court and it will take some time for judges, lawyers and petitioners to learn what use they can make of its case law and of all the remedies available before it. Another reason is the lack of institutional channels of communication between the Constitutional Court and the ordinary judiciary and, in particular with the Supreme Court. As it will be recalled from chapter 1, the Constitutional Court was added to the existing ordinary judiciary and no institutional link between the Court and the ordinary judiciary was provided for in the 1989 Constitution. In fact, the Constitutional Court is clearly cut off from the ordinary judiciary in Hungary, as it is in many of the other post-communist countries too. Moreover, in terms of personnel there is no connection between the two types of judges, as a seat in the

---

[8] B Pokol, 'Statutory Interpretation and Precedent in Hungary' [2000] *OsteuropaRecht* 267–68.

Constitutional Court does not necessarily reward a successful career in the ordinary judiciary. Moreover, the criteria for appointing constitutional judges were devised to ensure that the Court would be staffed by independent judges, ie those who had managed to maintain some distance from communist implementation of law. In contrast, there was no move to renew the body of ordinary judges completely and systematically. Retraining them is a lengthy process which only started some time after the change of regime. This meant that, for a number of years, judicial reasoning went along different tracks: one West-oriented opened by the Constitutional Court through law importation and the other following its own logic.

Moreover, the language of rights spoken by the Constitutional Court arguably made more sense to Westerners, as well as to the élite involved in those changes, than to most ordinary judges, as they were not necessarily familiar with it. More specifically, judicial reasoning in cases involving human dignity is familiar to German lawyers and to the Hungarian lawyers acquainted with German law. It is less sure that ordinary judges, most of whom, in the early years of the transition, had been trained under communism, understood them in the same way.

(c) Beyond Elite Importers: Sharing the Knowledge

As it will be recalled from chapter 2, importers of law are part of an élite char-acterised by its education, its easy access to Western knowledge and networks and its involvement in the decision-making process of political importance. This raises at least two questions. The first is an issue of generation, namely, the need to replace the generation of the élite who made the transition happen with people who can make the transition continue. This is perhaps particularly visible for the Constitutional Court whose judges are elected for a term of nine years: by 1999, all of the judges who sat in the first Court had retired. This in turn raises the question of continuity in the judicial spirit of the first Court, which was very favourable to law importation and committed to introducing new liberal rights and values.[9] In addition, the strategy of importation was supported by a particular constellation of élites in power, which were initially moving in broadly the same direction. The renewal of these élites, including that of politicians and government members, is bound to lead to a different configur-ation, with new élites seeking to implement different agenda.

The second issue raised in relation to the élite of importers is its enlargement so as to encompass more people, perhaps at first all professionals and in particu-lar the ordinary judiciary. If it is going to operate and to make sense, imported law, ie the new values and concepts imported with it, has to be supported and relayed by the perhaps mythical and yet very necessary ingredient of liberal

---

[9] KL Scheppele, 'The New Hungarian Constitutional Court' (1999) 8 *East European Constitutional Law Review* 81–87.

democracies: civil society. Without engaging too much with this complex issue, a word of caution in relation to its existence and its ability to carry forward the process of transforming post-communist societies into liberal democracies is necessary here[10]. Although the collapse of communism in Central Europe was heralded as the 'people's revolutions,'[11] it now appears that the process of transformation itself was undertaken by a tiny minority of people: those directly involved in the decision-making process. Sociologist Bill Lomax noted with some concern the elitist character of the change of regimes in Hungary:

> Far from 'the people' emerging victorious from these so-called revolutions, it has been the cultural élites, the educated classes, intellectuals, technocrats and politicians who have come to dominate political life and monopolise social and educational opportunities and life chances for themselves and their families, while in the field of economic activity, wealth creation and property ownership a stratum of 'new rich' is emerging comprising a range of entrepreneurs from former state managers, technocrats and party bureaucrats, to cowboys, gangsters, criminals and mafiosos from formerly less privileged backgrounds.[12]

Many observers of post-communist transitions have a rather pessimistic view on the strength of civil society and the ability of wider sections of the population to engage with the changes and to participate in them.[13] Appropriating the law imported from the West and making sense of it is absolutely crucial for the complete transformation of post-communist systems into working liberal democracies. The ability of imported law to put down roots in its new legal soil is vital in all situations of legal developments through legal importation. In the context of post-communist transitions, this is perhaps even more important because of the risk that the whole process of law importation might develop a bitter taste of *déjà-vu*. After all, it is the second time in a century that law importation has been used for redeveloping the law of Central and Eastern countries. After the war, Soviet law was spread to the newly created communist legal systems in a not too dissimilar way: it was imported from the Soviet Union and implemented by an élite of lawyers whose training and selection ensured that they would enforce it.

---

[10] See eg JL Cohen and A Arato, *Civil Society and Political Theory* (Cambridge, MIT Press, 1992) and J Keane (ed), *Civil Society and the State* (London, Verso, 1988).

[11] See eg TG Ash, *We the People: the Revolutions of 1989* (Cambridge, Penguin/Granta, 1990).

[12] B Lomax, 'The Strange Death of "Civil Society" in Post-Communist Hungary' [1997] *Journal of Communist Studies and Transition Politics* 40–41.

[13] M Szabó, 'Changing Patterns of Mobilisation in Hungary within New Social Movements' in Gy. Szoboszlai (ed), *Democracy and Political Transformation* (Budapest, Hungarian Political Science Association, 1991), 310; T Cox and L Vass, 'Civil Society and Interest Representation in Hungarian Political Development' in T Cox and A Furlong (eds), *Hungary: The Politics of Transition* (London, Frank Cass, 1995), 162; F Miszlivetz, 'Participation and Transition: Can the Civil Society Project Survive in Hungary?' [1997] *Journal of Communist Studies and Transition Politics* 31; JJ Linz and A Stepan, *Problems of Democratic Transitions and Consolidation, Southern Europe, South America and Post-Communist Europe* (Baltimore and London, Johns Hopkins University Press, 1996), 314: 'Here we have a bit of a paradox. Some Hungarian analysts called 1988 the year of civil society and 1989 the year of the political society. This should have prepared the ground for a mutually supportive relationship. . . . However, political society after 1989 effectively demobilised civil society.'

In addition, the law imported from the West has had to face 'centuries-old legal nihilism' which renders the function of civil society in making sense of this law even more important, as Schwartz pointed out in his study of post-communist constitutional courts:

> There is probably a-chicken-and-egg relationship between the establishment of a civil society on the one hand and making the rule of law a reality on the other. The non-governmental institutions essential to both a civil society and the economic transitions to a market cannot function except in a setting in which the actors develop respect for the law and obey it as a matter of course. But developing such respect in turn depends on the participants in the economy and in the institutions of civil society realising that they need stable and enforceable rules on which they can rely in order to function. All that can take a long time under the best of circumstances, and in Eastern Europe, the circumstances have been far from the best. It is particularly difficult for most of the peoples of Eastern Europe because of a pervasive and centuries-old legal nihilism, the conviction that legal rules have almost no influence on how officials behave. *Scepticism about the efficacy of legal norms has been reinforced over the years by the widespread corruption present not only before and during the Communist period but persistent even now throughout the area.*[14] (emphasis added)

Law importation on its own and even if it were enthusiastically carried out by lawyers in the early years of the transition, cannot turn the former communist legal systems into liberal democracies overnight. Its success greatly depends on a number of factors over which the importers have little control, such as economic prosperity, the renewal of élites and wide-spread retraining of the legal community. While law importation clearly sped up the early stages in the creation of this new legal system, it also made it fragile. As a result, the time which was apparently gained in the early years of the transition, thanks to the importation of ready-made rights, together with other components of a legal system, might become very precious in later stages of legal developments.

The success of law importation, as discussed above, largely depends on how the imported law is being understood and appropriated beyond the use that the Constitutional Court made of it. Law importation was clearly an attempt by the Hungarian Constitutional Court to raise itself to the level of its Western counterparts, to demonstrate its ability to speak their language and to take part with them in the elaboration of a common body of law. In so doing, the importers of law sought to redress the poor image that (post)communist countries generally had in the eyes of the West and to become its equal partners in Europe. The image that the West has of these countries was, however, far less affected by the efforts made by the East to shake off the burden of the communist past, with its ghosts and stigma. In fact, despite post-communist countries' endeavour to

---

[14] H Schwartz, *The Struggle for Constitutional Justice in Post-Communist Europe* (Chicago and London, University of Chicago Press, 2000) 2.

become mainstream democracies, they still suffer from being considered as 'backwards and turbulent' by the West.[15]

Finally, as law importation was a two-way process which was greatly encouraged by Western democracies, its ultimate success also depends on sustained Western involvement in the process of transformation taking place in Eastern Europe and in particular on the ongoing credibility of the 'West is best' mantra. However, the process of enlargement of the European Union has revealed a different picture of the West, which together with the cost of accessing the EU for the candidates has proved much more difficult than envisaged in the early stages of the transition. While 'the ordeal of enlargement' may nevertheless not lead the candidates to withdraw from this process,[16] it is certainly affecting their representation of the West and leading them to see their relationship with Western democracies in a different light and perhaps to rethink the choice of their model. These developments seem to contrast with the very beginning of post-communist legal systems, when people had a considerable faith in law.

2. FAITH IN LAW AND THE MIGHT OF WORDS

The genesis of law in post-communist countries was characterised by a tension between, on the one hand, a difficulty in adopting a legal logic of reasoning and on the other, a considerable faith in law and the power of words to transform reality. Chapter 2 highlighted the spirit of institutional optimism of the early years of the transition. The previous section has shown that to a great extent law importation was about speaking the right language, ie the language which would open the way to the West. The logic of law importation was driven by a very strong faith in the ability of law alone to create and foster democracy after decades of despotic communist rule and in the power of words to achieve this. The Hungarian Constitutional Court's strength essentially lay in its ability to convince parliament and the government, as well as petitioners and, of course, the judiciary. Its case law was absolutely fascinating (albeit very complex) and reflected the Court's clear sense of the importance of creating a new language of law and a new law through its language. In this respect, the separate opinions occasionally joined to individual cases only give a weak indication of the legal discussions which must have raged during the preparatory stages of cases, as well as during the plenary sessions.

As the Court operated in a context which was more like a giant legal building site than a well-oiled and predictable machine, its most powerful tools were its words. Of course, in all situations of legal interpretation, words matter and sophisticated arguments can go on for ever about which particular shade of

---

[15] B Kovrig, 'Marginality Reinforced' in Z Barany and I Volgyes (eds), *The Legacies of Communism in Eastern Europe* (Baltimore, Johns Hopkins University Press, 1995), 41.

[16] See the special issue 'The Ordeal of EU Enlargement: Enlargement as Seen from the East' (2000) 9 *East European Constitutional Review* 62–91.

meaning to give to particular rights. However, in the context of post-communist transitions, words preceded legal reality and created it—that is, the words used by the Court in its reasoning brought the rights listed in the Constitution to life. In the absence of historical traditions, or solid doctrinal support for constitutional rights, it was the Constitutional Court's interpretation which turned the constitutional provisions into actual rights. The Court followed a recurring pattern which consisted in enunciating a very strong and comprehensive definition, as with human dignity in case 8/1990, where the Court asserted the link between human dignity and the general personality right. In so doing, the Court turned a group of letters into a very specific legal reality. Repetition of legal definitions, in a manner similar to some magical incantation, was part of the reification process through which words became law. In the context of post-communist transitions, the words referring to the new law were often the same as those used for the pre-1989 law and in this sense words carried with themselves the history and the ideology of a particular term. It is not surprising therefore, that in order to renew the constitutional foundations of the legal system after the demise of communism, the Hungarian Court chose to speak a foreign language, ie the language of Western liberal legal systems. For instance, while there is more than one way to name the rights protecting the personality, the Court chose a phrase which was disconnected from Hungarian law and hence did not carry any memory of communist times—that is, for the purpose of interpreting Article 54(1) of the Constitution, the Court chose to refer to '*általános személyiségi jog*' (general personality right) which in most lawyers' minds is instantly associated with the German '*allgemeines Persönlichkeitsrecht*'. In choosing this phrase, the Court excluded another possible phrase, also well-known to Hungarian lawyers, '*a személyhez füzödö jogok*' (the rights related to the personality) which is used by the Hungarian Civil Code.

Furthermore, as it will be recalled from chapter 6, the Court had to give certain words—which were also used under communism—a very different meaning. With these words, the Court was fighting decades of communist language of law and of rights in particular. Winning this fight with words was particularly important because for an unknown period of time in the early stages of the change of system, the new reality of law would be essentially made of words, before they could be turned into consistent and generalised practice. Finally, the uncertainty surrounding the beginning of the new Hungarian legal system meant that for some time, borrowed legal vocabulary provided the only stable points of reference for orienting the course of the transition and this is why words had such a potent aura in the law.

3. THE IMPORTANCE OF PERSONALITIES

Surprisingly few people were part of this gigantic task of creating the new legal system. As a result their personalities were so influential on the development of law in the early years of the transition that the law was closely associated with them in the early stages of its formation. One such dominant personality was the president of the Court, László Sólyom, whose name has frequently been mentioned in this study. He was one of the main architects of Hungarian constitutional justice, always seizing the opportunity of separate opinions to hammer a point home or to discuss the theoretical basis of a particular argument. Moreover, Sólyom contributed to making the Court known both inside and outside Hungary. For the most important and controversial cases, such as the death penalty case and the cases decided on the austerity laws, the Court under Sólyom invited experts and members of government and parliament to present their views. In addition, the ruling in some of these cases was delivered publicly and was heavily mediatised. Abroad, the president of the Court actively promoted it through his participation in countless conferences and seminars and as a result, many academics in Europe have had the opportunity to meet him and to learn about the Constitutional Court. Although his colleagues also greatly contributed to the promotion of the Court inside and outside Hungary, the first Court is known as the Sólyom Court.

Sólyom is not an isolated example of the importance of personalities in the creation of new law and in fact post-communist transitions were marked by a number of prominent personalities, the best known generally being the politicians: for instance, one might wonder what would have happened to Central Europe without people like Walesa, Havel and Gorbachev. Similarly, the 'first' Constitutional Court of Hungary would not have been the same with a different president, and indeed the 'second' Court under the presidency of Németh is quite different. George Schöpflin has referred to a similar phenomenon in the political realm as 'the personalisation of politics' and sees a number of problems deriving from it:

> The present political system in Central and Eastern Europe should be understood as functioning in three dimensions—ideological, institutional and personal. These three overlap and interlock, and crucially the codes appropriate to one are regularly used in another context. It is important that, where the institutional level is weak, there will be a much more direct relationship between persons and ideologies, and it will be far easier for individuals to use ideology to disguise their bid for personal power or for defence of a personal privilege. . . . The overall difficulty with this situation is that it promotes confusion and also cynicism, because institutions will be perceived as nothing more than façades hiding different personal interests and hence nothing will be done to strengthen institutionalisation.[17]

Personalisation of politics certainly has problems, as highlighted by Schöpflin, and again it raises the issue of the renewal of key personalities (Yeltsin after Gorbachev for instance). Personalisation can also arguably be understood as a typical characteristic of the early stages of the development of a legal system, that is before the legal features of an institution are firmly and

---

[17] G Schöpflin, *Politics in Eastern Europe* (Oxford, Blackwell, 1993), 276.

precisely defined.[18] In other words the law, before becoming entirely self-referential, may need the support of strong personalities in order to develop fully. However, it falls beyond the scope of this study to consider whether judges used 'ideology to disguise their bid for personal power.' Nevertheless, one can fairly safely say that without Sólyom, constitutional justice would not have developed in Hungary in the way it did and the Court would not have played the role it did in the transformation of the Hungarian legal system.

4. NO BIG BANG IN THE CREATION OF A NEW LEGAL SYSTEM

The last remark about the birth of a legal system is that there is no Big Bang: the law does not emerge *ex nihilo* and there is not a situation of *tabula rasa* upon which new law can appear, untouched by the past. The creation of new law is a very incremental process: even the post-communist systems which emerged after a legal and ideological rupture have carried with them some of the law which existed before. This raises at least two issues.

4.1. Importation versus Innovation

Although, as seen in chapter 5, law importation does not amount to some mechanical imitation of a body of foreign law, it does not encourage legal innovation. Indeed, one of the driving motivations for law importation was the desire and the need to comply and to conform with the Western model of law. The fall of the Berlin Wall, which was so full of promise and hopes that a third way between communism and liberalism might come into existence including (perhaps for the dreamers) the best of both worlds, in fact led to the reproduction of Western-type democracies. This lack of substantial innovation has at least two consequences for post-communist law and, in particular, for the political institutions. The first consequence is the adaptation of the imported law to the post-communist situations. For instance, fundamental rights, as seen with the example of human dignity, have been interpreted and enforced in a very individualistic and liberal way, erasing in many cases most of the pre-existing social rights. The disappearance of these rights has considerably fragilised the daily lives of many people who relied on state support in case of illness or retirement or for more generally affordable education. Furthermore, the absence of properly implemented social rights has perhaps slowed the process of developing people's identification with their new set of institutions and their acceptance of what post-communist democracy meant for them.

---

[18] It has to be noted, however, that an institution will always be influenced by the personalities of those who represent it.

The second consequence of the lack of innovation is that post-communist democracies have imported political institutions without really improving them. Many of these Western institutions are now being heavily criticised and questioned for their inability to respond to the challenges of wide-scale corruption and institutionalised racism and xenophobia, not to mention their inability to represent and engage the entire community living in a particular state. The European Union itself is currently facing substantial institutional reformation (which has only partially been triggered by the prospect of enlargement). It might be that, from a pessimistic point of view, post-communist countries imported outdated institutions from the West, which 10 years after their incorporation into post-communist legal systems show some serious sign of dysfunction in their original setting.

4.2. Going Towards the Future Without a Past?

In general, while the collapse of communism created one of the first opportunities in centuries for people in Central and Eastern Europe to re-examine and assess their past, little has been done so far to address the past.[19] It is true that some major historical events, such as the 1956 Revolution in Hungary, were officially requalified and its main official actor, Imre Nagy, was rehabilitated. In terms of what is now called 'lustration,' that is the process by which the communist files on individuals are opened and the informers working for the various systems of secret police are named and/or filtered out, this has mainly remained at a superficial level in most countries, except perhaps in the former Democratic Republic of Germany.[20] This, however, should not close the debates on the past and Istvan Pogany advocates 'moral rather than material restitution, except in cases of genuine need' and wide-ranging education about the past.[21]

Law importation has encouraged a development of law turned towards the outside and the future, without coming to terms with the past. It is difficult to

---

[19] A Barahona de Brito, C González-Enríquez and P Aguilar (eds), *The Politics of Memory: Transitional Justice in Democratizing Societie*s (Oxford, Oxford University Press, 2001). See also G Brunner (ed), *Juristische Bewältigung des kommunistischen Unrechts in Osteuropa und Deutschland* (Berlin, Arno Spitz, 1995) and in particular the contribution of G Brunner and G Halmai on 'Hungarian Law', 9.

[20] C González-Enríquez, 'De-communization and Political Justice in Central and Eastern Europe' in Barahona de Brito, González-Enríquez and Aguilar, above n 19, at 244 and J-W Müller, 'East Germany: Incorporation, Tainted Truth and the Double Division', in *ibid*, 248.

[21] I Pogany, *Righting Wrongs in Eastern Europe* (Manchester, Manchester University Press, 1997): 'Moral restitution would require something altogether different, a shift in public attitudes towards groups which have traditionally been perceived as lying outside the "nation"—whether Hungarians in Slovakia, Romania or Serbia, Germans in the Czech Republic, Romania and Poland, or Jews and Gipsies almost everywhere in the region. . . . This can be accomplished, if at all, only through intensive and wide-ranging education—focusing on the "real" history of the nations of East Central Europe and offering some insight into the lives of those peoples who coexist(ed) in the countries of the region' (at 217–18).

decide which came first: the desire to turn to the outside world or the discomfort with the past which made it easier to look outside for inspiration. In Hungarian constitutional case law, this unease with the past is palpable. It is exacerbated, as it was explained in the previous chapter, by the difficulty in directly addressing issues of an ideological nature. Although the Court did filter out a number of past institutions, rules and norms (many of them because they did not comply with human dignity and the related rights or with the new principle of the rule of law), it never really addressed the past directly. In fact the Court seemed to make a point of considering that there was nothing particularly special nor problematic with this past and that its adjudication function was as normal as in any other Western country.

More generally, law importation was grounded on a sort of *tabula rasa* fiction, in that the importation was based on the belief (or the assumption) that incorporation of new external institutions would be enough to start afresh on a strong basis. This amounted to negating the inherited institutions, rules, practice and in one big phrase 'legal culture'. It was perhaps hoped that the new imported law and institutions would as such cancel out all the undesirable effects of the past. In so doing, however, importers forgot that confronting the past was part of moving towards the future.

Select Bibliography

POST-COMMUNIST TRANSITIONS

Ash, TG, *We the People: the Revolution of 89 Witnessed in Warsaw, Budapest, Berlin and Prague* (London, Granta Books, 1990).

Barany, Z and Volgyes, I (eds), *The Legacies of Communism in Eastern Europe* (Baltimore, Johns Hopkins University Press, 1995).

Batt, J, White, S and Lewis, PJ (eds), *Developments in East European Politics* (Basingstoke, Macmillan Press, 1993).

Belohradsky, V, Kendé, P and Rupnick, J (eds), *Democrazie da inventare* (Torino, Edizioni della Fondazione Giovanni Agnelli, 1991).

Beyme, K v, *Systemwechsel in Osteuropa* (Frankfurt/Main, Suhrkamp, 1994).

Bozoki, A, 'Political Transition and Constitutional Change in Hungary' [1990] *Südosteuropa* 538.

Dawisha, K and Parrot, B (eds), *The Consolidation of Democracy in East-Central Europe* (Cambridge, Cambridge University Press, 1997).

Elster, J (ed), *The Roundtable Talks and the Breakdown of Communism* (Chicago, Chicago University Press, 1996).

Elster, J, Offe, C, and Preuß, UK, *Institutional Design in Post Communist Societies: Rebuilding the Ship at Sea* (Cambridge, Cambridge University Press, 1997).

Goldwin, RA and Kaufman, A (eds), *Constitution-Makers on Constitution-Making: the Experience of Eight Nations* (Washington DC, American Enterprise Institute, 1988).

Gremion, P and Hassner, P, *Vents d'Est, vers l'Europe des États de droit?* (Paris, Presses Universitaires de France, 1990).

Grilli di Cortona, P, 'Dal communismo alla democrazia in Europa Centrale, Ungheria e Cecoslovachia' [1991] *Rivista Italiana di Scienza Politica* 281.

Howard, DAE (ed), *Constitution-Making in Eastern Europe* (Washington DC, Woodrow Wilson Center Press, 1993).

Jozsa, Gy, *Von der Implosion des politbürokratischen Systems in Ungarn zum Rechtsstaat und zum Parteipluralismus* (Köln, Bundesinstitut für ost-wissenschaftlichen und internationalen Studien, 1992).

Kendé, P and Smolnar, A, *La grande secousse en Europe de l'Est, 1989–1990* (Paris, CNRS, 1990).

Kis, J, 'Between Reform and Revolution: Three Hypotheses about the Nature of the Regime Change' (1995) 3 *Constellations* 399.

Lhomel, É and Schreiber, T (eds), *L'Europe Centrale et Orientale* (Paris, La Documentation Française, 1999).

Lijphart, A, 'Democratization and Constitutional Choices in Czecho-Slovakia, Hungary and Poland, 1989–1991' (1992) 4 *Journal of Theoretical Politics* 207.

Linz, JJ and Stepan, A (eds), *Problems of Democratic Transition and Consolidation: Southern Europe, South America and Post Communist Europe* (Baltimore, Johns Hopkins University Press, 1996).

Ludwikowski, R, 'Searching for a New Constitution in East Central Europe' (1991) 17 *Syracuse Journal of International Law and Commerce* 90.

McWhinney, E, *Constitution-Making: Principles, Process, Practice* (Toronto, University of Toronto Press, 1981).

Milacic, S (ed), *Démocratie constitutionelle en Europe Centrale et Orientale: Bilans et perspectives* (Bruxelles, Bruylant, 1998).

Molnar, M, *La démocratie se lève à l'Est: Société civile et communisme en Europe de l'Est* (Paris, Presses Universitaires de France, 1990).

Offe, C, 'Capitalism by Democratic Design: Democratic Theory Facing Triple Transition in Eastern Europe' (1991) 58 *Social Research* 865.

Potel, J-Y, *Les Cent Portes de l'Europe Centrale et Orientale* (Paris, Les Éditions de l'Atelier, 1998).

Pridham, G and Vanhaven, T (eds), *Democratization in Eastern Europe: Domestic and International Perspectives* (London, Routledge, 1994).

Przeworski, A, *Democracy and the Market: Political and Economic Reforms in Eastern Europe and Latin America* (Cambridge, Cambridge University Press, 1991).

Schmitter, PhC, O'Donnell, G and Whitehead, L, *Transitions from Authoritarian Rule: Prospects for Democracy* (Baltimore, Johns Hopkins University Press, 1986).

Schmitter, PhC and Santiso, J, 'Three Temporal Dimensions to the Consolidation of Democracy', (1998) 19 *International Political Science Review* 69.

Schöpflin, G, *Politics in Eastern Europe* (Oxford, Blackwell, 1993).

Stokes, G, *The Walls Came Tumbling Down* (Oxford, Oxford University Press, 1993).

Tökés, R, *Hungary's Negotiated Revolution: Economic Reform, Social Change and Political Succession* (Cambridge, Cambridge University Press, 1996).

HUNGARIAN HISTORY

General

Barta, I *et al*, *Histoire de la hongrie des origines à nos jours* (Budapest, Editions Horváth, 1974).

Gerö, A, *Modern Hungarian Society in the Making: the Unfinished Experience* (Budapest, Central European University Press, 1995).

Molnar, M, *A Concise History of Hungary* (Cambridge, Cambridge University Press, 2001).

Constitutional/Legal History

Hantos, E, *The Magna Carta of the English and the Hungarian Constitution* (London, Kegan Paul, French, Trubner and Co, 1904).

Horváth, E, *L'Angleterre, Genève et la Hongrie: élaboration d'un système constitutionnel, 1748–1848* (Budapest, Sarkany, 1938).

Kovács, I, *La formation et l'évolution du droit constitutionnel de la République Populaire Hongroise* (Szeged, Acta Juridica et Politica, 1973).

Marczali, H, *Ungarische Verfassungsgeschichte* (Tübingen, Verlag von JCB Mohr, 1910).

Radó-Rothfeld, S, *Die ungarische Verfassung geschichtlich dargestellt. Mit einem Anhang: die wichtgsten Verfassungsgesetze* (Berlin, Putkammer und Mühlbrecht, 1898).

Timon, A v, *Ungarische Verfassungs-und-Rechtsgeschichte mit Bezug auf die Rechtsent-wicklung der westlichen Staaten* (2nd edn, Berlin, Putkammer und Mühlbrecht, 1909).
Török, B, 'Die ungarische Verfassung und die autoritäre Neuordnung Europas' (1942) 3 *Auswärtige Politik* 189.
Toulmin Smith J, *Parallels Between the Constitution and Constitutional History of England and Hungary* (London, Effingham Wilson, 1849).

HUNGARIAN CONSTITUTIONS

Constitution of 1989

Blaustein, AP and Flanz, GH (eds), *Constitutions of the Countries of the World* (New York, Oceana Publications, 1977, with updated inserts).
Lesage, M (ed), *Constitutions d'Europe Centrale, Orientale et Balte* (Paris, La Documentation Française, 1995).
Masing, A (ed), *Die Verfassung der Republik Ungarn, Zweisprachige Ausgabe* (Berlin, Arno Spitz, 1995).
Website of the Constitutional Court: www.mkab.hu

Constitution of 1983

Ungarische Volksrepublik, Staat, Demokratie, Leitung, Dokumente (Staatsverlag der DDR, Berlin, 1985), 137.

Constitution of 1975

Simons, WB (ed), *The Constitutions of the Communist World* (Alphen aan den Rijn, Sijthoff and Noordhoff, 1980), 182.

Constitution of 1949

Brunner, G and Meissner, B (eds), *Verfassungen der kommunistischen Staaten* (München, Paderborn, 1979), 476.
Kneif, T, 'Die Entwicklung des Verfassungsrechts in Ungarn seit 1945' (1959) 8 *Archiv für öffentliches Recht* 365.
Triska, JF (ed), *Constitutions of the Communist Party-States* (Stanford, The Hoover Institution Publications, 1968), 196.

HUNGARIAN LEGAL SYSTEM

Before 1989

Socialist Law

Ajani, G, *Diritto dell'Europa Orientale* (Torino, Utet, 1996).
Bihari, O, *Le sens et les formes de l'unité de la législation et de l'exécution dans l'État socialiste aujourd'hui* (Budapest, Akadémiai Kiadó, 1970).

Bihari, O, *The Constitutional Models of Socialist State Organisations* (Budapest, Akadémiai Kiadó, 1979).

Brunner, G (ed), *Before Reforms: Human Rights in the Warsaw Pact States, 1971–1988* (London, Hurst and Co, 1990).

Charvin, R, *Les États socialistes européens* (Toulouse, Dalloz, 1975).

Collins, H, *Marxism and Law* (Oxford, Clarendon Press, 1982).

Hazard, JN, *Communists and their Law: A Search for the Common Core of the Legal Systems of the Marxian Socialist States* (Chicago, University of Chicago Press, 1969).

Kopp, FO, 'Das Verfassungsverständnis in den sozialistischen Staaten' in *Recht und Staat: Festschrift f. Günther Küchenhoff* (Berlin, Duncker und Humblot, 1972), 573.

Nelson, D and White, S, *Communist Legislatures in Comparative Perspectives* (London, Basingstoke, McMillan Press, 1982).

Pashukanis, E, *Law and Marxism: a General Theory* (Worcester, Pluto Press, 1989).

Péteri, Z, 'Problems of the Legislative Process in the Socialist Countries of Europe' in Pizzorusso, A (ed), *Law in the Making* (Berlin, Springer Verlag, 1988), 306.

Stoyanovitch, K, *La pensée marxiste du droit* (Paris, Presses Universitaires de France, 1974).

Hungarian Law, General

Ádám, A, 'Entwicklungstendenzen der Verfassung und der Verfassungsmäßigkeit in Ungarn' (1985) 34 *Jahrbuch für Öffentliches Recht* 567.

Antalffy, Gy, 'Les bases théoriques de l'amendement de la Constitution' [1974] *Revue de Droit Hongrois* 29.

—— 'Sur l'amendement de la constitution de la République Populaire Hongroise' (1975) 24 *Jahrbuch für Öffentliches Recht* 287.

—— 'Modification de la constitution en Hongrie' [1984] *Revue de Droit Hongrois* 5.

Bihari, O, 'Constitutionalism and Legality' [1964] *Acta Juridica Academiae Scientiarum Hungaricae* 99.

Brunner, G, 'Neuere Tendenzen in der verfassungsrechtlichen Entwicklung Osteuropäischer Staaten' [1974] *Jahrbuch für Öffentliches Recht* 209.

—— 'Rechtssprechung und Richterrecht in Ungarn' [1980] *Osteuropa Recht* 1.

Eörsi, Gy (ed), *Introduction au Droit de la République Populaire Hongroise* (Paris, Pédone, 1974).

Kneif, T, 'Die Entwicklung des Verfassungsrechts in Ungarn seit 1945' (1959) 8 *Jahrbuch für Öffentliches Recht* 365.

Kovács, I, *New Elements in the Evolution of the Socialist Constitution* (Budapest, Akadémiai Kiadó, 1968).

—— 'Le droit constitutionnel' in Gy Eörsi (ed), *Introduction au droit de la République Populaire Hongroise* (Paris, Pédone, 1974), 33.

—— 'Du droit public hongrois au droit constitutionnel socialiste hongrois' (1987) 29 *Acta Juridica Academiae Scientiarum Hungaricae* 321.

Kurtan, S (ed), *Vor der Wende: politisches System, Gesellschaft und Reformen im Ungarn der 80. Jahre* (Wien, Studien zur Politik und Verwaltung, 1993).

Majoros, F, *Änderung der ungarischen Staats-und-Verfassungsordnung bis Oktober 1989* (Köln, Bundesinstitut für Ostwissenschaftlichen und Internationalen Studien, 1990).

Rácz, G, *Die neue Rechtsentwicklung in Ungarn* (Budapest, Danubia, 1943).

——'Einführung der Verfassungsnormenkontrolle in Ungarn' [1984] *Juristenzeitung* 879.

——'L'introduction du contrôle constitutionnel des normes juridiques en Hongrie' [1985] *Revue Internationale de Droit Comparé* 136.

Szabó, I, *Trends and Problems of Development of Law in Hungary* (Budapest, Akadémiai Kiadó, 1974).

Szikra, J, 'Die Rechtsentwicklung in der Sowjetunion: Das kommunistische Verfassungssystem Ungarns' (1961) 10 *Schriftenreihe des Schweizerischen Ostinstituts* 50.

Takács, A, 'Problems of the Protection of the Constitution, with Special Regard to the Constitutional Law Council' (1987) 29 *Acta Juridica Academiae Scientiarum Hungaricae* 165.

Takács, I, 'Les bases théoriques de l'amendement de la Constitution' [1974] *Revue de Droit Hongrois* 29.

Zajtay, I, *Introduction à l'étude du droit hongrois* (Paris, Pédone, 1953).

Rights

Ádám, A, *Verfassungsmäßigkeit und Verfassungsschutz in der ungarischen Volksrepublik* (Pécs, Studia Iuridica Auctoritate Universitatis Pécs Publicate, 1975).

Csizmadia, A, 'Les déclarations des droits de l'homme et leur place dans l'histoire de la constitution hongroise' in Z Péteri (ed), *La comparaison du droit, IXème Congrès de Droit Comparé* (Budapest, Akadémiai Kiadó, 1974), 11.

Halász, J, *Socialist Concept of Human Rights* (Budapest, Akadémiai Kiadó, 1966).

Kovács, I, *Les libertés démocratiques de la République Populaire Hongroise* (Budapest, Association des juristes hongrois, 1953).

Péteri, Z, 'The Declarations of Rights of Man and the Citizens and the Hungarian Constitution' (1991) 33 *Acta Juridica Hungarica* 57.

Rácz, A, 'Protection of the Fundamental Rights of the Citizens in Hungary' [1987] *Études de Droit Constitutionnel Hongrois* 40.

Sólyom, L, *Die Persönlichkeitsrechte: Eine vergleichend-historische Studie über ihre Grundlage* (Budapest, Akadémiai Kiadó, 1984).

Szabó, I, *Cultural Rights* (Budapest, Akadémiai Kiadó, 1974).

Szilagyi, I, 'Los Derechos Humanos y los Derechos de Libertad en Hungria: Ayer y Hoy' (1993) 3 *Cuadernos de la Catedra Fabrique Furio Ceriol* 53.

Törö, K, 'Protection of the Personality within the Hungarian Legal System' in M Katona Soltész (ed), *Human Rights in Today's Hungary* (Budapest, Mezon, 1990), 87.

Hungarian Law Since 1989

Ádám, A, 'Tendances du développement de l'ordre constitutionnel en Hongrie' (1990) 120 *Studia Iuridica Auctoritate Universitatis* 13.

——'Lo sviluppo costituzionale in Ungheria dopo il crollo del regimen comunista' (1992) 3 *Quaderni Costituzionali* 413.

Arato, A, 'The Constitution-Making Endgame in Hungary' (1996) 5 *East European Constitutional Review* 31.

Bartole, S, *Riforme costituzionali nell'Europa Centro-orientale: da satelliti comunisti a democrazie sovrane* (Bologna, Il Mulino, 1993).

Bartole, S, 'Organising the Judiciary in Central and Eastern Europe' (1998) 7 *East European Constitutional Review* 62.

Bringmann, O, 'Die Ungarische Verfassung: die rechtliche Stellung der Streitkräfte und weitere sicherheitspolitische Aspekte' [1998] *Recht im Ost und West* 205.

Brunner, G, 'Die neue Verfassung der ungarischen Republik: Entstehungsgeschichte und Grundprobleme' [1991] *Jahrbuch für Politik* 297.

Halmai, G, 'Einleitung zur ungarischen Verfassungsrevision' (1990) 39 *Jahrbuch für Öffentliches Recht* 235.

—— 'Von der gelebten Verfassung bis zur Verfassungsstaatlichkeit in Ungarn' [1990] *Osteuropa Recht* 1.

Harmathy, A (ed), *Introduction to Hungarian Law* (The Hague, Kluwer Law International, 1998).

Hiller, K, 'Neue Verfassung für Ungarn' [1998] *Recht im Ost und West* 74.

Holmes, S, 'Conception of Democracy in the Draft Constitutions of Post-Communist Countries' in B Crawford (ed), *Markets, States and Democracy* (Boulder, Westview Press, 1995), 71.

Katona Soltész, M (ed), *Human Rights in Today's Hungary* (Budapest, Mezon, 1990).

Kilényi, G, 'Ungarn schreitet in Richtung Rechtsstaatlichkeit' [1989] *Europäische Grundrechtszeitschrift* 513.

Kiss, L, 'Einige aktuelle Fragen der Rechtssetzung und des Rechtsquellsystems in der ungarischen Republik' [1989] *DeutschesVerwaltungsblatt* 918.

—— 'Einige Fragen der Rechtsstsaatlichkeit und Gesetzgebung in Ungarn' [1990] *OsteuropaRecht* 12.

Kuss, K-J, 'Rechtsstaatliche Wurzeln in den osteuropäischen Staaten', (1985) 34 *Jahrbuch für Öffentliches Recht* 589.

Lipschit, G, 'Prime considerazioni sugli amendamenti della costituzione ungherese' [1983] *Rivista Trimestriale di Diritto Pubblico* 830.

Majoros, F, 'Ungarns neue Verfassungsordnung: die Genese einer neuen demokratischen Republik nach westlichen Maßstäben' [1990] *OsteuropaRecht* 164.

—— 'Zur Entwicklung der Verfassungsgerichtsbarkeit in Ungarn' [1993] *OsteuropaRecht* 106.

Paczolay, P, 'The New Hungarian Constitutional State' in DAE Howard (ed), *Constitution-Making in Eastern Europe* (Washington DC, Woodrow Wilson Center Press, 1993), 21.

—— 'La Jurisprudence de la Cour Constitutionnelle en Matière de Séparation des Pouvoirs' in *Rapport Général de la Dixième Conférence des Cours Constitutionnelles Européennes* (Budapest, May 1996, on file with the author).

Péteri, Z, *Einige Fragen zur Verfassungsgebung in Ungarn* (paper presented at the Academy of Sciences, Budapest, March 1995, on file with the author).

Pogany, I, 'Human Rights in Hungary' [1992] *International and Comparative Law Quarterly* 676.

—— 'Constitutional Reform in Central and Eastern Europe: Hungary's Transition to Democracy' (1993) 42 *International and Comparative Law Quarterly* 332.

—— (ed), *Human Rights in Eastern Europe* (Coventry, Elgar Publishing, 1995).

—— *Righting Wrongs in Eastern Europe* (Manchester, Manchester University Press, 1997).

Priban, J and Young, J (eds), *The Rule of Law in Central Europe* (Dartmouth, Ashgate Publishers, 1999).

Schanda, B, 'Rechtsstaatlichkeit in Ungarn' in R Hofmann *et al*, *Rechtsstaatlichkeit in Europa* (Heidelberg, CF Müller Verlag, 1995), 219.

Szikinger, I, 'The Procuracy and its Problems, Hungary' (1999) 8 *East European Constitutional Review* 85.

Weller, M, 'Application of the European Convention on Human Rights in the Hungarian Legal System' [1999] *Acta Juridica Hungarica* 105.

Weller, M and Bokor-Szegö, H, 'Hungary' in R Blackburn and J Polakiewicz (eds), *Fundamental Rights in Europe: the ECHR and its Member States, 1950–2000* (Oxford, Oxford University Press, 2001), 383.

HUNGARIAN CONSTITUTIONAL COURT

Case Reports and Summaries

Alkotmányos elvek és esetek (*Constitutional Cases and Principles*) (Budapest, Constitutional and Legislative Policy Institute (COLPI), 1996).

Annuaire International de Justice Constitutionnelle (Economica, Presses Universitaires d'Aix Marseille, yearly volume).

Balogh, Zs, Holló, A, *Az értelmezett alkotmány* (*The Interpreted Constitution*) (Budapest, Közlöny és Lapkiadó, 1995).

Bulletin de jurisprudence constitutionnelle, Commission de Venise, Conseil de l'Europe.

Magyar Közlöny (*Official Gazette of the Republic of Hungary*).

Sólyom, L and Brunner, G (eds), *Verfassungsgerichtsbarkeit in Ungarn: Analysen und Entscheidungssammlung, 1990–1993* (Baden-Baden, Nomos Verlag, 1995).

—— and —— (eds), *Constitutional Judiciary in a New Democracy: the Hungarian Constitutional Court* (Ann Arbor, University of Michigan Press, 2000).

Academic Studies

Ádám, A, 'Der Schutz der Grundrechte durch die Verfassungsgerichtsbarkeit in Ungarn' in G Brunner (ed), *Politischer Pluralismus und Verfassungsstaat in Deutschland und in Ungarn* (München, Südosteuropa Gesellschaft, 1992), 23.

—— 'Le contrôle de la constitutionnalité des actes adminisratifs et gouvernementaux en Hongrie' (1992) 121 *Studia Juridica* 3.

—— 'Constitutions: interprétations et interprètes, rapport national hongrois' in *Quatrième Congrès Mondial de l'Association Internationale de Droit Constitutionnel* (Tokyo, 1995).

Brunner, G, 'Development of a Constitutional Judiciary in Eastern Europe' (1992) 6 *Review of Central and East European Law* 535.

—— 'Zweieinhalb Jahre ungarische Verfassungsgerichtsbarkeit' (1993) 32 *Der Staat* 287.

Brunner, G, and Halmai, G, 'Die juristische Bewältigung des kommunistischen Unrechts in Ungarn' in G Brunner (ed), *Juristische Bewältigung des kommunistischen Unrechts in Osteuropa und Deutschland* (Berlin, Arno Spitz, 1995), 9.

Dupré, C, 'Le droit à la dignité humaine: emblème de la transition constitutionnelle en Hongrie?' in K Tóth (ed), *Changement de régime politique et le développement de la constitution en Europe Centrale et Orientale* (Kecskemét, Karoli Gáspár Reformed University Press, 1995), 67.

Halmai, G, 'Ein neues Menschenrechtsverständnis in Ungarn am Beispiel der Vereinigungsfreiheit' (1990) 36 *Jahrbuch für Öffentliches Recht* 12.

—— 'Protection of Human Rights in Poland and Hungary', in I Pogany (ed), *Human Rights in Eastern Europe* (Coventry, Elgar Publishing, 1995).

—— (ed), *The Constitution Found? The First Nine Years of the Hungarian Constitutional Review on Fundamental Rights* (Budapest, INDOK, 2000).

Halmai, G and Scheppele, K-L, 'Constitutional Protection for Homosexuality in Hungary' [1997] *East European Human Rights Review* 17.

Halmai, G, Scheppele, K-L, and Majtényi, L, 'Confronting the Past: the Hungarian Constitutional Court's Lustration Decision of 1994' (1995) 1 *East European Human Rights Review* 111.

Horváth, T, 'Abolition of capital punishment in Hungary' (1991) 33 *Acta Juridica Hungarica* 153.

Klingsberg, E, 'Judicial Review and Hungary's Transition from Communism to Democracy: the Constitutional Court, the Continuity of Law and the Redefinition of Property Rights' (1992) 44 *Brightam Young Law Review* 41.

Küpper, H, 'Der Sparkurs der ungarischen Regierung auf dem Prüfstand des Verfassungsgerichts' [1995] *Recht im Ost und West* 101.

—— 'Die Grundrechte des Kindes in der ungarischen Verfassungsrechtssprechung' [1996] *Recht im Ost und West* 274.

—— 'Das zweite Abtreibungsurteil des ungarischen Verfassungsgerichts' [1999] *OsteuropaRecht* 155.

Lábady, T, 'Über die Richtungen der Weiterentwicklung der Verfassungsgerichtsbarkeit' [1991] *Monatshefte für osteuropäisches Recht* 368.

—— 'Constitutional Protection of Privacy (Protection of Marriage and the Family, Right to Privacy)' (1995/96) 37 *Acta Juridica Hungarica* 23.

Paczolay, P, 'Judicial Review of the Compensation Law in Hungary' (1992) 13 *Michigan Journal of International Law* 806.

Pajor-Bytomsky, M, 'Einführung in die ungarische Verfassungsgerichtsbarkeit' [1993] *Europa Grundrechtzeitschrift* 220.

Pataki, J, 'Hungary: the Constitutional Court in Search of Identity' (1991) 25 *Report on Eastern Europe* 5.

Rácz, G, 'Une nouvelle cour constitutionnelle en Hongrie' [1990] *Revue Internationale de Droit Comparé* 1329.

Sajó, A, 'On Old and New Battles: Obstacles to the Rule of Law in Eastern Europe' (1995) 22 *Journal of Law and Society* 97.

—— 'Reading the Invisible Constitution' (1995) 15 *Oxford Journal of Legal Studies* 253.

—— 'How the Rule of Law Killed Hungarian Welfare Reform' (1996) 5 *East European Constitutional Review* 31.

Sajó, A and Sándor, J, 'Legal Status of the 'Terminally Ill' under Hungarian Law' (1995/96) 37 *Acta Iuridica Hungarica* 1.

Scheppele, K-L, 'The New Hungarian Constitutional Court' (1999) 8 *East European Constitutional Law Review*, 81.

Sólyom, L, 'The First Year of the Constitutional Court' (1991) 33 *Acta Iuridica Hungarica* 5.

—— 'The Hungarian Constitutional Court and Social Change' (1994) 19 *Yale Journal of International Law* 223.

—— 'Aufbau und dogmatische Fundierung der ungarischen Verfassungsgerichtsbarkeit' [2000] *OsteuropaRecht* 230.

Spuller, G, *Das Verfassungsgericht der Republik Ungarn: Zuständigkeiten, Organisation, Verfahren, Stellung* (Frankfurt/Main, Peter Lang, 1998).

—— 'Der Einfluß des ungarischen Verfassungsgerichts auf das Gesetzgebungsverfahren des Parlaments der Republik Ungarn' [2000] *Jahrbuch für Öffentliches Recht* 35.

Takács, A, 'Dilemmas of Constitutionalism in the Decisions of the Hungarian Constitutional Court' [1991] *Acta Juridica Hungarica* 217.

HUMAN DIGNITY AND GENERAL PERSONALITY RIGHT

Hungarian Law

Biskey, B, *Az élethéz és az emberi méltósághoz való jog elöfordulása és értelmezése az Alkotmánybíróság gyakorlatában (1990–1994)* (*The Interpretation of the Right to Life and Human Dignity by the Constitutional Court*) (Masters dissertation, manuscript, Law Faculty, ELTE, Budapest, 1995).

Dupré, C, 'The Right to Human Dignity in Hungarian Constitutional Case Law' in *The Principle of Respect for Human Dignity* (Strasbourg, Council of Europe Publishing, 1999), 68.

Törö, K, *Szemelyiségvedelem a polgari jogban* (*The Protection of the Personality by the Civil Law*) (Budapest, Közgazdász és Könyvkiadó, 1979).

—— 'Protection of the Personality within the Hungarian Legal System', in M Katona Soltész (ed), *Human Rights in Today's Hungary* (Budapest, Mezon, 1990), 87.

Zoltan, Ö, 'Az emberi méltóságról' (Human Dignity) [1996] *Magyar Jog* 531.

German Law, General

Bettermann, KA, Neumann, FI and Nipperdey, HC, *Die Grundrechte, Handbuch der Theorie und Praxis der Grundrechte* (Berlin, Duncker und Humblot, 1962).

Hesse, K, *Grundzüge des Verfassungsrechts der Bundesrepublik Deutschland* (Heidelberg, CF Müller Juristischer Verlag, 1982).

Mangoldt, H v, Klein, F and Starck, C, *Das Bonner Grundgesetz* (München, Vahlen, 1999).

Maunz, T and Zippelius, R, *Deutsches Staatsrecht* (Munich, CH BeckVerlag, 1998).

Münch, I v (ed), *Grundgesetzkommentar* (München, CH Beck Verlag, 1985).

Wassermann, R (ed), *Kommentar zum Grundgesetz der Bundesrepublik Deutschland* (Darmstadt, Luchterhand, 1984).

Case Law of the Federal Constitutional Court

Bundesverfassungsgericht (ed), *Nachschlagewerk der Rechtsprechung des Bundesverfassungsgerichts* (Heidelberg, CF Müller Verlag, R v Decker's Verlag, 1978, looseleaf edition, regularly updated).

Kommers, D, *The Constitutional Jurisprudence of the Federal Republic of Germany* (Durham and London, Duke University Press, 1997).

Richter, I and Schuppert, GF (eds), *Casebook, Verfassungsrecht* (München, Verlag CH Beck, 1996).

Human Dignity

Dürig, G, 'Die Menschenauffassung des Grundgesetzes' [1952] *Juristen Zeitschrift* 259.

—— 'Der Grundrechtssatz von der Menschenwürde' (1956) 81 *Archiv für Öffentliches Recht* 117.

Geddert-Steinacher, T, *Menschenwürde als Verfassungsbegriff: Aspekte der Rechtssprechung des Bundesverfassunsgerichts zum Art. 1 Abs 1* (Berlin, Duncker und Humblot, 1990).

Küchenhoff, G, 'Persönlichkeitsschutz kraft Menschenwürde' in *Menschenwürde und freiheitliche Rechtsordnung: Festschrift für W. Geiger zum 65. Geburstag* (Tübingen, JC Mohr, 1974), 45.

Podlech, A, 'Art. 2 GG' in R Wassermann (ed), *Kommentar zum Grundgesetz der Bundesrepublik Deutschland* (Darmstadt, Luchterhand, 1984), 317.

Starck, C, 'Menschenwürde als Verfassungsgarantie im modernen Staat' [1981] *Juristen Zeitschrift* 457.

Stern, K v, 'Menschenwürde als Wurzel der Menschen-Grundrechte' in *Recht und Staat im sozialen Wandel: Festschrift f. H. U. Scupin* (Berlin, Duncker und Humblot, 1983), 627.

Vitztum, GW, 'Die Menschenwürde als Verfassungsbegriff' [1985] *JuristenZeitschrift* 201.

Walter, C, 'The Principle of Human Dignity in German Constitutional Law' in *The Principle of Respect for Human Dignity* (Strasbourg, Council of Europe Publishing, 1999), 25.

Wertenbruch, W, *Grundgesetz und Menschenwürde: ein kritischer Beitrag zur Verfassungswirklichkeit* (Köln, Carl Heymanns Verlag, 1958).

Free Fulfilment of the Personality

Amelung, K, 'Die zweite Tagebuchentscheidung des BVerfG' (1990) 29 *Neue Juristische Wochenschrift* 1753.

Benda, E, 'Privatsphäre und Persönlichkeitsprofile' in *Festschrift f. W. Geiger* (Tübingen, JC Mohr, 1974), 23.

Haas, D 'Freie Entfaltung der Persönlichkeit' [1954] *Die Öffentliche Verwaltung* 70.

Jarass, H D, 'Das allgemeine Persönlichkeitsrecht im Grundgesetz' [1989] *Neue Juristische Wochenschrift* 857.

Nipperdey, HC, 'Freie Entfaltung der Persönlichkeit' in KA Bettermann, FI Neumann and HC Nipperdey (eds), *Die Grundrechte, Handbuch der Theorie und Praxis der Grundrechte* (Berlin, Duncker und Humblot, 1962), vol 2, 751.

Scholz, R, 'Das Grundrecht auf freie Entfaltung der Persönlichkeit in der Rechtssprechung des Bundesverfassungsgerichts' (1975) 100 *Archiv für Öffentliches Recht* 80.

Wehrhahn, H, 'Systematische Vorfragen einer Auslegung des Art. 2 Abs.1' (1957) 82 *Archiv für Öffentliches Recht* 250.

Wintrich, J, 'Zur Auslegung und Anwendung des Art. 2 Abs.1' in *Staat und Bürger, Festschrift f. Apelt* (Berlin, Verlag E H Beck, 1958), 1.

MOVEMENT OF LAW BEYOND STATE BORDERS

Ajani, G, 'By chance and prestige: Legal Transplants in Russia and Eastern Europe' [1995] *American Journal of Comparative Law* 43.

Arnaud, A J, *Pour une pensée juridique européenne* (Paris, Presses Universitaires de France, 1991).

——*Modernité et mondialisation: Cinq leçons d'histoire de la philosophie du droit et de l'État* (Paris, LGDJ, 1998).

Badie, B, *L'État importé: essai sur l'occidentalisation de l'ordre politique* (Paris, Fayard, 1992).

Bugnicourt, J, 'Le mimétisme administratif en Afrique: un obstacle majeur au développement' (1973) 6 *Revue Française de Sciences Politiques* 1239.

Burley, AM, 'Law among Liberal States: Liberal Internationalism' (1992) 92 *Columbia Law Review* 1916.

Cappelletti, M, *New Perspectives for a Common Law of Europe* (Leyden and Bruxelles, Sijthof & Bruylant, 1978).

Cappelletti, M and Adams, JC, 'Judicial Review of Legislation, European Antecedents and Adaptations' (1966) 79 *Harvard Law Review* 207.

Coing, H, 'Europäisierung der Rechtswissenschaft' (1990) 15 *Neue Juristische Wochenschrift* 937.

Davison, 'America's Impact on Constitutional Changes in Eastern Europe' [1992] *Alb. Law Review* 793.

Dorandeu, R, 'Les pélerins constitutionnels' in Y Mény (ed), *Les politiques du mimétisme institutionnel* (Paris, L'Harmattan, 1993), 3.

Dupré, C, 'Importing German Law: the Interpretation of the Right to Human Dignity by the Hungarian Constitutional Court' [2000] *OsteuropaRecht* 144.

——'Importing German Case Law: the Right to Human Dignity in Hungarian Constitutional Case Law' in G Halmai (ed), *The Constitution Found? The First Nine Years of Hungarian Constitutional Review on Fundamental Rights* (Budapest, INDOK, 2000), 215.

Ewald, W, 'The Logic of Legal Transplants' [1995] *American Journal of Comparative Law* 489.

Feher, F, 'Imagining the West' (1995) 42 *Thesis Eleven* 52.

Friedman, L, 'Borders: on the Emerging Sociology of Transnational Law' [1996] *Stanford Journal of International Law* 64.

Gaudemet J, 'Les transferts de droit' [1976] *Année Sociologique* 29.

Glendon, MA, *Rights Talk: The Impoverishment of Political Discourse* (New York, Toronto, Free Press, 1991).

Grugel, J (ed), *Democracy Without Borders: Transnationalisation and Conditionality in New Democracies* (London and New York, Routledge, 1999).

Guénaire, M et al, 'Droit Romain, Common Law: quel Droit Mondial?' [2001] *Le Débat* 48.

Hartkamp, AS, Hesselin, MW and Hondius, EH, *Towards a European Civil Code* (Nijmegen, Ars Aequi Libri, 1994).

Howard, DAE, 'How Ideas Travel' in DAE Howard (ed), *Constitution-Making in Eastern Europe* (Washington DC, Woodrow Wilson Center Press, 1993), 9.

Kendé, P, 'L'optimisme institutionnel des élites post communistes' in Y Mény (ed), *Les politiques du mimétisme institutionnel* (Paris, L'Harmattan, 1993), 237.

Kovács, JM, 'Pardigmen des Übergangs, westliches Theorieangebot und östliche Nachfrage in den Wirtschaftswissenschaften' (1995) 9 *Transit* 54.

Langrod, G, 'Genèse et conséquence du mimétisme en Afrique' (1973) 2 *Revue Internationale des Sciences Administratives* 119.

Legrand, P, 'European Systems Are Not Converging' (1996) 45 *International and Comparative Law Quarterly* 52.

—— 'The Impossibility of "Legal Transplants"' [1997] *Maastricht Journal of European and Comparative Law* 111.

Lester, A, 'The Overseas Trade in the American Bill of Rights' [1988] *Columbia Law Review* 537.

Loveland, I (ed), *Importing the First Amendment: Freedom of Expression in American, English and European Law* (Oxford, Hart Publishing, 1998).

Lowenthal, A (ed), *Exporting Democracy: the United States and Latin America* (Baltimore, Johns Hopkins University Press, 1991).

Mattei, U, 'Efficiency of Legal Transplants' [1994] *International Review of Law and Economics* 3.

Mény, Y (ed), *Les politiques du mimétisme institutionnel* (Paris, L'Harmattan, 1993).

Örücü E, 'A Theoretical Framework for Transfrontier Mobility of Law' in R Jagtenberg, E Örücü and A J De Roo (eds), *Transfrontier Mobility of Law* (The Hague, Kluwer International, 1995), 5.

Pejovich, S, 'Der Markt der Institutionen, Osteuropa zwischen Nationalismus und Liberalismus' (1995) 9 *Transit* 44.

Perry, 'Constitutional Johnny Appelseeds: American Consultants and the Drafting of Foreign Constitutions' [1992] *Alb. Law Review* 767.

Pescatore, P, 'Le recours dans la jurisprudence de la CJCE à des normes déduites de la comparaison des droits des États membres' [1980] *Revue Internationale de Droit Comparé* 337.

Polakiewicz, J, 'The European Human Rights Convention in Domestic Law' (1991) 12 *Human Rights Law Journal* 125.

Rose, R, *Lesson Drawing in Public Policy: a Guide to Learning Across Time and Space* (Chatham, Chatham House Publishers, 1993).

Rotunda, R, 'Exporting the American Bill of Rights: The Lesson from Romania' [1991] *University of Illinois Law Review* 1065.

Sacco, R, 'Modèles français et modèles allemands dans le droit civil italien' [1976] *Revue Internationale de Droit Comparé* 225.

Sajó, A, 'Universal Rights, Missionaries, Converts and "Local Savages"' (1997) 6 *East European Constitutional Review* 44.

Sartori, G, *Comparative Constitutional Engineering: An Inquiry into Structures, Incentives and Outcomes* (London, Macmillan, 1994).

Seidman, A and R, 'Drafting Legislation for Development: Lessons from a Chinese Project' [1996] *American Journal of Comparative Law* 1.

Slaughter, A-M, 'A Typology of Transjudicial Communication' (1994) 29 *University of Richmond Law Review* 99.

Sólyom, L, 'Sur la coopération des cours constitutionnelles', *Introduction à la Conférence des Cours Constitutionnelles Européennes* (Budapest, May 1996, on file with the author.)

Stein, E, 'International Law in Internal Law: Toward Internationalization of Central-Eastern European Constitutions?' (1994) 88 *American Journal of International Law* 427.

Steinberger, H, *Modèles de Juridictions Constitutionnelles* (Strasbourg, Conseil de l'Europe Publishing, 1998).

Teubner, G, 'Legal Irritants: Good Faith in British Law and How Unifying the Law Ends Up in New Divergences' [1998] *Modern Law Review* 11.

Timsit, G, 'Modèles administratifs et pays en voie de développement' (1976) 4 *Revue Internationale de Sciences Administratives* 349.

Waelde, TW and Gunderson, J, 'Legislative Reform in Transition Economies: Western Transplants, a Short-cut to Market Economy Status?' [1994] *International and Comparative Law Quarterly* 345.

Watson, A, *Legal Transplants: an Approach to Comparative Law* (Edinburgh, Scottish Academic Press, 1974).

—— 'Legal Transplants and Law Reform' (1976) 92 *Law Quarterly Review* 79.

—— 'Aspects of Reception of Law' (1996) 2 *American Journal of Comparative Law* 333.

Weiler, JHH, 'Transformation of Europe' (1991) 100 *Yale Law Journal* 2403.

—— 'A Quiet Revolution: the European Court of Justice and its Interlocutors' (1994) 26 *Comparative Political Studies* 510.

Whitehead, L, 'The Imposition of Democracy' in A Lowenthal (ed), *Exporting Democracy: the United States and Latin America* (Baltimore, Johns Hopkins University Press, 1991), 216.

Zajtay, I, 'La réception des droits étrangers et le droit comparé' [1957] *Revue Internationale de Droit Comparé* 686.

Zlinsky, J, 'Two Questions about the Adaptation of Juridical Models: the XII Tables and Hungarian Reception' (1991) 33 *Acta Juridica Hungarica* 39.

COMPARATIVE LAW

General

Ancel, M, 'La tendance universaliste dans la doctrine comparative française au début du XX' in *Festschrift f. E. Rabel* (Tübingen, JC Mohr, 1953), 17.

—— *Utilité et méthodes du droit comparé, éléments d'introduction à l'étude comparative générale des droits* (Neuchâtel, Éditions Ides et Calendes, 1971).

Constantinesco L-J, *Traité de droit comparé*, I (Paris, LGDJ, 1972).

—— *Rechtsvergleichung: Die rechtsvergleichende Methode*, II (Köln, Carl Heymanns Verlag, 1972).

—— *Traité de droit comparé, la science des droits comparés*, III (Paris, Économica, 1983).

David, R, 'Le droit comparé, enseignement de culture générale' [1950] *Revue Internationale de Droit Comparé* 682.

David, R, *Les grands systèmes de droit contemporains* (9th edn, Paris, Dalloz, 1988).

De Cruz, P, *Comparative Law in a Changing World* (London, Cavendish, 1999).

Dupré, C, 'The Perspective of Law Importation: the Hungarian Experience' in A Harding and E Örücü (eds), *Comparative Law in the 21st Century* (The Hague, Kluwer Law International, 2002), 267.

Glendon, MA, Gordon, WM and Osakwe, C, *Comparative Legal Traditions* (Saint Paul, West Publishing, 1982).

Harding, A and Örücü, E (eds), *Comparative Law in the 21st Century* (The Hague, Kluwer Law International, 2002).

Harmathy, A, 'Comparative Law and the Changes of Law' [1999] *Acta Juridica Hungarica* 159.

Hermet, G and Badie, B, *Politique comparée* (Paris, Presses Universitaires de France, 1990).

Kahn-Freund, O, 'On Uses and Misuses of Comparative Law' (1974) 1 *Modern Law Review* 1.

Kiirkeri, M, *Comparative Legal Reasoning and European Law* (Dordrecht, Kluwer Academic Publishers, 2001).

Markesinis, B, *Foreign Law and Comparative Methodology* (Oxford, Hart Publishing, 1998).

Nelken, D, *Comparing Legal Cultures* (Aldershot, Dartmouth, 1997).

Örücü, E, *Critical Comparative Law: Considering Paradoxes for Legal Systems in Transition* (Deventer, Kluwer Law International, 1999).

Øyen, E (ed), *Comparative Methodology, Theory and Practice in International Social Research* (London, Sage, 1990).

Sacco, R, *La comparaison juridique au service de la connaissance du droit* (Paris, Économica, 1991).

Zweigert, K and Kötz, H, *An Introduction to Comparative Law* (Amsterdam, North Holland, 1977).

Socialist Conception of Comparative Law

Ancel, M, 'La confrontation des droits socialistes et des droits occidentaux' in Z Péteri (ed), *Legal Theory, Comparative Law: Études en l'honneur du Professeur I. Szabó* (Budapest, Akadémiai Kiadó, 1984), 13.

Lamm, V and Péteri, Z (eds), *Legal Development and Comparative Law: Selected Essays for the International Congress of Comparative Law* (Budapest, Akadémiai Kiadó, 1974).

Péteri, Z, *Some Aspects of the Sociological Approach in Comparative Law* (Budapest, Akadémiai Kiadó, 1972), 75.

—— (ed), *La comparaison du droit* (Budapest, Akadémiai Kiadó, 1974).

—— *Goals and Methods of Legal Comparison* (Budapest, Akadémiai Kiadó, 1974).

—— (ed), *Legal Theory, Comparative Law: Studies in Honour of Prof I. Szabó* (Budapest, Akadémiai Kiadó, 1984), 317.

Szabó, I, 'Les buts et la méthode de la comparaison du droit' in *Rapports généraux du IX Congrès International de Droit Comparé, Téhéran* (Bruxelles, Bruylant, 1977), 157.

CONSTITUTIONAL JUSTICE

General

Brewer-Carias, AR, *Judicial Review in Comparative Law* (Cambridge, Cambridge University Press, 1989).

Cappelletti, M, 'Nécessité et légitimité de la justice constitutionnelle' [1981] *Revue Internationale de Droit Comparé* 625.

Kelsen, H, 'La garantie juridictionnelle de la constitution' (1928) 44 *Revue du Droit Public* 197.

Landfried, C (ed), *Constitutional Review and Legislation: An International Comparison* (Baden-Baden, Nomos Verlag, 1988).

McWhinney, E, *Supreme Courts and Judicial Law-Making: Constitutional Tribunals and Constitutional Review* (Dordrecht, Nijhof, 1986).

Rousseau, D, *La justice constitutionnelle en Europe* (Paris, Montchrestien, 1992).

Schwartz, H, 'The New East-European Constitutional Courts', in DAE Howard (ed), *Constitution-Making in Eastern Europe* (Washington DC, Woodrow Wilson Center Press, 1993), 163.

——*The Struggle for Constitutional Justice in Post Communist Europe* (Chicago, University of Chicago Press, 2000).

Stone, A, *The Birth of Judicial Politics in France* (Oxford, Oxford University Press, 1992).

Verdrussen, M (ed), *La justice constitutionelle en Europe Centrale* (Bruxelles, Bruyland and Paris LGDJ, 1997).

Vergottini, G de (ed), *Giustizia Costituzionale e Sviluppo Democratico nei Paesi dell'Europa Centro-Orientale* (Torino, G Giappichelli, 2000).

Unwritten Constitutional Rights and Creative Interpretation

Barak, A, 'Constitutional Law without a Constitution', in S Shetreet (ed), *The Role of Courts in Society* (Dordrecht, Martinus Nijhoff Publishers, 1988), 448.

Bourcier, D and Mackay, P (eds), *Lire le droit, langue, texte, cognition* (Paris, LGDJ, 1992).

Cappelletti, M, 'The Law-Making Power of the Judges and its Limits: A Comparative Analysis' (1981) 8 *Monash Law Review* 15.

Corwin, ES, 'The Higher Law: Background of American Constitutional Law' [1928] *Harvard Law Review* 152.

Denninger, E, 'Constitutional Law Between Statutory Law and Higher Law' in A Pizzorusso (ed), *Law in the Making* (Berlin, Springer Verlag, 1988), 103.

Dworkin, R, *Taking Rights Seriously* (London, Duckworth, 1977).

Grey, T, 'Do We Have an Unwritten Constitution?' (1978) 27 *Stanford Law Review* 703.

——'The Origins of the Unwritten Constitution' (1978) 30 *Stanford Law Review* 843.

Grisel, A, 'Droit public non écrit' in *Mélanges Max Imboden* (Bâle, Verlag Helbing und Lichtenhahn, 1972), 139.

Huber, H, 'Über die Konkretisierung der Grundrechte' in *Mélanges Max Imboden* (Bâle, Verlag Helbing und Lichtenhahn, 1972), 191.

Kirby, MD, 'The Role of the Judge in Advancing Human Rights by Reference to International Human Rights Norms' (1988) 62 *Australian Law Journal* 514.

Klein, E, 'Human Rights of the Third Generation', in C Starck (ed), *Rights, Institutions and Impact of International Law According to the German Basic Law* (Baden-Baden, Nomos, 1987), 63.

Lenoble, J and Ost, F, *Droit mythe et raison: essai sur la dérive mythologique de la rationnalité juridique* (Bruxelles, Publications des facultés universitaires de Saint Louis, 1980).

Macdonald, RA, 'Procedural Due Process in Canadian Constitutional Law: Natural Justice and Fundamental Justice' (1987) 39 *University of Florida Law Review* 217.

Mota, H, 'Le principe de la liste ouverte en matière de droits fondamentaux', in P Bon *et al* (eds), *La justice constitutionnelle au Portugal* (Économica-PUAM, 1988), 177.

Perry, MJ, *The Constitution, the Courts and Human Rights: An Inquiry Into the Legitimacy of Constitutional Policy-Making by the Judiciary* (New Haven, Yale University Press, 1982).

Ponthoreau, M-C, *La reconnaissance des droits non écrits par les cours constitution- nelles italienne et française: essai sur le pouvoir créateur du juge constitutionnel* (Marseille, Économica, 1994).

Rivero, J, 'Vers de nouveaux droits de l'homme' [1982] *Revue des Sciences Morales et Politiques* 673.

—— 'Déclarations parallèles des droits de l'homme' [1990] *Revue Trimestrielle des Droits de l'Homme* 323.

Rossinelli, M, *Les libertés non écrites: contribution à l'étude du pouvoir créateur du juge constitutionnel* (Lausanne, Payot, 1987).

Rubio-Llorente, F, 'Constitutional Jurisdiction as Law-Making' in A Pizzorusso (ed), *Law in the Making* (Berlin, Springer Verlag, 1988), 156.

Natural Law

Barnett, RE, 'Getting Normative: the Role of Natural Rights in Constitutional Adjudication' in RP George (ed), *Natural Law, Liberalism and Morality* (Oxford, Clarendon Press, 1996), 151.

Bloch, E, *Naturrecht und menschliche Würde* (Frankfurt/M, Suhrkamp, 1961).

George, RP (ed), *Natural Law, Liberalism and Morality* (Oxford, Clarendon Press, 1996).

Kamenka, E and Erh-Soon Teh, A. (eds), *Human Rights* (London, Edward Arnold, 1978).

Passerin D'Entrèves, AP, *Natural Law: An Introduction to Legal Philosophy* (New Brunswick, Transaction Publishers, 1994).

Rommen, H, 'Natural Law in the Decisions of the Federal Supreme Court and the Constitutional Courts in Germany' (1959) 4 *Natural Law Forum* 1.

Schneider, P, 'Naturrechtliche Strömungen in deutscher Rechtsprechung' [1959] *Archiv für Recht und Sozialphilosophie* 98.

Tuck, R, *Natural Rights Theories: Their Origin and Development* (Cambridge, Cambridge University Press, 1979).

DICTIONARIES

Doucet, M, *Dictionnaire juridique et économique, allemand-français* (2nd edn, München, CH Beck, 1966).

Eckhardt, S, *Magyar-Francia kéziszótár* (9th edn, Budapest, Akadémiai Kiadó, 1992).

Herbst, R (ed), *Wörterbuch der Handels-Finanz-und-Rechtssprache, Deutsch, English, Französich* (Zoug, Translegal, 1975).

Karcsay, S, *Wörterbuch der Rechts-und-Verwaltungssprache, Ungarisch-Deutsch* (2nd edn, München, CH Beck, 1969).

Sherwood, PA (ed), *A Concise Hungarian-English Dictionary* (Budapest, Akadémiai Kiadó, 1999).

Index